LIBERALISM

Liberalism

Politics, Ideology and the Market

JOHN A. HALL

THE UNIVERSITY OF
NORTH CAROLINA PRESS
CHAPEL HILL

First published in the United States in 1988
by the University of North Carolina Press

Originally published in Great Britain in 1988
by Paladin, Grafton Books
A division of the Collins Publishing Group
8 Grafton Street, London W1X 3LA

The paper in this book meets the guidelines for
permanence and durability of the Committee on
Production Guidelines for Book Longevity of the
Council on Library Resources.

92 91 90 89 88   5 4 3 2 1

Library of Congress Cataloging-in-Publication Data

Hall, John A., 1949–
Liberalism: politics, ideology, and the market.

Published simultaneously in London by
Paladin Grafton Books.
Bibliography: p.
Includes index.
1. Liberty—History. 2. Liberalism—History.
3. Capitalism—History. I. Title.
JC585.H175   1988   320.5′1′09   88-40140
ISBN 0-8078-1812-7 (alk. paper)
ISBN 0-8078-4235-4 (pbk.: alk. paper)

For Catherine and Liz

ACKNOWLEDGEMENTS

The comments, conversation and writings of several friends and colleagues have been of the greatest help, and I particularly want to thank Bennett Berger, Justin Wintle, Steve Krasner, Patricia Crone, Bill Jordan, Carlos Waisman, Tony Rees, Susan Strange, Nicos Mouzelis, José Merquior, Ralf Dahrendorf, Michael Freeden, Stanley Hoffman, Jeff Frieden, David Lake, Judy Goldstein, David Riesman and Michael Mann. The writings of Sir Karl Popper, Ernest Gellner and Raymond Aron, to my mind the greatest liberals of the post-war period, have long been fundamental to my own work, and it is a pleasure to attest here to the weight of their contribution to modern thought. I owe a particular personal debt to Caroline Thomas and Molly Hall who provided the emotional support without which it would not have been possible to write this book.

CONTENTS

Contents

In Praise of Masks
Recapitulation
The Betrayal of the Intellectuals

viii

Contents

A Liberal World Order?
Conclusion

FOREWORD

There have been many books on liberalism, some of them very distinguished, so it is important to characterize the approach adopted here, not least to alert the reader to the nature of the argument which follows. This can best be done by considering the thesis so passionately sustained by Anthony Arblaster in *The Rise and Decline of Western Liberalism*.[1]

Arblaster offers us a definition of liberalism, an account of its historical career and, upon that basis, the judgement that liberalism no longer deserves our respect. Arblaster's views are inspired by Marxism. In consequence, 'liberalism' is defined in terms of its protection of private property; this is to claim that liberalism and capitalism go hand in hand. Following Marx and the Hungarian Marxist philosopher György von Lukács, Arblaster considers that the historical career of liberalism sees a move from progressivism to reaction. Where once the bourgeoisie had fought for new freedoms, it became fearful, once it was the dominant class of a rising proletariat; in consequence, in or about the year 1848, it became politically reactionary – a movement which Lukács saw represented in literature in terms of a change from Stendhal to Flaubert and modernism.[2] Arblaster does not believe that liberalism has recovered its nerve: he sees its continued loyalty to capitalism as evidence that it could again embrace authoritarianism, and he generally remarks on modern liberalism's effete spinelessness.

These charges are so serious that the argument is largely structured so as to confront them head on. Let me begin

1

with an alternative definition. Liberalism considers individuals, seen as the seat of moral value, as of equal worth; it is held to follow from this that the individual should be able to chose his or her own ends in life.[3] It is important to emphasize one point immediately: liberalism may be morally neutral in regard to the ends people choose for themselves, but it is not morally neutral about the view that such choice is desirable. Liberalism is a view of the world, an ideology, and to adopt it is to take a stand. More particularly, an open society based on premises of negative liberty is held to be superior to all others on offer; particular suspicion is shown to those in which some *totalizing ideology* tries to lay down patterns of behaviour in every aspect of life. Beyond this, of course, liberalism has had many detailed attitudes towards morality, epistemology and politics. Arblaster is right to argue that there has been a close association between liberalism and capitalism, that the former has long considered the latter an appropriate means to realize its ends. But these are *secondary* matters; changes in characteristic liberal views in these areas may be necessary in order most effectively to achieve the core of the liberal vision. To distinguish between core intent and means has one particular advantage to it, namely that it points to the amount of calculation that a liberal vision requires. There are manifest tensions inside liberalism, notably between wealth and freedom and between knowledge and morality, and continual, complex assessment is required if the liberal aim is to be best served. There are very complex questions of 'trade-offs' here, some of which I shall point to rather than solve; they fully deserve analytic treatment in their own right.[4]

All this is to say that my analysis will be of liberalism in a generic sense. However, as Arblaster is correct in noting change and development in liberal doctrines and institutions, it is only sensible to make the analysis historical. In the first part of this book two facets of liberalism are introduced, and they remain at the centre of attention thereafter. The presence of a chapter on knowledge and morality indicates a weakness in Arblaster's account; namely its failure to consider the link between liberalism and science. The Focus then turns to the relationship between liberalism and capitalism. Particular attention is paid to the fact that capitalism was endorsed less for economic reasons than as a means by which political power could be controlled. In the last analysis, I am not of Arblaster's party because the need to control political power seems to me to be a permanent problem facing human society.

The second part of this book examines the slide of Europe into reaction in the later nineteenth and early twentieth centuries. Did liberalism contribute, knowingly or unknowingly, to this slide? Chapter 3 examines the strengths and weaknesses of liberal ideology. The remaining two chapters ask whether capitalism, to which liberalism was so closely linked, brought with it reaction. Chapter 4 examines the claim that the working class wanted revolution; Chapter 5 analyses the hugely important thesis that capitalists create war. My argument in all of these cases is similar. Liberalism has considerable debits to its name; in particular, Arblaster is quite right to question the equation, so often and so easily accepted, that the bourgeois economic class is necessarily and automatically politically liberal. However, these debits are not so great as to entail the complete abandonment of liberalism. In this part of the book, it will be seen that a greater weakness of liberalism – and of Marxism! – has been its attitude to geopolitics rather than to property. Underlying this is the sociological realization that modern history has been quite as much affected by the behaviour, in turns foolish and prudent, of political elites as by that of social classes.

A general theory of liberalism is offered in the last part of the book. Liberalism is not necessarily supine, self-satisfied and finished: it can retain vitality if it learns from its mistakes. Such a theory requires a restatement of philosophical premises *and* a much greater awareness of social and political issues. More is involved here than a better understanding of geopolitics. Any theory of modern liberalism must systematically consider the situation of the Third World. Let me stress one characteristic of this general theory – indeed, of the book as a whole. It will be seen that a weakness of much liberalism has been that of excessive moralism. Liberals, and perhaps especially those with a Nonconformist background, often treat political life as if it were but a branch of private morality. Although there are dangers to 'realism', Raymond Aron was right to insist, against all the friends of his youth, that politics is not moral, and that a liberal should always be concerned with the consequences of action.[5] Social and political theorists, in other words, need both to specify a desirable society and to inquire into the means by which it can be realized; they should, in other words, offer intelligent views of theory and practice. The general theory of liberalism offered here is designed to be at once philosophically sound and sociologically realistic; indeed, the rather low-powered philosophical validation for liberalism makes it necessary to place great emphasis on potential social developments. It is only honest to admit at this point that behind my insistence that liberalism could develop in a particular direction lies the hope that it will in fact do so. The reader will want to bear this in mind since it is possible that my hopes have distorted my sociological analysis.

The huge diversity of the liberal tradition, the fact that it is at once a civilization and a doctrine, together with its involvement in economics, epistemology, geopolitics, ethics and politics, makes it very difficult to write about liberalism in a short compass. Added to this is the further problem that liberalism has had enemies whose comments about it are often acute, interesting and, in a book written as a polemic on behalf of liberalism, in need of consideration. The centre of the Marxist critique is that there is a clear imbalance between the freedoms enjoyed by capital and by labour; conservatism has stressed that liberalism leaves the individual isolated and bereft of necessary social support. At least as important, however, is the critique offered by 'reactionary modernists', that is, by those who combined respect for hierarchy with a futuristic appreciation of the powers of modern science.[6] Little attention is paid here to conservatism since it is impossible to arrest social change in modern circumstances; in contrast, extensive analyses of Marxism and fascism are offered, with concentration, for reasons to be explained, on the sociological presuppositions of the former and the philosophical bases of the latter.

There is simply not sufficient space in a book of this sort to offer a complete history or an exhaustive account of every facet of liberalism. Nevertheless, this book does have historical points to make and it does at least hint at the diversity of the liberal tradition. Three characteristics of this book are designed to help the reader through the material discussed. First, discussion concentrates on the relationship between ideology, politics and the market. Secondly, this book offers an interpretation. This interpretation of liberalism's content, career and most desirable future will not meet with the approval of all who consider themselves liberals – and especially not with those who have recently argued that the heart of liberalism *should be* an appreciation of capitalist mentality and institutions.[7] Finally, at every point I have sought to explain the relevance of the particular topic under discussion to the general argument; this may at times be slightly tendentious, but it seemed preferable to being elliptical.

NOTES

1. A. Arblaster, *The Rise and Decline of Western Liberalism* (Oxford: Basil Blackwell, 1984). For another interpretation from the left, see the various works of C. B. MacPherson, most famously *The Political Theory of Possessive Individualism* (Oxford: Oxford University Press, 1962).

2. G. Lukács, *The Meaning of Contemporary Realism* (London: Merlin Press, 1963); *Studies in European Realism* (London: Hillway Press, 1950).

3. My position is very close to Ronald Dworkin, particularly as he expresses it in 'Liberalism', in S. Hampshire (ed.), *Public and Private Morality* (Oxford: Oxford University Press, 1978).

4. We can look forward to Michael Freeden's forthcoming book on this topic.

5. For an account of Aron's views in this important matter, see my *Raymond Aron* (Oxford: Polity Press, to be published 1988).

6. J. Herf, *Reactionary Modernism, Technology, Culture and Politics in Weimar and the Third Reich* (Cambridge: Cambridge University Press, 1984).

7. I have in mind here various thinkers on the right, notably Friedrich von Hayek, Milton Friedman and Murray Rothbard. Their views inform J. Gray, *Liberalism* (Milton Keynes: Open University Press, 1986).

I
CONFIDENT ORIGINS

1
KNOWLEDGE AND MORALITY

What is the nature of a good life? A fundamental characteristic of liberalism has been that it has sought to answer this question by making use of the cognitive practices of modern science. In fact, liberalism's admiration for science is sometimes so great as to result in the very strong thesis of an identity between science and liberalism. If that claim is allowed, liberalism will be able to bask in the glow to be derived from the success story of modern cognition; it will appear less a way of ordering the world than the inevitable and proper one. In the interests of honesty, it may as well be said that I consider there to be some substance to this argument.

In order to get to grips with this claim, it is obviously necessary to gain some appreciation of the epistemological principles on which modern science depends. There are long historical roots to the take-off into sustained cognitive growth that took place in Western European society. The combination of Judaic and Greek culture led to a view of the world functioning according to laws of nature with which God did not interfere; it has been claimed that this allowed and encouraged – as, for example, the absolutist monotheism of Islam did not – investigation of the world.[1] Moreover, the emergence of natural science probably relied upon pre-existent notions of the right to question; in this connection, it is worth noting that many early scientific advances took place in countries where some respect was shown for freedom of opinion.[2] This is an important point since it suggests that much modern epistemology is dependent on already existing norms which it in part codifies, in part takes for granted. Nevertheless, it is broadly correct to argue that a fundamental revolution in cognition results from the adoption of strategies which make it possible not just to question, but to establish a measure of certainty.[3] Those strategies are best examined through analysis of the empiricism of David Hume and the mechanism of Immanuel Kant, and of the way in which these strategic approaches to knowledge were able to work together. The ability to discover a great deal about the natural world did not, it is important to stress, lead to the creation of a large measure of certainty in moral affairs. The thinker of greatest relevance in this respect is John Stuart Mill. Analysis of an important but revealing weakness in Mill's work will make it necessary to question the putative science–liberalism nexus, but not to dismantle it altogether.

Nothing Exists but Sensation

David Hume gave his major philosophical work a long title which is, unfortunately, not always cited in full: *A Treatise of Human Nature: Being an Attempt to introduce the experimental Method of Reasoning into Moral Subjects*. This title is reflected in the three volumes of the treatise, one on the understanding, a second on the passions and a third on morality. We need to have some grasp of the way in which these volumes are linked to each other if we are to make real sense of what Hume was seeking to achieve.

The first volume of the treatise is the best known. Hume makes it clear that his intention is to place the study of the human mind on a scientific basis, just as Bacon was held to have placed the study of the natural world on a firm and scientific basis. It is to this end that he uses an experimental or observational method, and his imitative intent explains his wish to reduce the complex to the simple; that is, the desire to build up a general picture on the basis of firm and reliable building blocks. The nature of his argument as a whole results from the conclusion that the building blocks he adopts are none too firm and reliable.

The building blocks are, of course, the human senses. For Hume, nothing exists but sensation. It is important to be clear about the nature of this claim. Many thinkers offer some allegiance to the senses; Hume's position is original, rigorous and brilliantly sustained because it seeks to rule out anything else whatsoever. He insists, for example, that there is no such thing as autonomous human reason; in so far as we can use this term, it is as a description of certain workings of the mind occasioned by the senses. Reason is thus seen by Hume as being only 'a slave to the passions'. The nature of sensation is carefully and subtly expounded by Hume, utilizing the method of an appeal to reasoned introspection. He distinguishes between impressions and ideas, the latter being the aftertaste of the former and reducible to them. We gain a picture of the human mind as a type of assembly kit piecing together a picture of the world, from the base up.

The trouble with this careful constructivism is that it led Hume to a position of great anxiety. This can be most clearly seen in his own famed questioning of the notion of causation. In the background of his argument there is the awareness that the mere observation of one thing following another is no real basis upon which to erect laws of nature. The most fundamental reason for this is that we can have no final certainty that a different result may not happen on the next occasion. We may believe, to take Popper's much trumpeted example, that all swans are white, only to have our expectations overturned by the discovery of black swans – which do indeed exist! (Is the sudden appearance of black swans in city parks a sign of the influence of Popper's work?) We can have no firmly inductive science. Our sensations are incapable of guaranteeing that the sun will come up tomorrow, and of assuring us that nature will continue to operate in the same manner as it is doing at present. A further and more substantial difficulty follows from this. If all that we have are impressions, how can we be sure that there is any constancy to the external world at all? Indeed, how can we be sure that the external world really exists?

There is a sense in which the first volume of the treatise leads logically to a sense of despair and anxiety which the remaining volumes then try and remove. The core of Hume's thought is best conveyed in his own words:

The *intense* view of these manifold contradictions and imperfections in human reason has so wrought upon me, and heated my brain, that I am ready to reject all belief and reasoning, and can look upon no opinion even as more probable or likely than another. Where am I, or what? From what causes do I derive my existence, and to what condition shall I return? Whose favour shall I court, and whose anger must I dread? What beings surround me? and on whom have I any influence, or who have any inflence on me? I am confounded with all these questions, and begin to fancy myself in the most deplorable condition imaginable, inviron'd with the deepest darkness, and utterly deprived of the use of every member and faculty.

Most fortunately it happens, that since reason is incapable of dispelling these clouds, nature herself suffices to that purpose, and cures me of this philosophical melancholy and delirium, either by relaxing this bent of mind, or by some avocation, and lively impression of my senses, which obliterate all these chimeras. I dine, I play a game of backgammon, I converse, and am merry with my friends; and when after three or four hour's amusement, I wou'd return to these speculations, they appear so cold, and strain'd, and ridiculous, that I cannot find in my heart to enter into them any farther.[4]

However, Hume tells us that eventually even these pleasant distractions pall; when they do so the attractions of philosophy become apparent once again.

Hume considered his position to be that of moderate scepticism. His naturalistic view of human nature convinced him that human beings simply do not tolerate absolute scepticism; his position as a whole depends upon this. When discussing the theory of knowledge, he argues that it is a natural propensity of the imagination to *presume* that the world will continue to work on regular lines, even though there is no rigorous proof of this being so; that this is so is seen as inevitable, and as happily beneficial since it makes it possible for us to live. Upon this basis Hume seeks to build up a view of moral and political institutions. His account continues to be naturalistic and descriptive. Thus, property is held to be justified because of the strong feeling that those who own it have for it. His conclusions in these realms are moderate, and it is, in general, fair to say that he effectively endorses the progressive commercial institutions of his own society, in this both influencing and echoing his close friend Adam Smith. Hume's insistence that we must accept ourselves for what we are is scarcely terrifying given that the portrait of what we are so heavily reflects Hume's own warm and balanced personality.

One final point must be made about Hume's position before seeking to assess it. Although Hume's descriptive naturalism should rule out any active moralizing or interference, he introduces, as Smith was also to do, a certain measure of activism in a back-handed way. Hume does this in his account of judgement. There is a distinction to be drawn, in his view, between the vulgar and the wise – terms which reveal how anchored he was in eighteenth-century assumptions. Hume's distinction can be illustrated by means of a fanciful example. A vulgar man with a passion for alcohol might drink so much that he would kill himself in a short time; in contrast, a wise man, aware of the regrettable weakness of the liver, might drink less, with the happy result that, over a lengthier life, his total consumption would be greater. The trouble with this sort of argument is that it introduces by the back door some conception of reason and reflection, minimal perhaps and certainly class-based, but definitely present.

Commentators on David Hume have been split when assessing his work as a whole.[5] John Stuart Mill felt that Hume's volumes on the passions and on morals followed naturally from that on the understanding; it was precisely because of his fears of darkness that Hume grabbed at the comfort of settled life. In a somewhat similar vein, members of the Frankfurt School of Social Research have argued that acceptance of a positivist (i.e. an empiricist) ethic is bound to lead to a conservative acceptance of society: positivism can only describe what is, and has nothing to say about rational standards by which we might gain some purchase on what ought to be. Bertrand Russell, however, contrasted the exceptional radicalism of Hume's epistemology with his acceptance of the social order; Russell accepted the former but rejected the latter as complacent and without real philosophical weight. What is the proper position to take when considering these views?

If we start with Hume's own corpus of work, it is clear that he was by no means a traditional conservative. It is true that he was distressed when he was once accused of propagating ideas dangerous to social order, but that he makes an uneasy bedfellow for traditional conservatism becomes obvious once we note how rarely Hume figures in any pantheon of conservative thinkers. Three general considerations justify this judgement. The most obvious concerns religion. Hume insisted that if we seriously believed that the world was based upon a reliable regularity of nature, then there was no reason whatsoever for us to have any religious belief. Although he *was* fairly well settled into his society, he would not bend on this point and it certainly adversely affected his chances of employment. In this matter he differed from Edmund Burke. When the Irish intellectual sought to defend, in *Reflections on the Revolution in France and on the Proceedings in Certain Societies in London Relative to that Event*, the combination of hierarchy and capitalism of which most eighteenth-century British thinkers approved, he did so by saying that it was divinely ordained. Had Hume been alive in 1790, and thereby forced to defend the principle of hierarchy, he would surely not have been able to make use of this argument! For there is an air of unmistakable sulphur about his work:

Knowledge and Morality

When we run over libraries, persuaded of these [epistemological] principles, what havoc must we make? If we take in our hand any volume; of divinity or school metaphysics, for instance; let us ask, *Does it contain any abstract reasoning concerning quantity or number?* No. *Does it contain any experimental reasoning concerning matter of fact and existence?* No. Commit it then to the flames: for it can contain nothing but sophistry and illusion.[6]

Secondly, we cannot help but note that acceptance of the empiricist ethic is deeply corrosive of certain types of order. That this was and is so can neatly be seen when thinking again about Burke's defence of the established British social order. If one of his principal arguments was that of the divine plan, another line of defence was that it was impossible to reform one institution without damaging others with which it was linked. Such social orders were, in other words, packages; to touch one part would lead to the unravelling of the whole. This *is* a very striking and essentially correct way of understanding the corrosive effect of allowing any piecemeal social reform in societies based on totalizing ideologies. The point to be made is that the empiricist injunction to respect the facts, and more particularly the insistence that *facts are separable, and should only be considered one at a time*, served as a terrible humbler of traditional orders. Empiricism made it necessary for such orders to defend themselves in terms which were not their own; it shifted the ground of battle from a place where evidence could be controlled, i.e. the insistence that this is the way we do things here, to one where a more neutral calculus could hold sway. The real justification for saying all this is provided by the history of nineteenth-century British social thought. The utilitarianism most fully spelled out at the end of the eighteenth century by Jeremy Bentham amounts to being the translation into moral and social theory of the core of Humean empiricism. The principal reason for saying this is that utilitarianism sought to establish this-worldly moral standards, thereby abandoning

15

ineffable, religious or Platonic judgements about human behaviour. What was important about the felicific calculus introduced by the utilitarians, i.e. the practice of judging a policy by its capacity either to increase aggregate pleasure or to diminish aggregate pain, was less any particular notion of happiness than the fact that the examination of institutions in terms of calculation took place one at a time.

Finally, political radicalism was helped by the spirit of empiricism. Hume was certainly no democrat. In his early years, Bentham was not a democrat either: why should a reformer, possessed of knowledge about what men really need, bother actually to consult individuals? Bentham became a convert to democracy when he discovered that the aristocracy was selfish and would not act in the general interest of the body politic. However, I want to claim that, in the long run, the link between empiricism and democracy is more than contingent. There was a genuine 'elective affinity' between styles of thought. What is crucial here is an implicit egalitarianism at work in Humean and utilitarian naturalism. All human beings have the same passions. There is a fundamental democratic impulse in Bentham's philistine comment that pushpin is as good as poetry, and it is no surprise to find that in the felicific calculus of the utilitarians every individual is presumed to count as one.

The Pure Thought of Duty

Immanuel Kant tells us that it was reading David Hume which wakened him from his slumbers and forced him to philosophize. Hume was an exceptionally amiable human being, and an orderly one too, and it is in consequence possible to forget how very worrying and destructive his thought was for men of the eighteenth century. Kant faced two ways as the result of his encounter with Hume. On the one hand, he wished to protect our reason from Hume's naturalism so as to allow for agency and therefore morality; it is this side of his work that is best known, even if its character is not always properly appreciated. On the other

16

hand, he stood in many ways as an ally of Hume. Both appreciated the impact and importance of modern science; Kant was at one with Hume in seeking to theorize something which they both admired. Kant's opposition to Hume in moral matters did not mean for a moment that he wished somehow to undermine the cognitive claims and power of science. It was Kant's intention to provide firmer grounds for knowledge than Hume had been able to offer.

How did Kant go about 'grounding' knowledge? He began by making it clear that he wished to rescue us from the formless and chaotic world with which sensationalism had threatened Hume – at least before he dined and played backgammon. Above all, Kant felt it necessary to restore some sense of objectivity, and he insisted that this could be done only by redeeming the notion of causation from Hume's attack. Kant's restoration of a notion of causation did not try and disprove Hume's contention that our senses cannot guarantee causal processes or the regularity of nature; that Kant left this alone is meritorious because the Humean position is not open to refutation. Kant's strategy was to argue that the notion of causality and objectivity result from the structures of our mind, from the sort of conceptual spectacles with which we approach the world. The human mind was not a passive receptacle of sensation; its experience of the external world – investigation of which remained at the forefront of Kant's programme – was shaped by pre-existent mental categories. The most important of these concerned objectivity and causality. Perhaps the deep structure of the external world *is* chaotic, but in that case we will never, according to Kant, be able to appreciate it.

We can gain further purchase on Kant's philosophy by considering his related views on the nature of explanation. A proper explanation centres on the establishment of structures, or mechanisms; it depends upon specifying patterns which are open to public examination. Explanation *is* reductionist: it is the attempt to explain surface phenomena, sensations if you like, in terms of a deep structure which specifies why it is that they work in the way in which they do. This is not to say that Kant rejected the experimental method, merely that he added to it the understanding that science is also based on the search for structure or mechanism; Kant's argument is that science has to be involved in this search for explanation if it is to progress beyond the futility of endlessly repeating the same experiment to find out whether nature is going to remain regular or not. As scientists do not win Nobel prizes for checking that water still boils at 100 degrees Celsius, it seems that he was on to something.

The way in which Kant dealt with the problem of causation dictated a certain style to his moral philosophy. If he wanted to save science by establishing a basis for objective knowledge, he also wanted to preserve humanity itself from being utterly causally explained. Kant had a greater appreciation of human virtue than did Hume. He was favourably impressed with Rousseau's proto-romantic view of man, whereas Hume, in part because of a disastrous but revealing encounter, deeply distrusted the apostle of sincerity and authenticity.[7] This need to 'protect' humanity was very real, as we can see by examining two problems in Hume. First, we can recall the wobble in Hume's thought when he distinguished between the wise and the virtuous, and thereby suggested that 'reflection' may play a positive role in life. This is a most unsatisfactory *ad hoc* argument which runs counter to the spirit of his naturalism. Even if Hume scholars can find a way around this prevarication, the problem for classical empiricism remains. There is something comic about the way in which naturalistic theorists write books surely designed – or else why bother – to make us change our minds in one way or another; such books represent an appeal to thought, reason and reflection on the part of those who would deny their existence. There is, then, everything to be said for Kant's attempt to preserve an element of reason and to explain its limitations.

18

Secondly, it is worth drawing attention to a standard charge against the classical utilitarian version of empiricism. If a hospital ward full of sick people were to share the limbs and bodily organs of one healthy orderly, the criticism goes, utilitarian values, that is, the greatest good of the greatest number, would be served. In many ways this is a very silly and misleading example: the utilitarians lived *inside* a world in which personal rights were protected. That a type of egalitarianism was a background assumption to their work can be seen by recalling that everyone is to count as one in the felicific calculus. Nevertheless, a Kantian version of such human rights is fundamentally necessary so as to justify openly what had remained implicit in utilitarianism. His defence of the basic liberal aim of considering individuals to be of moral worth remains high-powered and absolutely central to liberalism.

The nature of Kant's attempt to protect the elements of morality from the logic of a fully mechanistic universe has been neatly captured by Ernest Gellner:

Kant . . . falls back in the fact that it is not the nature of things, but the nature of our thought, which had imposed this inexorable order on the world. But if this is so, he argues, and if we find that our humanity requires that we have at least a partial exemption from this cold world, may we not grant ourselves such an exemption? *We* imposed the order; it was not in the nature of things. Why should we suffer from a vision imposed by ourselves?

This is a desperate remedy, and Kant does not use it lightly. It is only because, without such an assumption, and without such an exemption, all morality and freedom would disappear, that we must in his view assume, in the interest of preserving this absolute minimum which gives meaning to our lives, that we are indeed exempt from the vision we have ourselves imposed.[8]

It is worth underlining two points made here. First, this *is* a desperate remedy for Kant as it goes against the consistent ethic of his work *not* to make exceptions on an *ad hoc* basis. Second, Kant preserved only the barest minimum. This can be clearly seen in a passage in the *Ground-*

work of the Metaphysic of Morals in which he argued against a critic who had complained that moral teaching is ineffective:

[T]he teachers themselves do not make their concepts pure, but – since they try to do too well by hunting everywhere for inducements to be moral – they spoil their medicine altogether by their very attempt to make it really powerful. For the most ordinary observation shows that when a righteous act is represented as being done with a steadfast mind in complete disregard of any advantage in this or in another world, and even under the greatest temptations of affliction or allurement, it leaves far behind it any similar action affected even in the slightest degree by an alien impulsion and casts it into the shade: it uplifts the soul and rouses a wish that we too could act in this way. Even children of moderate age feel this impression, and duties should never be presented to them in any other way.[9]

This passage contains in it the germs of a simple idea of morality, that of 'the pure thought of duty'. Several elements make up this idea. It is not appropriate to base morality on anything contingent or empirical, and this means that inducements to morality must be rejected as mere bribes. Kant tells us to associate ourselves with duty rather than with our senses; importantly, duty is not tied to the obligations of a particular social order; morality must be based upon what is pure and unsullied in a single human being. From this follows a categorical imperative that we should seek to treat others as capable of similar pure rationality, that is, we should act on the view that our best selves are universalizable and treat others as ends in themselves rather than as means or objects for us to use.

Kant's moral vision has only been hinted at, as must be the case given the complexity and rigour of the argumentation he uses to safeguard free will, rationality, obligation, causation – and precious little else. Critics, either endorsing or seeking to go beyond Kant, have rightly pointed out the sparseness of his vision,[10] and there is no doubt at all but that it is the product of a rigorous and puritanical *Weltan-*

schauung. We are really being offered the advice of Luther in philosophic garb: examine your conscience and then act only according to your better self.

A Sense of Order

The title of this section is designed to point to the fact that there is a rapprochement between empiricism and mechanism despite the obvious ways in which they stand opposed to each other. It has already been seen that Kant's concern with the categories of our mind was not such as to lead him to reject the lessons of empiricism. A moment's thought will make us realize that the empiricist tradition did not, as a matter of fact, disintegrate into mere descriptive reporting of sensations; empiricism did not become phenomenology. The reason for this was that the empiricists were attracted to mechanism from the start, as these words of David Hume make clear:

> Could men anatomise nature, according to the most probable, or at least the most intelligible philosophy, they would find, that . . . causes are but the particular fabric and structure of the minute parts of their own bodies and of external objects; and that, by a regular and constant machinery, all the events are produced, about which they are most concerned.[11]

This is to say that the empiricists chose to investigate an orderly structure of the world. Underlying this is an assumption shared with Kant which can best be described by noting a certain illogicality about the approach to ethics of classical empiricist philosophy. If nothing exists but sensation, surely we ought to maximize such sensations: we should eat, drink and be merry in as many ways as we can discover, and as often as we can. What is noticeable in David Hume is the relative orderliness of the sensations he describes; the passions that drive the individual happily lead him towards a settled, moderate and civilized life. Similarly, the utilitarians sought to improve the quality of life in this world in a rather high-minded and ascetic manner. They did not seriously entertain the idea of pleasure-seeking as the chief end of human beings because they had an inbuilt sense of duty. Equally, we have seen that they took for granted the liberal rights of the citizen. Just as Kant did not wish to abandon the empiricist ethic, so the empiricists took for granted many of the things that Kant felt he had to spell out.

All this is to say that there was a certain ethical rapprochement between these sets of thinkers. Utilitarianism had a respect for all individuals; its calculus operated on the basis of an assumption that Kant explicitly justified. Similarly, its passions were as orderly as Kant could have wished. In turn, the British empiricists could welcome Kant's respect for empirical evidence. Kant and the British empiricists inhabited the same world, and merely articulated different parts of it. But to stop at this point would be unsatisfactory since it would ignore certain ways in which the two approaches co-operated in scientific inquiry.[12] These two approaches were allies in the Enlightenment's battle against religion and obscurantism in general; there was a certain coming together as the result of sharing the same enemies. But the nub of the matter lay in a certain division of labour between the two approaches.

Clearly, truly sceptical and rigorous empiricism would undermine science by descending into passive description of events. But to say this is not, for a single moment, to imply thereby that empiricism has no role to play in modern science: its unsettling tendency to reduce the world into a mass of confusing and buzzing feelings, that is, its lack of a decent model of explanation, should not hide its supreme efficacy as a selector or tester of theories. We have already pointed to this role when referring to the manner in which the atomistic metaphysic at the heart of empiricism subtly but totally undermines philosophies and views which seek to survive as unexamined packages. There is, in fact, no certainty among modern philosophers of science about the way in which science functions, and there are some very silly viewpoints on offer which *must* be false given that their epistemologies would not allow science to work – which it very clearly does![13] The seat of much present confusion results from the observation that scientific theories control a surprising amount of their evidence, or, more technically, from the discovery that 'facts' are not pure but are 'theory-laden'. Nevertheless, certain theories have been conclusively, once and for all, disproved by means of empirical evidence. However, the Kantian-type argument stressing that we see the world through our theories also holds water in many and obvious examples. To say this is not to allow that the empiricist injunction is thereby without significance. All theories may control their facts to a certain extent, and some may do so a great deal, but there is no doubt about the wide acceptance of the empiricist injunction that a theory deserves support only if it can marshal factual evidence. As long as theories are used to investigate the world, rather than as safe houses from which one need never stir, scientific knowledge seems to grow.

The final point in need of emphasis about the rapprochement over the nature of science is that mechanism has as important a role to play as does empiricism. Mechanism gives us the model of an explanation that empiricism lacks, and without which modern science would be unimaginable. It is the creation of models, and the testing of their validity, that comprises the scientific enterprise. Mere empiricism would lead to confusion or to endless repetition of the same experiment, while the construction of models without testing would equally by no means guarantee cognitive progress: it is the combination of the two that seems to work.

Kant and Hume are exceptionally powerful thinkers, and we have not yet exhausted the implications of their work for a proper understanding of the nature of science. But even to this point, it is clear that the practices of science and liberalism support each other in three fundamental ways. First, it is worth emphasizing that the ability to ask questions and to seek for explanations was itself dependent upon a relatively liberal society in which a measure of freedom of opinion was respected. Secondly, Hume and Kant wielded powerful weapons of destruction; their cognitive practices undermine established certainties and allow that much more room not just for science but for an open society in general. Finally, it is extremely important to stress that both Hume and Kant do not replace old certainties with ones that are morally equivalent. Kant established a measure of certainty concerning the individual as a rational knowing subject, but the measure was small. Of course, Hume claimed that his work led to an underwriting of much of his social order, but in this he was surely wrong. What matters about empiricism is its fundamental opposition to totalizing ideologies *per se*. This is a contentious matter. Further light can be thrown upon it by means of an analysis of the work of John Stuart Mill.

John Stuart Mill's Real Problem

Mill is generally considered, and with good reason, as the most important single theorist of liberalism. His range of work was huge – from his *Autobiography* to *Principles of Political Economy* and from *The System of Logic* to *Utilitarianism* and *The Subjection of Women* – and its consistently high-powered reasoning is remarkable. As is well known, Mill sought to add to basic Benthamism a fuller appreciation of the capacity of human beings as creative individuals. He was influenced less by Immanuel Kant than by Wilhelm von Humboldt; but this German thinker's notion of *Bildung* – perhaps best translated as the moral development of the personality – had Kantian overtones. Now it is this attempt to improve on basic Benthamism which is often seen as the Mill problem. But much interesting exegesis has resulted in the fairly clear demonstration that he did not add much to or depart far from the initial vision which he received as a child; this problem has been much exaggerated. But there is a second Mill problem: did his thought justify licence or brainwashing?

The first of these positions focuses on his *On Liberty*, a defence of freedom that has rightly received canonical status within the liberal tradition. The arguments of this treatise are well known, and they remain moving:

The object of this Essay is to assert one very simple principle . . . that the sole end for which mankind are warranted, individually or collectively, in interfering with the liberty of action of any of their number, is self-protection. That the only purpose for which power can be rightfully exercised over any member of a civilised community, against his will, is to prevent harm to others. His own good, either physical or moral, is not a sufficient warrant. He cannot rightfully be compelled to do or forbear because it will be better for him to do so, because it will make him happier, because in the opinions of others, to do so would be wise, or even right. These are good reasons for remonstrating with him, or reasoning with him, or persuading him, or entreating him, but not for compelling him, or visiting him with any evil in case he do otherwise. To justify that, the conduct from which it is desired to deter him, must be calculated to produce evil to someone else. The only part of the conduct of anyone, for which he is amenable to society, is that which concerns others. In the part which merely concerns himself, his independence is, of right, absolute. Over himself, over his own body and mind, the individual is sovereign.[14]

A considerable part of the emotional force of *On Liberty* results from a perceived threat to the sovereign individual. Mill, perhaps as the result of adopting the more romantic views of Harriet Taylor, suggested that there was a danger of social conformity such that the truly outstanding individual could be silenced by some sort of tyranny of the majority. The passage cited might give the impression that Mill felt it necessary to produce some theory of human natural rights in order to defend the individual. But in fact his utilitarian preconceptions were so deeply rooted as to close off this Kantian route to him, and the defence of individual liberty takes on an entirely different character. Society will benefit from such freedom in intellectual terms – and these terms are implicitly held to be related to the larger success of society. Thus we should not suppress a

view in case it is right and our own wrong; if a view is wrong, however, we should still not suppress it since it is only in debate that we sharpen our position and make it live. There should, in other words, be sustained debate very largely for epistemological reasons.

It is only recently that Mill's argument has been accused of leading to libertinism.[15] This accusation suggests that Mill is envisaging a world in which anything goes, and in which one can 'do one's own thing'. The charge, in a nutshell, is that Mill is tacitly embracing relativism and abandoning any objective morality. There seems to me no real justification for such an interpretation of *On Liberty* since Mill envisages intellectual debate *in order that the best idea may actually win*. None the less, the treatise *is* a sustained attempt to protect the individual; it is this which gives exceptional pungency to a second interpretation of Mill.

The interpretation in question is that of Maurice Cowling's *Mill and Liberalism*.[16] This polemic asserts sharply that Mill was not really in favour of freedom at all, and it offers several considerations in defence of this heresy. Most obviously, Mill was continuously fascinated, most obviously in *Considerations on Representative Government*, with electoral matters, and a keen advocate of weighting the electoral system – which was to exclude a large proportion of people 'unfit' to vote – so that the voice of 'the educated' could be heard. Such a line of argument in fact follows rather naturally from his fear of the majority. If the majority were muddled at best, vicious at worst, then they were scarcely likely to read and be influenced by such a high-minded tract, let alone understand, as Mill thought necessary, the laws of political economy; hence the educated needed a realistic mechanism by means of which to protect themselves. Cowling also points out that Mill, for all his protestations about the desirability of a pluralistic schooling system, never doubted the necessity for 'a general improvement of morals', and this view of the 'illiberal', moralizing tendency of nineteenth-century British thought, and in particular its relation to state-building, has been made much of in a remarkable recent book by Philip Corrigan and Derek Sayer, two Marxisant authors poles apart from Cowling's wildly idiosyncratic conservatism.[17] Mill did wish to extend the provision of state schooling in order morally to 'integrate' the 'masses' into 'society'; he did *not*, in other words, plan to leave people as they were but rather planned to mould them in a very decided manner. Finally, Cowling even queries the depth of Mill's commitment to dissentient intellectual opinion. Once all the scientific methods recommended in *The System of Logic* had been used to resolve a particular dispute, did it not behove the proponent of the defeated opinion to see the error of his ways?

To stress only one of these poles seems to me absolutely to misunderstand John Mill. Both are present. Cowling is correct in his observations. Mill was a social reformer and as such sought to create the human material to man a particular type of social order: he wished to spread literacy, remove poverty and destroy the gin palaces of the new urban centres. He sought to spread what a recent author has termed an 'extended code' of language and citizen-ship.[18] If we look at the whole question from the other point of view we can see that the liberal society of free debate that Mill admired could work only if the right sort of human material was available, prepared to debate openly and without recourse to force when defeated. Such an institutional frame is exceptionally rare in history, and it is scarcely surprising that Mill was prepared to accept that it might have to be engineered.

However, Cowling does not consider everything; his argument suffers from grievous sins of omission. There remains something highly distinctive about the world which Mill was trying to create, and we can highlight exactly what it was by recalling his study of *Comte and Positivism*. Mill had admired the early Comte, but became more and more distant from the French sociologist as Comte moved towards setting up a permanent clerisy in which the enlightened few would rule. Mill rejected this view in Comte, and he rejected it equally firmly in certain of his contemporaries. If he was creating a world, it remained a distinctive world in which, within prescribed limits, genuinely open debate would be possible and in which the individual would have the right institutional surround in which to 'develop'. A social order was to be created in which, in a nutshell, the intellectuals would not have permanent control of power or opinion. This is not to deny his tinkering with electoral politics, merely to place it within a proper perspective.

The case being made deserves summary. Mill's praise for liberty was slightly disingenuous and exaggerated. He did think that an open society had certain virtues, *but this is not to say that he was 'open-minded' about everything*. Specifically, he took for granted that there was a social framework within which uncertainty could be best dealt with, and which would allow for intellectual progress. Mill's argument amounts to providing an epistemological underpinning to liberalism. This underpinning is, in a sense, negative: we must respect the right to question in an open society because we cannot know everything. However, *On Liberty* contains other arguments, not always properly spelled out, which support Mill's general view of liberalism. Mill's case is not simply a facilitative one, i.e. that certain arrangements will allow for cognitive growth; it does not necessarily depend, in other words, on the negative notion that nobody knows everything, and that we should therefore turn uncertainty into a positive virtue. The notion of *Bildung* has importance at this point. An open society is an end in itself because it is a necessary condition for the moral development of the individual. Mill sought, in other words, to go beyond the fact that we are individuals to a notion of individuality, i.e. a view which stressed that the individual could develop an identity and thereby move beyond mere egoism so as to become a responsible member of an open society. This is the height of liberal optimism.

All this is to say that there is an answer to Mill's second problem. But a third problem arises from this that Mill was not able to deal with at all. The fact that Mill was creating a world meant that he had to try and justify it, i.e. to find some way of grounding his preferences for this particular way of conducting our social and epistemological life. Mill was optimistic about being able to provide such justification. That Mill's liberalism represents a high point of confidence can be particularly clearly seen in his *Considerations on Representative Government*. It is well known that this book is schizophrenic in its division between a plan for personal moral development and the desire to create institutions designed to prevent the abuse of power. I do not see anything wrong with *trying* to combine these two values.[19] How striking is the optimism and democratic feeling in Mill's belief that all are capable of being able to participate in this liberal social order! And what a social order! Mill's society contains not just free speech, but human moral development and a parliamentary system. Nevertheless, it is certainly true that Mill offers anything but a really firm combination of these factors, and this is neatly captured in the formulation proposed by Collini, Winch and Burrow:

[T]he old question concerning the logical status of the premises about human behaviour from which at various points thereafter he deduces the need for certain kinds of institutions then comes back to haunt him. There is a pervasive ambiguity in the book on this point: it purports to consider the arguments for the various features of representative government *sub specie aeternitas*, and yet one has the nagging feeling that a society bearing an alarming resemblance to Britain circa 1860 is being assumed throughout. In fact, the fourth chapter explicitly excludes most known historical societies as unsuitable . . .[20]

This can be put in another way. Mill felt that his prescriptions were firmly based upon a proper description of the natural propensities of mankind; he believed, in other words, that a consideration of human history would allow him to sift out the genuine characteristics of an ideal–

29

typical human being. In fact, this noble vision is essentially prescriptive for a straightforward reason. Mill's planned 'science of ethology', that is, his view of human nature considered in the light of history, was never forthcoming. We are thus offered a picture of the good society without firm ontological rooting. At the end of a consideration of Mill's work, one is left in a position in which liberalism is but one ideology amongst others.

Conclusion: The Spectre of Relativism

A moment's reflection makes it obvious that not just Mill but also Hume and Kant were not, as they thought, describing human nature, but a measured, calculative and puritanical type of social character. This raises a terrible question for liberals. *Why* should we be puritanical accountants? Wordsworth certainly scorned this ethic and spoke scathingly, in his sonnet 'The World is too much with us', of how 'getting and spending we lay waste our powers'. Elsewhere he offered this advice:

> Give all thou cans't; High heaven rejects the lore
> Of nicely calculated less and more.[21]

Is not Karl Marx right to attack an insipid view, the dull dream of deadly bureaucrats? Liberal morality scarcely warms the heart like wine, at least for those with more romantic yearnings.

The theories of Kant, Hume and Mill are prescriptive rather than descriptive. This means that science is based on cognitive *norms*.[22] We have seen this particularly clearly in the case of empiricism. This cognitive style – for it is a style, an ethic, rather than something somehow written into the law of nature – *presumes*, i.e. it takes for granted in an *a priori* way, an atomistic quality to the world. There is no absolute defence available for this position, although it seems to me to have a certain inherent plausibility. It may be that empiricism falsifies reality: facts may not be separable from each other and the world might be some sort of glutinous mass. Similarly, it may be that the world does *not* function according to the orderly Protestant terms that Kant specifically ascribed to our minds; if this is so, it is unlikely, if we accept Kant's general position, that we will ever understand reality.

This means that we are faced with the spectre of relativism. If there are different and alternate worlds, then how is it possible to say that one is preferable to another? In this situation, thought has two possible options. One option is simply that of accepting relativism, of saying that this is our vision, that we are used to it and like it, and intend to defend it against all comers. There can be a brutal self-awareness about this position which lends it an air of appeal. But its general drive is, of course, absolute anathema to liberals. What *right* do liberals have to tell others to behave? To boss people around and to indoctrinate them is surely a travesty of the most basic of liberal aims.

It is probably a positive advantage to recognize openly the presence of competing visions. Such recognition will force us to search for reasons why we should choose between various options. The obvious reason for adopting science is simple. We should (and in fact do) accept the cognitive norms of empiricism and mechanism because they have been responsible for a type of sustained scientific advance that eluded the primitive belief-system of magic – just as it surely would any 'Wordsworthian' scientist. Might is right in this area, not least for the excellent moral reason that modern science has the capacity to deliver a high standard of living.

To put matters this way is to raise an extremely important problem. To speak about norms is to imply a society. But who belongs to the society which pays attention to the cognitive norms in question? What does it mean to say, as I have just done, that *we* accept cognitive norms? Obviously, the ideal of liberalism is precisely that everyone should share these norms. But a different strategy is in principle possible. The norms in question could be reserved to a body of scientists separate from the rest of society; it might be possible, in other words, to combine high levels of technology with a morality derived from some totalizing ideology. Such a combination is likely to have especial appeal to those societies which did not in the first place have any notable measure of freedom of opinion and which complain, in a sense rightly, that the morality engendered by science/liberalism is, so to speak, thin and bloodless. It takes only a moment's thought to realize that fascism represents such a combination, as do attempts to combine Islam with technology in the modern world. Both these combinations habitually consider science as mere technology, and relegate it to a mere means. However, it is also sometimes claimed that a totalizing ideology is justified on scientific grounds: this occasionally occurs with fascism, but is most fully the case with Marxism.

It is now possible to draw the argument to a close. It has been argued that empiricism and mechanism depended upon the proto-liberalism of a civilization which respected freedom of opinion and the right to raise questions; these techniques then provided the means that led to a further institutionalizing of liberalism. However, other civilizations did not have this background, and it is immediately apparent that they may wish to combine technological power with the preservation of customary belief. There is no logical nexus, as Mill had claimed, between the two. This leads to the interesting and open question as to whether it is possible to segregate scientists in the manner noted over an extended period of time. Liberalism clearly wishes the nexus with science to be restored or, better, more firmly cemented. For this to take place, it will be necessary to show that alternative visions are neither morally superior nor sociologically practical.

NOTES

1. J. Milton, 'The Origin of the concept "Laws of Nature"', *European Journal of Sociology*, 22 (1982); P. Crone and M. Cook, *Hagarism* (Cambridge: Cambridge University Press, 1977).

2. L. Greenfeld, 'In the Service of the Nation: An Alternative Explanation of the Institutionalisation of Modern Science', forthcoming in *Minerva*, 25 (1987).

3. E. Gellner, *Legitimation of Belief* (Cambridge: Cambridge University Press, 1974). I am heavily indebted to this book throughout this chapter. For a commentary on Gellner's social philosophy, see my *Diagnoses of Our Time* (London: Heinemann Educational, 1981).

4. D. Hume, *A Treatise of Human Nature: Being an Attempt to introduce the experimental Method of Reasoning into Moral Subjects* (Harmondsworth: Penguin, 1985), p.316.

5. The views of John Mill and Bertrand Russell are cited and analysed in David Miller's lucid and helpful *Philosophy and Ideology in Hume's Political Thought* (Oxford: Oxford University Press, 1981), p.13. The clearest expression of the view of the Frankfurt School in this matter remains Herbert Marcuse's *Reason and Revolution*, 2nd edition (London: Routledge and Kegan Paul, 1969).

6. D. Hume, *An Inquiry concerning Human Understanding*, in *Essays, Literary, Moral and Political* (Chicago: Henry Regnery, 1965), p.173.

7. For this revealing story, see E. C. Mossner, *The Life of David Hume* (Oxford: Oxford University Press, 1954).

8. Gellner, op. cit., p.187.

9. I. Kant, *Groundwork of the Metaphysic of Morals*, in H. J. Paton, *The Moral Law* (London: Hutchinson, 1978), p.75.

10. M. J. Sandel, *Liberalism and the Limits of Justice* (Cambridge: Cambridge University Press, 1982).

11. Hume, *A Treatise of Human Nature*, op. cit., p.209.

12. In this whole discussion of rapprochement I am drawing heavily on Gellner, op. cit.

13. I am thinking here of Thomas Kuhn's *The Structure of Scientific Revolutions* (Chicago: University of Chicago Press, 1962). Kuhn argued that scientists live in and through their paradigms, and this position effectively made him a relativist. However, Kuhn clearly prefers some paradigms rather than others – most notably that of Einstein in preference to that of Newton. His preferences are right, and his epistemology, despite its many striking virtues, ultimately wrong.

14. J. S. Mill, *On Liberty* (Oxford: Oxford University Press, 1966), pp.14–15.

15. G. Himmelfarb, *On Liberty and Liberalism: The Case of John Stuart Mill* (New York: Knopf, 1974).

16. M. Cowling, *Mill and Liberalism* (Cambridge: Cambridge University Press, 1971).

17. P. Corrigan and D. Sayer, *The Great Arch* (Oxford: Basil Blackwell, 1985).

18. B. Bernstein, *Class, Codes and Control*, 3 vols (London: Routledge and Kegan Paul, 1971–5).

19. The accusation of inconsistency in *Considerations on Representative Government* is made particularly clearly by J. Dunn in his *Western Political Theory in the Face of the Future* (Cambridge: Cambridge University Press, 1979), p.52.

20. S. Collini, D. Winch and J. Burrow, *That Noble Science of Politics* (Cambridge: Cambridge University Press, 1983), p.153.

21. W. Wordsworth. 'Inside of King's College Chapel, Cambridge', *Ecclesiastical Sonnets*, 111, xliii, in E. Dowden (ed.), *The Poetical Works of Wordsworth*, Vol. 4 (London: Bell and Sons, 1905), p.133.

22. In the rest of this chapter I draw upon E. Gellner, 'An Ethic of Cognition', in his *Spectacles and Predicaments* (Cambridge: Cambridge University Press, 1979). Cf. J. A. Hall, Haberinas and Gellner on Epistemology and Politics, or, Need We Feel Disenchanted?', *Philosophy of Social Sciences*, 12 (1982).

2
COMMERCE AND LIBERTY

There is little agreement as to the chronological point at which the history of liberalism as a social and political movement begins. The epithet 'liberal' was first used in 1812 to describe a Spanish political party. However, varying attempts have been made to discover a more venerable ancestry. Perhaps the most interesting attempt has been Gore Vidal's argument, in his novel *Creation*, that a fundamental softness of life was most clearly available in the high cultures of pre-industrial empires before the emergence of those world religions whose universalist monotheism he sees, with some justification, as inherently totalitarian.[1] There is much sociological sense here: pre-industrial rule was incapable of controlling civil society to any marked extent while, in the long run, monotheism's egalitarianism towards members of a society was counterbalanced by deeming other societies to be altogether outside the pale of civilization.[2] Nevertheless, this view is, on balance, too eccentric: the hierarchical nature of belief systems before the emergence of the great religions offends too deeply against the core intent of liberalism, and it is proper to see Christianity as playing a key part in 'the discovery of the individual', i.e. in treating each individual as of equal spiritual worth.[3] A further and crucial uniqueness of the West may well lie in that concept of freedom which arose – ironically, as Orlando Patterson has shown – out of the dialectics of slavery: only a society based on slavery has fully elaborated the notion of freedom.[4] Finally, it is worth remembering that the concept of toleration, so central to liberalism's insistence that the individual choose his own purposes in life, developed out of the wars of religion that decimated European civilization in the sixteenth and seventeenth centuries.[5]

A history of liberalism would have to evaluate these contributions. But attention here will be focused on the nature of the relationship between liberalism and capitalism, not least for the simple reason that liberalism has, as we shall now see, considered capitalism a suitable means to achieve its own ends. I shall concentrate most on the claim that there is a relationship between commerce and liberty. Montesquieu's work centres on this, as does that of Richard Cobden and a whole galaxy of thinkers who insist that trading nations tend to be constitutional and free. This is obviously a highly contentious assertion. On the one hand, Karl Marx and those indebted to his work, including Arblaster, insist that capitalism is a threat to liberty, that the formal freedoms of liberal society mask exploitation which can be ended only by abolishing capitalism and creating substantive freedom.[6] On the other hand, those modern conservative thinkers who confusingly call themselves liberals have claimed to accept the equation, and have insisted bluntly that freedom and capitalism always go in tandem.[7] The position that I shall develop in this book will argue that capitalism can help but may hinder liberal aims.

In order to cast some light on the whole matter, a detailed discussion of one of the clearest proponents of the view in question suggests itself; this will allow assessment of arguments for and against the liberty-with-commerce equation. So let us consider Adam Smith. The purpose of this discussion is not, it should be noted, to present a fully rounded portrait of Smith; it is rather that of drawing upon recent, high-powered scholarship of the Scottish Enlightenment in order to underline key issues which must be at the centre of our attention throughout this book.

Wealth and Virtue

The thinkers of the Scottish Enlightenment were exceptionally sophisticated, and were well aware of the nature of the intellectual enterprise upon which they were engaged. In particular, they sought to distance themselves from the mainstream assumptions about politics and society prevalent in their day. They sought to replace a tradition concerned with virtue with a new one focusing on wealth; we need to understand their reasons for this.[8]

The tradition of civic virtue has its roots in the Greek city states, and it received a new lease of life at the hands of the intellectuals of Rome and of the northern Italian city states of the Renaissance. The model of a virtuous man is the citizen of a city state who participates in civic or 'political' affairs. It is very important to note that such citizenship depended upon, and was seen to depend upon, living a frugal and orderly life so that it was thereby possible to serve in the militia: it was very largely through popular participation in infantry warfare that rights of citizenship were first gained. This image of republican nobility and simplicity was attached to a theory of history. The state was held to be safe as long as the citizens remained virtuous; but virtue is transient, and a cyclical motion affects society whereby virtue is followed by corruption, and thence again by a moral revival. It was in the light of this theory that Polybius wrote of the movement of Roman politics, and Machiavelli of the fate of Italian city states.

Smith and Hume refused to endorse the civilization of the ancient Greek world on the grounds that it was dependent upon slavery; they would not accord this civilization the status of a model since it was based upon exploitation. As I consider the core of liberalism to lie in its respect for the moral worth of every individual, this seems to me wholly admirable. This is why this discussion of liberalism's social and political theory begins with eighteenth-century thinkers rather than, say, the pre-Socratics. However, it is certainly not my intention to limit discussion, and the extent to which this is a good starting point for liberalism, and most particularly the extent to which liberalism is right to connect itself with capitalism, will be kept constantly under review.

The rejection of the tradition of civic humanism was not only dependent upon a rejection of slavery. The eighteenth-century aristocratic elite, which had the civic humanist tradition as its principal political language, was not based upon slavery. But eighteenth-century Britain had much poverty, and the aristocratic elite tended to scorn 'the dangerous classes'. Poverty was as much disliked as slavery by members of the Scottish Enlightenment, and a baseline of their position was a desire to see all human beings provided with some sort of sufficiency. This is to say that a moral stance lay behind the adoption of a particular mechanism, a point worth making since the mechanism itself does not work according to moral principles. We can see this fundamental moral stance clearly in Smith's famous comment on the situation of the poorly paid labourer of Chinese civilization, whose static nature Smith deplored quite as much as did Karl Marx:

The poverty of the lower ranks of people in China far surpasses that of the most beggarly nations in Europe. In the neighbourhood of Canton many hundred, it is commonly said, many thousand families have no habitation on the land, but live constantly in little fishing boats upon the rivers and canals. The subsistence which they find there is so scanty that they are eager to fish up the nastiest garbage thrown overboard from any European ship. Any carrion, the carcase of a dead dog or cat, for example, though half putrid and stinking, is as welcome to them as the most wholesome food to the people of other countries. Marriage is encouraged in China, not by the profitableness of children, but by the liberty of destroying them. In all great towns several are every night exposed in the street, or drowned like puppies in the water. The performance of this horrid office is even said to be the avowed business by which some people earn their subsistence.[9]

38

The tone of moral outrage in this passage is unmistakable. Furthermore, the general point can be made equally firmly in slightly different ways. The central argument of *The Wealth of Nations* is that value, as Marx so stressed, rests upon labour: this is to talk about a contribution of 'workers' rather than the fecklessness of 'the dangerous classes'. Furthermore, Smith's sympathy for labour can be clearly seen in his fear that the character of labour in a commercial civilization might lead to a type of 'mental mutilation', a fear which has naturally been compared with Marx's early writings on the alienation of labour under capitalism.[10]

It is worth pausing to stress how remarkable was the rejection of civic humanism by Smith, Hume and many of their fellows. The scorn of Maynard Keynes for the acquisition of riches – 'a disgusting morbidity' in his view – is well known, but it is insufficiently appreciated that he was here, as elsewhere, merely echoing his Scottish predecessor. Smith had extremely harsh words for the evil effects of vanity. More important still, he believed that riches could not protect the individual from the real difficulties flesh is heir to:

They keep off the summer shower, not the winter storm, but leave him always as much, and sometimes more exposed than before, to anxiety, to fear, and to sorrow; to diseases, to danger, and to death.[11]

Nevertheless, these personal reservations did not make Smith blind to the fact that commercial society had the capacity to help the poor. Smith felt that various costs to commercial society were worth paying, especially as various reforms, notably an expansion of education together with service in the militia, would ease the situation. One reason for Smith's judgement was simply their insistence that commercial society would allow all to be properly fed. But much more than this was involved, and we must now turn to Smith's political theory so as to describe the manner in which commercial society was judged to be able to create liberal political rule.

Passion, Politics and Diamond Buckles

Samuel Johnson thought that 'there are few ways in which a man can be more innocently employed than in getting money'.[12] This seems an exceptionally odd sentiment to a post-Marxist age, but it is an important example of the main justification for the new liberal politics. There is no doubt that Johnson, one of the few major figures of the intellectual world of his time to have a genuine sense of tragedy, appreciated deeply the power of a range of human passions – indeed, he once shocked Adam Smith by falling to his knees in public to recite the Lord's Prayer, his characteristic method of avoiding the onset of madness. This makes his dictum comprehensible. The human mind was seen as being comprised of a set of forces whose power often made them unamenable to reason. When a particular passion was unleashed, however, there was something that we could do: we could try to counter its force by bringing another passion into play so as to diminish its intensity. Thus envy might be controlled by playing upon our own sense of pride. The general message is clear: if we cannot change human nature, we may at least be able to manage it. Crucially, money-making was seen as a 'calm' or 'soft' passion that would take the mind away from the gratifications that came from ruling other people. A social order which took money-making seriously thereby allowed for softer, more regular political life.

David Hume certainly saw the mind in these terms, even though he lacked Johnson's sense of the visceral power of passion. Adam Smith's ultimate originality in the history of ideas probably lies in the fact that he slowly undermined this subtle and neglected position, by reducing, in *The Theory of Moral Sentiments*, all the various passions to self-interest.[13] Nevertheless, Smith gave us the classical statement of the trading off of passions against each other in so far as it concerned the balance of activities, not within the human mind but within society. He tells us that David Hume shared his view that commerce was not just helpful in maintaining orderly but liberal government, but rather was the original creator of liberal rule.

Smith believed that history progressed through various stages quite as much as did Karl Marx, and it can be argued that his theory is in crucial respects superior to that of the German thinker. Most obviously, Smith has room in his scheme for pastoralism, where Marx does not. More importantly, the particular transition described in Book 3 of *The Wealth of Nations*, between agrarian and commercial society in north-west Europe after the fall of Rome, is distinctively characterized as something accidental and miraculous rather than necessary and unilinear. This is certainly the proper light in which to see the emergence of the modern world.[14] Smith is particularly concerned to explain the emergence of rule-bound societies since the absence of predation is a condition without which economic advance is impossible. The emergence of the rule of law, in Smith's explanation, is held to be the result of the relative weakness of the medieval monarch who, in order to gain revenue and in order to distance himself from baronial power, i.e. to make himself more than one among equals, allowed towns to purchase their independence. This small change is held to have had an enormous impact upon the feudal nobility. The king alone was incapable of controlling baronial power and of establishing the rule of law; he had insufficient military strength to counteract the barons when they were united, as King John discovered in 1215. But what the king could not achieve became a possibility as the result of the luxury goods produced by the productive and autonomous city. Hitherto, rich barons would spend their money – indeed *could only* spend their money – on the purchase of retainers. Smith waxed eloquent upon the way in which the production of luxuries, subtly and acciden-tally, changed the situation:

41

[C]ommerce and manufactures . . . gradually furnished the great proprietors with something for which they could exchange the whole surplus produce of their lands, and which they could consume themselves without sharing it either with tenants or retainers. All for ourselves and nothing for other people, seems, in every age of the world, to have been the vile maxim of the masters of mankind. As soon therefore, as they could find a method of consuming the whole value of their rents themselves, they had no disposition to share them with any other persons. For a pair of diamond buckles perhaps, or for something as frivolous and useless, they exchanged the maintenance, or what is the same thing, the price of the maintenance of a thousand men for a year, and with it the whole weight and authority which it could give them. The buckles, however, were to be all their own, and no other human creature was to have any share of them; whereas in the more ancient method of expense they must have shared with at least a thousand people. With the judges that were to determine this preference was perfectly decisive; and thus, for the gratifica-tion of the most childish, the meanest, and the most sordid of all vanities, they gradually bartered their whole power and authority.[15]

Smith rubs the point home that this process was not achieved by enlightened and rational action, but by the unintended consequences of very selfish social actors:

A revolution of the greatest importance to the public happiness was in this manner brought about by two different orders of people who had not the least intention to serve the public. To gratify the most childish vanity was the sole motive of the great proprietors. The merchants and artificers, much less ridiculous, acted merely from a view to their own interest . . . Neither of them had either knowledge or foresight of that great revolution which the folly of the one, and the industry of the other, was gradually bringing about.[16]

Even simple reflection shows how subtle is Smith's argu-ment and, more particularly, how very far removed it is from any naïve economic determinism. It is important to stress this since many commentators, including modern conservatives calling themselves liberals, have drawn atten-tion only to the last stage in Smith's account, namely the stage at which laissez-faire politics allows the economy to flourish. But we can now see that behind those politics lies the dissolution of power and glory by the productive city of the Middle Ages, and behind that the parcellization of sovereignty which called into being the autonomous city in the first instance: the causal chain at work, in other words, does not uniquely privilege economics.

There are extraordinary features to Smith's argument. Most obvious is the savage irony with which Smith treats the emergence of the rule of law: this was less the result of moral development than of the fortunate accidental result of base motives. Nevertheless, Smith's general contention is not in doubt. One particular blessing of commerce is its capacity to bring in its tail liberal political rule. Commerce is not always lovely or virtuous in its own right and it has many unfortunate side-effects. But it has an 'elective affinity' with liberal political rule, and that is what matters. There are, in other words, excellent moral reasons for approving of commercial society.

The Nature of the Wealth of Nations

The first chapter of *The Wealth of Nations* presents the famous paean to productivity. A single worker, forced to undertake every process involved in pin production, from mining to packing, might produce a pin a day. In contrast, the same man benefiting from the division of labour – the motor of productivity – would be capable of producing 4800 pins in the same period of time. This is well known; it is also true. But it is only one of the basic principles upon which Smith's economics rests. Equally central to his vision is the praise given to the market principle itself. The individual can choose for himself what he wants, and can conduct business with strangers on the basis of interest rather than of collective solidarity of any sort. Finally, it is well worth noting that there is an international dimension to Smith's argument. If rich nations avoided mercantilist 'errors of police' (to use Smith's words), there was no reason to believe that they could not continue to prosper.

It was perfectly acceptable that certain jobs should be taken over by countries with a comparative advantage in labour costs; the future of rich nations did not lie in cutting wages, but in increasing them so as to be able to produce, often by means of new technologies, more specialized and sophisticated goods. Rich nations could serve poor ones in this manner; the international economy could expand indefinitely so that world politics would not need to be conducted on a zero-sum basis.[17]

Two critical points must be made to bring out the presuppositions that lie behind these claims. First, Smith had decided views about the character of European civilization that made productivity possible. Shortly after his death, his friend Dugald Stewart reported that Smith had believed that:

[I]t was the general diffusion of wealth among the lower orders of men, which first gave birth to the spirit of independence in modern Europe, and which has produced under some of its governments, and especially under our own, a more equal diffusion of freedom and of happiness than took place under the most celebrated constitutions of antiquity.[18]

Stewart goes on to say that it was this diffusion of wealth among the people which accounted, in Smith's eyes, for the rapid diffusion of printing and literacy. Smith praised the virtues of the market but he was aware that, so to speak, you needed the right background to be able to participate in the market; only a particular type of citizenry had the capacity to flourish in this environment. There is an obvious resonance between this point and that right to question which provided a framework within which science could emerge, although Smith was rather more aware of the proto-liberalism of European society than were his epistemological colleagues. Smith's argument at this point has been lent much support by contemporary economic historians concerned to explain the economic dynamism that came to characterize European society. They point to a proto-industrial stage in European development which would be incomprehensible without a recognition of the energies of large numbers of people throughout society. Morever, it was these people, possessed of a certain amount of wealth, who created the high level of demand without which the industrial revolution would not later have been possible. The question of the right sort of human material for modern society will introduce complications for modern liberalism. Adam Smith did not have to think through a situation in which the requisite type of citizens had to be created rather than simply appreciated. Later in this book, Smith's views about the necessity of some diffusion of wealth in order that the market may work will seem important and full of resonance for contemporary life: the ethic to be derived from Adam Smith is one that allows for *entitlements*, something that has been utterly ignored by some of his professed recent admirers.

However, there is no doubt about how dated are his views on the second point in question. Smith wrote before the French Revolution, and his conception of liberty has in consequence very little to do with modern understanding of that term. Liberty for him meant soft political rule, i.e. freedom of opinion, the rule of law and a very few other, and circumscribed, matters. For all his sympathy with labour, Smith was not a democrat, and he had no experience of the entry of the people on to the political stage. His theory of society saw hierarchy working in tandem with capitalism, and *The Theory of Moral Sentiments* argued that this was the result of a natural propensity of the human mind. The lower orders would seek to emulate those above them; they would not seek to change the rules of the game in such a way that the freedom of capitalists, to invest and to take profits, would be removed. Capitalism went naturally with hierarchy. Smith never had to actually *defend* hierarchy: he produced a sociological, or 'natural jurisprudential', account of something which he considered to be firmly in place. Edmund Burke, whom Smith considered to

45

have reached similar conclusions about economic life without communication having passed between them, *was* forced to defend hierarchy.[19] As this defence of hierarchy was not intellectually powerful, capitalism was left with a besetting question: how was capitalism, which engendered social inequality, to be combined with the entry of the people on to the political stage?

Politics, Liberalism and the Market

Smith once said that he valued opulence *and* freedom. In what senses does this combination of values deserve to be called liberal? Let us consider both politics and the market. In doing so we shall learn something more about the nature of Smith's argument, and this too will prove relevant to our general consideration of liberalism. Most importantly, it is absolutely clear that Smith was a central member of that intellectual school, whose views have been identified, which admired capitalism because it served to control more vicious political passions. This is particularly apparent in Book 3 of *The Wealth of Nations*, where the role of the rise of commerce in establishing the rule of law is welcomed. There is no doubt that Smith appreciated the rule of law and freedom of expression as things to be valued in their own right, and a part of his praise for capitalism was given because it was such an efficient means to those ends. The mechanisms accounting for the rise of capitalism – and for its characteristic mode of operation – were amoral, but the reasons Smith had for adopting them were the result of a liberal moral stance.

This is a characteristically liberal position since it seeks to prevent the individual being subject to the exercise of arbitrary power. There is everything to be said on behalf of this position. Human beings face a permanent political problem because they are all too capable of oppressing each other. However, this assertion would not be accepted by all who have called themselves liberal. Nineteenth-century neo-classical economics lost much of Smith's appreciation of the danger of political power, and Herbert Spencer went so far as to toy with the hope that civil society might become so developed that the state would no longer need to exist.[20] As is well known, this is an idea that Karl Marx, despite his many other criticisms of the economic theory of capitalism, swallowed wholesale, as is apparent in his notion that the state would entirely 'wither away'. At the bottom of Marx's position was the view that the freedoms of capitalist society were merely formal, and that 'true' freedom would result from the establishment of a society in which economic exploitation – as much the sole source of evil in his mind as free exchange was of virtue in Spencer's – was abolished. Unfortunately for Marxism, it is entirely possible, both in principle and in practice, to have political suppression in combination with substantive equality, just as it is also possible to have political freedom with debilitating social inequalities. The problem that faces liberalism is precisely of trying to secure affluence *and* freedom.

The views of Marx and Spencer are mirror-images of each other. Both are excessively economistic and have little to recommend them. In contrast, Smith belonged to a tradition of thought which insisted that political passion could be as dangerous as exploitation by the rich, and the history of the twentieth century, and notably the fact that Hitler and Stalin were not 'in it for the money', would seem to suggest that there is everything to be said on behalf of this view. The tenets of the school as a whole deserve the final encapsulation they received at the hands of Maynard Keynes, a spiritual descendant of the Scottish Enlightenment whose own experience made it impossible to ignore the power of passion:

[D]angerous human proclivities can be canalised into comparatively harmless channels by the existence of opportunities for money-making and private wealth, which, if they cannot be satisfied in this way, may find their outlet in cruelty, the reckless pursuit of personal power and authority, and other forms of self-aggrandisement. It is better that a man should tyrannise over his

47

bank balance than over his fellow-citizens; and whilst the former is sometimes denounced as being but a means to the latter, sometimes at least it is an alternative.[21]

Something further is said in the next section of this chapter about the beneficial sociological consequences of recognizing that political power can have an autonomous effect upon history. But let us turn here immediately to a second liberal quality of Smith's argument. One reason that Smith praised the market was because of its economic efficacy, that is, because it was a fine mechanism for producing wealth. In his own time, there is no doubt that the emergence of capitalism increased the *substantive* freedoms of the people. The most serious defences of a continuing link between capitalism and liberalism, notably those of Maynard Keynes and Raymond Aron, centre themselves on the efficacy of the market; whether or not capitalism *is* efficacious in this way will be the subject of later consideration. It is important to stress again, however, that Smith believed that the market had proved so beneficial in European history because so many had been able to participate in it: this was made possible by the fact that even the lowly had a measure of wealth and property. It is not, in other words, simply that the market is a good means with which to care for basic needs but rather that it works well when people have the capacity to use the market.

This latter point is not without relevance for the next element of Smith's thought that deserves to be called liberal. If so far we have seen Smith praising the market for essentially pragmatic reasons, he also gave a liberal defence of the market in its own terms. Benjamin Constant memorably theorized the distinction between what have here been termed the traditions of wealth and virtue:

Liberty is every man's right to be subject to the law alone, the right of not being arrested, tried, put to death or in any way molested, by the caprice of one or more individuals. It is every one's right to express his own opinion, to attend to his own art, to come and go, to associate with others. It is, lastly, every one's right to influence the administration of the state either by nominating all or some of its officers, or by his advice, demands and petitions, which the authorities are in a greater or less degree obliged to take into account.

Let us compare this liberty with that of the ancients. That consisted in the collective but direct exercise of many privileges of sovereignty, deliberating upon the public welfare, upon war and peace, voting upon laws, pronouncing judgement, examining accounts and so forth; but while the ancients regarded this as constituting liberty, they held that all this was compatible with the subjection of the individual to the power of the community . . . Among the ancients, the individual, a sovereign in public affairs, is a slave in private relations. Among the moderns, on the contrary, the individual, independent in his private life, is even in the freest states a sovereign only in appearance. His sovereignty is restricted, and almost always suspended, and if now and again he exercises it, he does so only in order to renounce it.[22]

The modern, liberal conception of 'negative' liberty has a natural affinity with choice in the market. If the individual is sovereign, there is no other source of judgement capable of dictating to him any particular standard of need or taste. Although Smith would not have accepted Constant's application of this sort of doctrine to political life, it is obvious that there is a natural parallel between economic choice in the market and democratic choice via representative democracy.[23]

An important consideration follows from this discussion of the relationship between economics and politics in liberalism. In so far as capitalism was but a means to the rule of law and to the provision of a decent economic sufficiency, it deserved to have the approval of liberals. However, if circumstances changed and capitalism were no longer to provide a suitable means to such liberal goals, it could not be looked upon with such favour by liberals. There is a sense in which Smith was himself arguing something very similar to this. *The Wealth of Nations*, it must be remembered, was designed as a handbook for the legislator. In that treatise, Smith warned about the predatory instincts of tradesmen and merchants; they conspired against the public good by trying to gain monopolistic privileges which would distort the workings of the market in their own interest. Smith's book was addressed principally to those enlightened and improving landowners who dominated Parliament; he believed that they, guided by wise and impartial spectators such as himself, would ensure that the market was kept free from political pressures and special favours.[24] The moral of this is worth stressing: merchants and traders, i.e. the bourgeoisie, could not be trusted to create a decent world by themselves. All this must be borne in mind. Certainly the need to make the market work so as to serve the aims of liberalism has never, as we shall see, been more pressing than it is in the contemporary world. Of course, the very idea that politicians should make the market work suggests that the state needs autonomy from social classes. The extent to which particular states have had such autonomy, and the extent to which such autonomy *is* desirable, is examined below.

These are not idle considerations. A strong case can be made for the equation of liberty *and* commerce in the first emergence of industrial society, and reflections on this, the real European miracle, comprise the next section. But the history of the nineteenth and twentieth centuries has demonstrated that authoritarianism can be combined with capitalism, as in Imperial Germany and Imperial Japan in the past and as in South Korea and various Latin American countries in the contemporary world. Analysis of the combination of authoritarianism with capitalism will naturally be of crucial importance later in this book: to the extent to which that combination is firm then the claim of Arblaster, that capitalism is a hindrance to liberalism, obviously gains weight. As there most certainly have been states combining capitalism with despotism, it can be said immediately that liberals cannot simply rest on the laurels provided by the European miracle of the past and assume that it will again be repeated. The first emergence of liberalism did have

50

something to do with capitalism, but whether that 'elective affinity' has applied since and whether it may apply again can only be decided by means of empirical investigation.

A Positive Sociological Critique

Although Adam Smith *was* correct in arguing that there was a connection, in north-west Europe, between commerce and liberty, it does not follow that his account should be accepted as it stands. This is not to deny huge merits to Smith's account – indeed, the role of a commercial aristocracy in creating a liberal society will seem increasingly important. But if this is not the place to offer a full account of this phenomenon, key analytic issues to be discussed in the rest of this book can be developed by pointing to certain strengths of Smith's account as well as by remedying some of its weaknesses.

One considerable strength of Smith's general account is its concern with the role of different political forms in the rise of capitalism. The form of politics in the pre-industrial world was a crucial factor at work in allowing or blocking the rise of an economic dynamic of capitalist character. The fact of centralization of decision-making in the Chinese empire, for example, meant that certain developments of a capitalist character, as in Buddhism's monastic production and control of inner Asian trade routes and, more famously, in the explorations under eunuch admiral Cheng-Ho, were ended as the result of court intrigue and mandarin jealousy. In contrast, a multipolar system of political rule was, as we shall show, a necessary condition for the rise of capitalism. This straightforward appreciation of the role of politics stands, we can note in passing, in stark contrast to the terrible conceptual difficulties, consequent upon trying to ignore the impact of political power, encountered by the Marxist notion of the 'Asiatic Mode of Production'.[25] In a nutshell, if liberalism is to have genuine intellectual strength it must take into account the fact that politics can alter the shape of history.

51

It has already been noted that Smith favoured a role for an intelligent state. However, given the preconceptions that inform thought, both academic and popular, about the benefits of 'laissez-faire', it is useful to say something more about the state. This can be done by making use of Michael Mann's distinction between different facets of state power.[26]

FIGURE I
TWO DIMENSIONS OF STATE POWER

INFRASTRUCTURAL CO-ORDINATION

		Low	*High*
DESPOTIC	*Low*	Feudal	Bureaucratic
POWER	*High*	Imperial	Authoritarian

The face of state power that we know the best concerns the extent of despotism in political rule. But there is a second dimension of state power which deserves the appellation 'infrastructural' since it concerns the depth to which a state can penetrate its society, provide services and organize social processes. Interestingly, a state with high infrastructural capacity/control and low despotic power typically possesses greater final strength than one with high despotism but without the capacity to organize and thus to control society. The fact that the Chinese imperial state was centralized enabled it to block capitalism, but this is not for a moment to say that it had genuine strength. Similarly it is true to say, even though it goes against the grain of our normal use of language, that the British state of the eighteenth century was stronger than its French rival even though it had no Absolutist façade; the proof of this statement was the success that Britain, often through its proxy states, had in four of the five occasions on which the two states were at war during the period in question.

Capitalists do need a certain freedom from interference. But such freedom typically depends upon the presence of a strong government. Max Weber stressed that capitalists wished for an orderly environment in which to be able to calculate the best manner of running their affairs. One element of such regularity was the absence of occasionalistic government predation. But equally important, especially in the longer run, was a government which was capable of providing certain infrastructural services without which capitalism could not prosper. The state had to be strong enough to provide defence against external enemies and to ensure internal order, to provide decent credit and banking facilities, and to administer justice. By and large, the states of Europe took on more and more of these tasks, and they deserve – with two qualifications to be noted – to be termed 'capitalist states'. For what, for example, was the British state in the eighteenth century but the assembly at which the linked interests of landlords and merchants were promoted by parliamentary means?

We can further explain the character of this state by preferring to call it 'organic', rather than, as Mann has it, 'bureaucratic'.[27] This quality was lent to the state because the king had to co-operate with other sources of power, most notably church, towns and nobility, if he was, as was necessary given the rules of state competition, to gain revenue in order to fight wars. The state grew up within society and was not something imposed from the outside by a group of military experts; this is to say that European society has had a long tradition of pluralism, and that it was this 'civil society' that made European liberty more than a merely formal matter. There was, in other words, movement in terms of Mann's diagram, from the feudal to the organic/bureaucratic category. When kings tried to impose their own will, as did King John, they found that established power sources stood in their way; the only route forward was to gain revenue by co-operating with and providing services for the larger society. What was at work here is so important that it deserves to be characterized in a different way. What is striking about European society is not just the presence of strong and autonomous groups, but that such groups were capable of co-operating together; there were different sources of power but they pointed, perhaps miraculously, in the same direction. The contractualism of European society left a legacy of great importance. A first qualification to a complete acceptance of the Marxist idea of the 'capitalist state' lies in the importance of this legacy. The point is nicely put by Edward Thompson at the end of his study of the manner in which law served the interests of the eighteenth-century aristocracy:

I have shown . . . a political oligarchy inventing callous and oppressive laws to serve its own interests . . . for many of England's governing élite the rules of law were a nuisance, to be manipulated and bent in what ways they could . . . But I do not conclude from this that the rule of law itself was humbug. On the contrary, the inhibitions upon power imposed by law seem to me a legacy as substantial as any handed down from the struggles of the seventeenth century to the eighteenth, and a true and important cultural achievement . . .[28]

What has been said to this point has concerned what can be termed mechanics internal to nation-states, and the argument has been that Smith had, and was right to have had, a much more positive conception of the state than some of his latter-day liberal conservative admirers would have us believe. But the general metaphysical point, that capitalism needs freedom from interference *and* the provision of a certain type of order – that is, low despotism and high infrastructure – should be generalized outside the confines of any national society to a larger arena. Adam Smith's account of the transition to commercial society did not pay attention to this larger realm, but we must do so, both to understand what happened and in order to raise questions that will prove crucial when analysing the modern world and the options of liberalism within it.

The most immediately noticeable characteristic of the larger world of the European scene that helped the rise of capitalism was its political fragmentation. Had the Roman

Empire been restored, it is likely that some attempt would have been made to control the 'natural' processes of capitalism. The point is perhaps best illustrated by a consideration of the European city. All historians agree that both Adam Smith and Max Weber were correct in noting that the European city was unique in being autonomous and a centre for production.[29] The city was a space in which the merchant was king and in which bourgeois values could gell and solidify. What explains this autonomy? The most satisfying answer is probably that it resulted from the presence of power vacuums, most notably in that area of north Italy which stood between the areas controlled by Pope and Emperor. How much these cities owed to their freedom from interference and freedom to experiment is simply seen: once they became a part of the Spanish Empire they contributed virtually nothing more to European civilization. And much the same point could be made by a 'thought-experiment': had Philip II created a long-lasting empire based on his new Spanish possessions, what would have happened to the social experiments taking place in Holland and Great Britain? It seems likely that such experiments in peripheral regions would have been stopped. As it was, the presence of a set of states made it very hard to control capitalism. Thus Philip's abuse of Antwerp led within a matter of years to the rise of Amsterdam. In a brilliant passage making this point, W. H. McNeill has shown that time and again Philip wanted to behave like an autocrat but the mobility of capital defeated him.[30] This was particularly true of his relationship with Liège, the foremost cannon producer of late-sixteenth-century Europe. When Philip pressurized them too hard, artisans and capitalists simply went elsewhere. There was, in other words, a type of laissez-faire built into Europe as a whole, and there is a relationship between this and the creation of favourable climates for capitalists inside nations. For the states of Europe were in competition with each other.

A second qualification to calling the European state a capitalist state is that the causes of this competition had, at least most of the time, little to do with capitalism. They represented rather the search for precedence and glory, i.e. autonomous goals of states in their own right. But such competition necessitated the rationalization of societies by their states, or, in an alternative formulation, the adoption of the social practices of the leading power. Some of the practices in question had an indirect relationship with the rise of capitalism. Thus the abolition of serfdom in Prussia after defeat by Napoleon was designed to help produce citizen armies, but the creation of free labour also benefited commercial life. But other practices, notably the adoption of local agricultural societies and the attack on state interference in eighteenth-century France, were self-conscious attempts to copy capitalist innovations. Such emulation has a long history in European society for the very brutal reason that a state which did not advance its economy would not be able to pay for sufficient military might to survive in the competitive international state arena.

If Adam Smith said little about the relationship of multipolarity to the triumph of capitalism, he had no inkling of the fact that European society as a whole had functioned after the fall of Rome only because it had itself been rule-bound.[31] The European economic dynamic began to gain intensity in the years 800 to 1100, that is, before there were many significant states in place. This raises the interesting question as to how this revival was possible. In particular, why was it that Europe did not simply revert to the localism that had characterized it before Roman integration once the empire collapsed? Europe did not become localized in these years because the Christian Church acted, in Thomas Hobbes's phrase, as the 'ghost of the Holy Roman Empire'. The church bound people together in a single normative system, and thereby created the very possibility of interchange over large distances.

The point being made here is that, in the lapidary formulation of Emile Durkheim, consensus stands behind contract. The keeping of contracts inside national states had, in fact, much less to do with consensus than Durkheim suggested: it was rather the result of the power of the state to enforce decisions. But Durkheim's phrase has great meaning when applied to early Latin Christendom: here normative consensus in a very pure sense underlay the possibility of interchange. So if there was freedom from interference inside the larger international system, there were also rules of the system itself. Competition, in a nutshell, fares best within a larger cultural framework. After about 1300, the role of the church as the provider of the shell for Europe faded as states tended to 'nationalize' their religious practices, a process concluded by the Reformation. But a larger cultural frame took the place of Christianity, and it was comprised of international economic competition and balance-of-power politics, a component of which was the spread of diplomatic practices throughout Europe.

Conclusion: The Problem of Social Cohesion
This chapter has sought to portray that confident moment in which liberal social and political theory felt that the emergence of capitalism would create decent political rule in combination with, and in part as a consequence of, affluence. By and large this confidence was justified: commerce and liberty did go together. However, to mention Durkheim is to raise a key problem: liberalism encourages privacy, wealth and soft political rule. But how can social cohesion be created and maintained, especially in the face of less scrupulous enemies, if social actors are dedicated only to enhancing their own interests?

This problem affects international society. The practice of balance-of-power politics was a poor substitute for the consensual shell provided by Latin Christendom. There is a simple reason for this. The society of states is, to use

Kant's expression, fundamentally 'asocial', that is, no government stands above the different actors so as to make the recourse to war anything other than normal. War in European history has indeed been, as Clausewitz had it, 'politics continued by other means'. Writing after two world wars, we cannot help but see that what was remarkable about the asocial society of states in European history was the fact that it lasted for so long, and even aided social progress, without causing disaster.

There has been much discussion about the need for social cohesion inside national societies, and the issues involved are elegantly underlined by John Dunn in an essay comparing the liberalism of Locke with that of Hume and Smith.[32] Dunn first notes the fundamental break between the applied theology of Locke and the more sociological viewpoint of Hume and Smith. This break is neatly captured in the fact that property was less an economic category for Locke than something like an omnibus notion of rights, to which all men, in the sight of God and being vehicles of his purpose, had equal entitlement. Dunn finds Locke attractive because the sharing of morality such as this provides for social order. Tocqueville's insistence that the stability of American democracy rested upon religion has an affinity with Dunn's argument.[33]

The two pillars on which Smith's sociological optimism were based – the fact that the maintenance of social hierarchy was guaranteed by human psychology and the capacity of an enlightened elite to ensure that the market worked properly – both proved to be unrealistic. The first of these presuppositions was, as noted, destroyed by the French Revolution. The second can be seen to fall in the career of Jeremy Bentham. His plans for reform were, to his surprise, rejected by the aristocracy which thereby proved itself, in his eyes, no selfless pillar of a new social order. However, British intellectuals of the early nineteenth century did not fall a prey to pessimism: they believed that a sound sociological base for liberal society could be found in the people. We shall see that this view was not entirely without sociological substance.

Nevertheless, this is not to deny the cogency of the Dunn/ Tocqueville objection. The core of that objection can best be seen as a refusal to go along with Smith's belief that a society would necessarily work through self-interest. Smith praised self-interest, as noted, largely for moral reasons, but it remains the case that morality plays no part in the daily workings of society. The question that arises is whether it was wise to leave such moral presuppositions in the background. Three points which lead to later discussion can usefully be made in conclusion. First, a theological basis for liberalism *is not available*; it has been ruled out, as we have seen, less by capitalism than by the impact of modern science – as is witnessed by the fact that secular-ization is a recognizable social process.[34] Secondly, it has already been stressed that liberalism is an ideology among others; it may well be that it needs to be defended for moral reasons – which is to admit that capitalism as means may not be sufficient to preserve liberal society. Finally, how-ever, it is worth stressing that Dunn seems to suggest that only a set of values morally equivalent to religion can underwrite basic respect for others; a similar argument has been made by Daniel Bell.[35] I doubt very much whether any totalizing ideology can stand up to the epistemological standards of modern science, and anyway doubt that liberalism is compatible with any such complete world view. However, discussion of this problem can be delayed until an analysis of the drift of European society into illiberalism has been offered.

NOTES

1. G. Vidal, *Creation* (London: Heinemann, 1981).
2. For an analysis of one instance of this process, see R. W. Southern, *Western Views of Islam in the Middle Age* (Cambridge MA: Harvard University Press, 1962).
3. C. Morris, *The Discovery of the Individual 1050–1200* (London: SPCK, 1972,. Cf. N. Abercrombie, S. Hill and B. Turner, *Sovereign Individuals of Capitalism* (London: Allen and Unwin, 1986).
4. This argument is hinted at in the concluding chapters of O. Patterson, *Slavery and Social Death* (Cambridge MA: Harvard University Press, 1984). But Patterson's fully worked out thoughts on the nature of the idea of freedom will soon be available in a separate monograph from Basic Books.
5. H. J. Laski, *The Rise of European Liberalism* (London: Allen and Unwin, 1936), chapters 1 and 2.
6. A. Arblaster, *The Rise and Decline of Western Liberalism* (Oxford: Basil Blackwell, 1984).
7. The most important such thinker is Milton Friedman, whose *Capitalism and Freedom* (Chicago: Henry Regnery, 1960) makes the point at issue with great clarity.
8. M. Ignatieff and I. Hont, 'Need and Justice in the *Wealth of Nations*: an Introductory Essay', in I. Hont and M. Ignatieff (eds), *Wealth and Virtue* (Cambridge: Cambridge University Press, 1983).
9. A. Smith, *An Inquiry into the Nature and Causes of the Wealth of Nations* (London: Dent, 1981), p.64.
10. I owe the expression 'sympathy with labour' to Chuck Nathanson of the University of California at San Diego. See his book of this title, forthcoming from Yale University Press.
11. A. Smith, *The Theory of Moral Sentiments* (Oxford: Oxford University Press, 1976), p.183.
12. This remark was made on 27 March 1775 according to J. Boswell, *Life of Johnson* (Oxford: Oxford University Press, 1980), p.597.
13. This argument is made by A. O. Hirschman in his brilliantly evocative treatment of the whole theme, *The Passions and the Interests: Political Arguments for Capitalism before Its Triumph* (Princeton: Princeton University Press, 1977).
14. Cf. my *Powers and Liberties: The Causes and Consequences of the Rise of the West* (Harmondsworth: Penguin, 1986).
15. Smith, *The Wealth of Nations*, op. cit., pp.366–7.
16. Ibid., pp.369–70.

17. I. Hont, 'The "Rich Country–Poor Country" debate in Scottish Classical Political Economy', in Hont and Ignatieff, op. cit.

18. D. Stewart, 'Account of the Life and Writings of Adam Smith, Ll.D', in A. Smith, *Essays on Philosophical Subjects* (Oxford: Oxford University Press, 1980), p.313.

19. Interesting comparative remarks about Hume and Smith, on the one hand, and Burke, on the other, are made by D. Miller in *Philosophy and Ideology in Hume's Political Thought* (Oxford: Oxford University Press, 1981), Conclusion.

20. See on this matter the excellent intellectual biography by J. D. Y. Peel, *Herbert Spencer* (London: Heinemann Educational, 1971).

21. J. M. Keynes, *The General Theory of Employment, Money and Interest* (London: Macmillan, 1983), p.374.

22. B. Constant. 'Liberty Ancient and Modern', quoted in G. de Ruggiero, *The History of European Liberalism* (Oxford: Oxford University Press, 1927), pp.167–8. This passage is cited by J. Gray, *Liberalism* (Milton Keynes: Open University Books, 1986), pp.20–1.

23. I am drawing here upon R. Dworkin, 'Liberalism', in S. Hampshire (ed.), *Public and Private Morality* (Oxford: Oxford University Press, 1978).

24. Cf. N. Phillipson, 'Adam Smith as Civic Moralist', in Hont and Ignatieff, op. cit.

25. These difficulties are analysed by E. Gellner, 'Soviets against Wittfogel; or, the Anthropological Preconditions of Mature Marxism', in J. A. Hall (ed.), *States in History* (Oxford: Basil Blackwell, 1986).

26. M. Mann, 'The Autonomous Power of the State: Its Origins, Mechanisms and Results', in Hall, *States in History*, op. cit.

27. For a justification of this terminology see: Hall, *Powers and Liberties*, op. cit., chapter 5 and chapters 2–4.

28. E. P. Thompson, *Whigs and Hunters* (Harmondsworth: Penguin, 1977), p.265.

29. P. Burke, 'City States', in Hall, *States in History*, op. cit.

30. W. H. McNeill, *The Pursuit of Power* (Oxford: Basil Blackwell, 1982), chapter 1.

31. This Durkheimian argument was first suggested to me by Michael Mann, and it appears in Hall, *Powers and Liberties*, op. cit., part 1. See now, however, Mann's own statement in his *The Sources of Social Power, Vol. 1: From the Beginning to 1760 A.D.* (Cambridge: Cambridge University Press, 1986), chapters 10 and 11.

32. J. Dunn, 'From Applied Theology to Social Analysis: the Break between John Locke and the Scottish Enlightenment', in Hont and Ignatieff, op. cit. Dunn's *Western Political Theory in the Face of the Future* (Cambridge: Cambridge University Press, 1979), chapter 2, presents an interesting view of liberalism as a whole which is complementary to the essay comparing Locke and the Scottish Enlightenment.
33. A. de Tocqueville, *Democracy in America* (New York: Anchor Books, 1969); and *The Old Regime and the French Revolution* (New York: Anchor Books, 1955), especially part II.
34. D. Martin, *A General Theory of Secularisation* (Oxford: Basil Blackwell, 1978).
35. D. Bell, *The Cultural Contradictions of Capitalism* (London: Heinemann Educational, 1976).

II

DOUBTS (LARGELY MISTAKEN) AND CATASTROPHE

INTRODUCTION: FROM THE 'PEOPLE' TO THE 'MASSES'

The later nineteenth century sees a loss of confidence on the part of liberalism, and in particular of liberal intellectuals. By the 1930s liberalism was widely believed to be finished, squeezed as it then was between the two power systems of bolshevism and fascism. We must analyse the European drift into illiberal, anti-Enlightenment ways of thinking and acting. There is a host of interrelated questions which needs to be addressed. Most importantly, did liberalism, either through underestimating its enemies or through excessive sympathy for capitalism, create conditions that nearly caused its own death? Were there particular weaknesses in the ways in which liberals understood the world? Have liberal hopes been proved so mistaken or so over-ambitious by the events from the period from 1848 to 1945 that they should now be curtailed or even abandoned?

Part II addresses these questions. By way of introduction, it is useful to describe, with sustained reference to the British case, those fears of liberal intellectuals that replaced earlier hopes. John Stuart Mill's work stands poised between two periods. He was ambivalent about the working class. On the one hand, he feared the 'tyranny of the majority' if the franchise were to be extended too rapidly and without provision for the creation of the proper citizenry for modern society. On the other hand, skilful political rule could ensure that the extension of the franchise did go hand in hand with the spread of educational provision, and there was no reason to believe that the working class would not come to share in his noble and high-minded vision. History was, moreover, moving in essentially the right direction, and there was every reason to believe that his theory was practicable. Although there were significant differences inside the early-nineteenth-century intelligentsia, Mill's hopes and fears were quite generally shared. Intellectuals saw it as their task to try and educate the general reader. Dickens ruthlessly insisted that the authors he published in *Household Words* were aware of the limitations of the newly literate, and the melodrama of his own fiction probably partly resulted from the attempt to deal with this problem. Equally, however, his picture of trade union 'agitators' in *Hard Times* shows that he shared some of Mill's fears. Similarly, George Eliot has Felix Holt famously addressing other working men, and thereby mouthing middle-class views as to the nature of respectable reform. If this voiced fears, hope none the less remained predominant. Why should it have been otherwise? George Eliot's own fiction, seeking to map the human emotions and social change in as scientific a manner as was possible, was addressed to the general reader and it gained a happy reception; she was able to command a full £10,000 as an advance on her later novels, an extraordinary tribute to the seriousness of the reading public of her time.[1]

All this stands in extreme contrast to the self-doubts which plagued intellectuals by the end of the nineteenth century. By that time, a revolution had taken place in newspaper production. This was popularly, albeit inaccurately, associated with the name of Lord Northcliffe, first at *Tit-Bits* and then at the *Daily Mail*. What was involved here was the discovery that the newly literate did not want to read the long, balanced and entirely unbroken columns of *The Nineteenth Century* or *The Times*; many preferred short, snappy and entertaining stories, often minimal in news content. The effect of this change upon the intellectuals' perception of what was happening was dramatic, and it received immortal expression in George Gissing's *New Grub Street*.

Introduction: From the 'People' to the 'Masses'

The novel has at its centre a contrast between Jasper Milvain, prepared to accede to the new situation, and Edwin Reardon, who is not. The difference between the two is characterized by Milvain in these words:

But just understand the difference between a man like Reardon and a man like me. He is the old type of unpractical artist; I am the literary man of 1882. He won't make concessions, or rather, he can't make them; he can't supply the market. I – well, you may say at present that I do nothing; but that's a great mistake, I am learning my business. Literature nowadays is a trade. Putting aside men of genius who may succeed by mere cosmic force, your successful man of letters is your skilful tradesman. He thinks first and foremost of the markets; when one kind of goods begins to go off slackly, he is ready with something new and appetising. He knows perfectly all the possible sources of income. Whatever he has to sell he'll get payment for it from all sorts of various quarters; none of your unpractical selling for a lump sum to a middleman who will make six distinct profits.[2]

Reardon's wife Amy is equally hostile to his literary ambitions, and insists that he should abandon the 'three decker', that is, the three-volume novel that dominated the Victorian age until the mid-1890s:

Now let me advise you; put aside all your strict ideas about what is worthy and what is unworthy, and just act upon my advice. It's impossible for you to write a three-volume novel; very well, then do a short story of a kind that's likely to be popular. You know Mr Milvain is always saying that the long novel has had its day, and that in future people will write shilling books. Why not try? Give yourself a week to invent a sensational plot, and then a fortnight for the writing . . . Just make it a matter of business . . .[3]

The story proceeds with all the fatalism one expects from Gissing to a grim *dénouement*: Reardon, unable to adapt to commercial pressures, has died and Amy becomes the wife of Milvain. The interesting point about the novel for our purposes is the way in which the demands of the people, now increasingly seen as an ill-educated and indistinguishable 'mass', are linked to a decline in quality. It is not at all surprising to discover that Gissing increasingly abandoned his early radicalism to become a rather crotchety conservative. His last book, *The Private Papers of Henry Ryecroft*, looks back with fondness to a more settled age in which patrons looked after artists. The purpose of the artist is no longer that of educating the general public; it has become that of defending 'high' culture against the depredations of the 'low', meretricious but popular culture of the masses.

Gissing's perception was highly idiosyncratic in that he, and his mouthpieces, virtually wished to fail. But the general view about the changing role of the artist became something of a common denominator among the artists of the turn of the century. This was scarcely surprising. Whereas George Eliot had been confident of money and readers, T. S. Eliot published much of his most famous early work in small magazines whose circulation was below fifty copies. Virginia Woolf cemented the equation of popular with meretricious in a famous essay, 'Mr Bennett and Mrs Brown', in which she insisted that the work of Arnold Bennett reached a larger public than her own because it seemed worldly but was superficial; only more inquisitive, more complicated writing would really disentangle the nature of human feelings.[4] These attitudes, distinguishing and endorsing 'high' from 'low' culture, have remained with us and have proved exceptionally influential on our cultural life as a whole.[5]

The same set of attitudes was at work in political affairs. Christopher Harvie's study of the university liberals of the mid-nineteenth century, notably Dicey, Stephen and Bryce, describes the process of disillusion. These thinkers had imagined that the extension of the franchise in 1867 and 1884 would lead to them and their friends being elected as Members of Parliament. But the newly enfranchised did not choose these exceptionally high-minded intellectuals, opting instead for a new generation of politicians with a more popular touch. Many liberals felt disillusioned, and quite a few became conservative; their position was well captured in 1900 by one of their number, G. C. Brodrick, looking back on those hopes of the 1860s which had led to their criticism of Lowe, the conservative politician who had opposed the extension of the franchise in 1867:

I assumed too easily that candidates of the higher class would do their best to educate the new constituencies, and, without rising altogether superior to party bias, would appeal to the better feelings and aspirations of their hearers. Mr Lowe's acquaintance with demagogy in Australia had convinced him of the very reverse. He knew that men of ability and professing high principles would not scruple to flatter the prejudices, pander to the passions, and inflame the class antipathies of voters whom they might have educated, for the sake of winning their support. This is exactly what has occurred . . .[6]

The newly enfranchised voted for whom they liked quite as much as they read what they wanted to; the idea of political and intellectual life as a seminar conducted under the stern aegis of John Stuart Mill thereby disintegrated. Much the same suspicion of blacks and other minorities in the United States has recently been shown by those 'liberals' associated with the magazine *Commentary*.

The fear at the back of the minds of liberal intellectuals went very deep indeed. One of the most remarkable of modern liberals, J. A. Hobson, was hugely distressed by the popular joy shown when Mafeking was relieved during the Boer War, and wrote *The Psychology of Jingoism* in order to explain how the mass mind could have been so manipulated into supporting rabid nationalism and war. He argued on the basis of the theories of Trotter and Le Bon that the popular mind had reverted, as the result of urban living and because of the power of press barons, into a type of primitive savagery dangerous for modern civilization.[7]

The same picture of liberal intellectuals feeling threatened by the age of mass democracy could easily be drawn of the European scene as a whole, even though such a

69

portrait, given the weaker hold of liberalism in Europe in the first place, would have to be drawn in darker and harsher colours. To do so, however, would add nothing to the problem that has been raised. It is time instead to turn to analysis. The next two chapters spell out in detail liberal fears, first about the moral life of the individual and then about the working class. Chapter 5 examines the idea that capitalism was responsible for the wars that destroyed Europe's position in the world. If Chapters 3 and 4 have a unity in treating liberal fears, so do Chapters 4 and 5: in this latter pair, systematic consideration is given to the nature of modern social classes in order to see whether capitalism undermines liberalism and whether, in consequence, a Marxist alternative seems to be on the cards. In all these chapters, my argument is that the historical record is such that liberalism, despite severe weaknesses, is not *logically* flawed; it has lessons to learn which, if absorbed, allow it a future. The danger that attaches to discussion of 'mistakes' made by historical actors is that of confusing one's hopes with what actually happened. While I have sought to avoid such confusion, it is up to the reader to decide whether the attempt has been successful.

NOTES

1. For interesting information about several famous Victorian authors, see J. A. Sutherland, *Victorian Novelists and Publishers* (London: Athlone Press, 1976).
2. G. Gissing, *New Grub Street* (Harmondsworth: Penguin, 1968), pp.38–9.
3. Ibid., p.84.
4. V. Woolf, *Mr Bennett and Mrs Brown* (London: Hogarth Press, 1924).
5. J. A. Hall, *The Sociology of Literature* (Harlow: Longman, 1979), chapter 5.
6. G. C. Brodrick, *Memories and Impressions* (1900) cited by C. Harvie, *The Lights of Liberalism* (London: Allen Lane, 1976), p.173.
7. J. A. Hobson, *The Psychology of Jingoism* (London: Grant Richards, 1901).

3
PROBLEMS OF BEING

This chapter is concerned with various worries about liberalism's conception of the moral life. The first section describes very different, indeed seemingly opposed, fears about the classic liberal concept of the individual moral agent. I will argue that these fears combined in a dreadful but entirely comprehensible way to create the most repulsive of the great totalizing ideologies of this century. This ideology is not such as to undermine liberalism; understanding its nature proves useful here in allowing specification of the nature of liberalism's view of morality. That view of morality is illustrated at some length by means of a discussion of what is probably the central issue raised by the work of the late Erving Goffman. The chapter ends with an attempt at explaining why the fears in question arose. Beliefs which are analytically wrong still represent something, and our argument is much advanced by an explanatory excursus into the sociology of knowledge.

Friedrich Nietzsche, Emile Durkheim and Robinson Crusoe
What is noticeable, with historical hindsight, about David Hume, Adam Smith and their contemporaries is that their view of the taming of the passions did not involve, to use a colloquialism helpful in this context, all that much loss of sleep. The point in question has been neatly captured by Ernest Gellner:

Anyone not familiar with Hume's thought might well suppose . . . that Hume's vision of man was something like that of Dostoyevsky, that he saw man as possessed by dark, tortuous, mysterious, perverse and uncontrollable passions. Not a bit of it. To understand properly the true nature of the famous Humean enslavement to passion, you must conjure up a different picture altogether. Imagine yourself floating in a boat on an artificial lake in a landscaped park, say one designed by Capability Brown. The currents of the lake are the passions, and you are indeed their slave, for the boat has neither oars nor rudder . . . The vessel will follow the currents, for there simply are no other forces that can impel or impede it.

Will they propel the boat to its destruction, in some maelstrom or cataract? Not at all. These currents are mild, the shores of the lake are rounded and slope gently. The currents may take you to a picnic on an island with a grotto or, alternatively, to a musical performance of Handel on one of the shores . . . With such passions, who would not gladly be their slave?[1]

That this striking image is exactly apposite can be seen when recalling (as, recently and skilfully, has Michael Ignatieff) the story of James Boswell's reaction to the death of David Hume.[2] Boswell chose to visit the dying Hume in the hope that the renowned atheist would change his mind; for to die without religious consolation was something that Boswell found terrifying, indeed almost unimaginable. Hume refused to recant his views, and, to Boswell's utter consternation, remained his witty and entertaining self. What is striking about this is the calmness of Hume's disposition, the fact that he could face death without 'fear and trembling'.

Others were by no means so sanguine, and foremost among their number was Friedrich Nietzsche. This German philosopher had a naturalistic view of human beings quite as much as did David Hume. But he considered the passions in altogether harsher and largely Darwinian terms. Human beings do not, in this interpretation, really derive ultimate satisfaction or meaning from the mere calculation of matters of interest. What matters in contrast is the 'will to power' – the central, but exceptionally murky, notion at the core of Nietzsche's vision. *Some* things about 'the will to power', however, are clear. Our internal lives are not peaceful and well-ordered; they are spaces filled with confusion and the longing to be taken seriously. Equally clear is the belief that most humans hide from experience and from their real individuality. In this context, Nietzsche has vicious comments to make about those ideologies, most notably Christianity, which try and impose some pious morality upon us. These ideologies are merely the resentment of unsuccessful weaklings against powerful and distinctive individuals:

Wherever the will to power declines in any form there is every time also a physiological reaction, a *décadence*. The divinity of *décadence*, pruned of all its manliest drives and virtues, from now on necessarily becomes the God of the physiologically retarded, the weak. They do *not* call themselves the weak, they call themselves 'the good' . . .
    The Christian conception of God [. . .] is one of the most corrupt conceptions of God arrived at on earth: perhaps it even represents the low-water mark in the descending development of the God type. God degenerated to the *contradiction of life*, instead of being its transfiguration and eternal *Yes*! In God a declaration of hostility towards life, nature, the will to life![3]

Some men – and the masculine is for once justified! – do have the supreme courage to face their condition; they are supermen.

Nietzsche saw as his task the revaluation of all values; like Hume and Kant, he sought to see what we could believe in if we examined the world as rigorously as possible. Nietzsche certainly has interesting points to make against Hume's sensationalist psychology. Our sensations, he insists, do not come one at a time, but rather bunched together in a package; we learn most in traumatic situations. This is surely correct. More generally, genuine and sustained argument about strongly held personal beliefs cannot easily be conducted according to the dictates of sweet reason; to remove such a belief from a human being is to assault their sense of self. Nietzsche adds that the search for knowledge is not itself neutral, but rather a part of the will to power. When we see any intellectual product we should ask why it has been produced, why it has such and such a content, and, above all, what the author is seeking to gain as a result. All of this leads Nietzsche to question taken-for-granted utilitarian views about the importance of science:

What? The ultimate goal of science is to create for man the greatest amount of pleasure and the least possible amount of pain? But suppose pleasure and pain were so linked together that he who *wants* to have the greatest amount of the one *must* have the greatest possible amount of the other also [. . .]? And perhaps that is how things are! The Stoics, at any rate, thought so, and were consistent when they desired to have the least possible amount of pleasure in order to have the least amount of pain from life [. . .] Today, too, you have the choice: either *as little pain as possible*, in short painlessness [. . .] or *as much pain as possible* as the price of an abundance of subtle joys and pleasures hitherto rarely tasted![4]

What are we to make of this? At first sight Nietzsche is the great opponent of the Enlightenment. It is true that his conception of our needs is much more brutal than that of those eighteenth-century thinkers who so influenced liberalism. Nevertheless, there is much sense to the claim that Nietzsche wanted less to destroy liberalism than to carry it to its logical conclusions.[5] His criticism of Christianity centres on the fact that hiding from oneself, and refusing to accept and understand one's position in the world, leads to exceptionally nasty motivation. A puritan moralist hiding from his own desire may well, in Nietzsche's view, be more dangerous than people who joyfully and openly recognize their emotional drives, a view of human motivation soon to be turned into a scientific practice by Sigmund Freud.[6] His ethic as a whole is one that encourages the growth of individualism, but which insists that this involves struggle and difficulty. In the struggle, however, a human being may achieve 'perfect moments' of conscious self-creation. This sentiment places Nietzsche squarely in the midst of the romantic movement of the nineteenth century.

It is helpful at this point to recall Robinson Crusoe. Karl Marx noted that the Robinson Crusoe story deserved to be seen as the representative myth of capitalist society. There is an obvious justification for this in the fact that Robinson Crusoe, discovering himself alone on the island, organizes, works and accumulates. But the Crusoe myth goes well beyond capitalism: the notion that the isolated individual can judge between false and real knowledge makes Robinson Crusoe a central character in the drama of modern epistemology.[7] There is a sense in which Nietzsche and John Stuart Mill had something in common. Mill admired the liberal aim of divesting oneself of prejudice, in the political and in the cognitive fields, so that one could face the evidence just like Robinson Crusoe. The image that this conveys is that of peeling away the false layers of an onion, the assumption being that there is a golden centre in the middle of untrammelled and unquestioned selfhood. However, it was Nietzsche who proved to be the expert at self-dissection; he examined everything, admitted appalling truths about human nature and cut the ground away from several pieties which were indeed completely self-serving. It is entirely appropriate that many painters chose to visualize him on mountain tops, always alone and usually staring into the distance.

The drive for authenticity does represent an understandable progression from liberalism's view of individuality. The second fear about liberalism's view of the moral life, not much discussed by liberal thinkers, is very different. The view in question is best represented by Emile Durkheim. It seeks to question whether we have 'real selves' in any easy or recognizable sense whatever.

Durkheim's *Suicide* was designed to cause a certain type of offence. To kill oneself had been seen by a liberal age as the ultimate act of individual selfhood. Durkheim overturned this view: what had seemed unique and personal became a matter of the play of social forces, of whether one

was a Catholic rather than a Protestant, married rather than single, in work or unemployed – the individual being, of course, notably more prone to suicide if he fitted the second of each of these pairs. The point being made was that the individual was not the source of independent strength that classical liberalism, let alone Nietzschean romanticism, had imagined. Very much to the contrary, the individual, if ever bereft of social support, had little chance of survival. This point was made with marvellous acuity and force by Joseph Conrad, interestingly but not surprisingly an exile well aware of the costs of social marginality. Both Decoud (in *Nostromo*) and Axel Heyst (in *Victory*) simply do not have enough to tie themselves into society, and correspondingly are unable to hang on to life itself. The epigraph, from Novalis, to *Lord Jim* – 'It is certain any conviction gains infinitely the moment another soul will believe in it' – makes the same point.[8]

Durkheim's argument can helpfully be illustrated with reference to Robinson Crusoe. The French sociologist is, of course, the most complete of all opponents of Robinson Crusoe strategies of every sort. Durkheim's objections receive impressive support from Michel Tournier's *Friday or the Other Island*.[9] Robinson Crusoe's fate in this novel is altogether more realistic than that of the original by Daniel Defoe. Crusoe does not dominate his environment. He loses most of his sense of time and a great deal of his identity, and he indulges in curious copulations with the local flora. He seems, more or less, to lose his self in conjunction with the loss of society; he does not go mad, so much as steadily disintegrate. When Friday arrives he is appreciated for his humanity and beauty and not for his potential as a labourer. Tournier has his own axe to grind, that of a strange pantheism in combination with hopes for new types of human relationships, but this does not prevent the main thrust of his argument carrying great conviction. Without social constructions, of time, space and custom, a human being cannot survive. Durkheim had insisted precisely on the social nature of such basic concepts in the dazzling pages that open his masterpiece *The Elementary Forms of Religious Life*.[10] Perhaps it is no wonder Nietzsche, that ultimate Robinson Crusoe, went mad.

Authenticity with Gemütlichkeit

It might seem at first sight that the demand for authenticity and the realization that the individual needs social support are entirely incompatible. However, this is not the case, and this section describes the combination – a combination which is not accidental – of these two factors in fascist theory. The argument should not be misunderstood. I am not claiming that Durkheim was himself illiberal. Nor do I think that this term can easily be applied to Nietzsche. Our position in history makes it impossible to read Nietzsche without seeing proto-fascist overtones; they are particularly clear in those passages in which he orders the masses to obey some 'authentic' and charismatic leader. Nevertheless, a large part of the thrust of Nietzsche's position is best seen, as argued, as an extension of liberalism. Perhaps thinkers should be held responsible for the manner in which they argue; certainly it is the case that lesser minds could make use of Nietzsche's violent destructiveness, not to liberate man but to found a new social order supposedly true to his purposes.

The thinker who best helps us understand the nature of this combination is Martin Heidegger. This highly representative and influential philosopher helped spread the view that modern technology is morally empty and meaningless since it did not address the 'problem of being'. The social organization engendered by modern technology was held to be responsible, in other words, for a type of alienation of man; political theory needs therefore to concern itself once again with the search for an authentic world. It is interesting to note that Heidegger's conception of politics and morality derived essentially from the experience of the Greek city state. It stands therefore in absolute contrast to the position advocated for moral reasons by Hume and Smith. Heidegger's existentialism had considerable popularity in Germany in the years after the First World War, as too did expressionism, an artistic style largely concerned to show the emptiness and dullness of the modern world. Both intellectual movements created a shared cultural pool on which both left (most notably Herbert Marcuse) and right drew.[11] Heidegger himself was attracted by the Nazi appeal to restore moral values, and to place technology under human control; moreover, his work was part of a culture in which it seemed only natural to give power to those who stood out from the masses by reason of their courage and authenticity. Heidegger was, of course, exceptionally naïve in this and after a short period retreated from his initial active commitment to the Nazis. However, he never changed his negative view about the soullessness of 'mere' technology.[12]

The Nazi party was not so discriminating, and it created a popular totalizing ideology on the basis of which it claimed power. That ideology combined respect for an authentic leader with a type of mass communal *Gemütlichkeit*. It is scarcely surprising to discover that Joseph Goebbels wrote an expressionist/existentialist novel before becoming a convert to Nazi ideology. The process of conversion was, however, surely not very surprising. Where Nietzsche sought to find new values, his lesser disciples simply accepted nihilism; on the basis of cultural despair they offered a politics based on worship of the will. Probably there is here a general connection between dislike of and inability to withstand emptiness, and the likelihood of swallowing some total system. The total ideology that Goebbels admired was, of course, a 'catch all' philosophy combining elements of pre-industrial solidarity *with* modern industrial might.[13] The character of this ideology is best captured in the title of Jeff Herf's study of the phenomenon, *Reactionary Modernism*. Perhaps the most striking thinker of a 'school' which included Hans Freyer, Carl Schmitt and

Oswald Spengler was Ernst Junger. Herf cites a revealing passage:

> But haven't we, who of course are not materialists, but instead label ourselves realists, already felt the experience of mathematical precision and magical background during the war. Didn't phenomena such as the modern battleship arouse the same impression in us. *This embodiment of an icy will*, all coal and steel, oil, explosives and electricity, manned by specialised positions from admiral to boiler heater, the image of the latest precision mechanics, served by workers and directors, functional in the highest degree, composed of millions of objects – this whole apparatus is sacrificed in seconds for the sake of things which one does not know but rather in which one can only take on faith. It goes down burning, shot to pieces, sinking with flags flying, perishing forever, in moments in which destiny itself appears to intoxicate the blood amid the cries of the dying, sacrificed in a sea most distant from one's fatherland, which perhaps will belong to history tomorrow, but perishing amid a 'hurrah' that must shake every individual wherever he may stand, to the core of his heart, because in this cry the whole tension between two worlds is illuminated as by a moving lightning bolt – yes, isn't all this taken together not the image of a contradiction which has captured every one of us between its poles, from the last office girl to the very last factory worker.[14]

The appalling intellectual poverty of some of the thought of reactionary modernism is evident in Herf's summary list of the way in which his thinkers viewed their thought as being opposed to liberalism.[15]

German 'Kultur'	*Liberalism*
Soul	Mind
Feeling	Intellect
Community	Society
Blood	Intellect and/or money
Life	Death
Will	Passivity
Productivity	Parasitism
Germany the *Kulturnation*	America and Russia

79

Liberalism

Creative labour	Finance capital
Worker-soldier	Citizen
Anticapitalism	Capitalism
German socialism	International socialism
Sacrifice	Self-interest
Primacy of politics	Primacy of the market
Will towards form	Parliamentary confusion
German	Jew
Beauty	Ugliness

The best summary of this whole mood remains the comment given by Leon Brunschvicq after he had witnessed the worship of the Führer at a Nuremburg rally to his student Raymond Aron: 'religion according to Durkheim, society worshipping itself'.[16]

A Preliminary Assessment

The historical consequences of reactionary modernism are well known. Rather than repeat them let us move on instead to an assessment of these critiques of liberal individualism, taking each of them in turn. Both have kernels of truth; equally, both offer social and political prescriptions of which we need to be most suspicious.'

Liberals have been so disturbed by the discovery of Nietzschean instinctual desires that they have tended to turn their backs upon them. One striking example of this is that of the scorn habitually shown for the work of Rudyard Kipling. A story such as 'Mary Postgate' – in which a simple and loyal servant happily watches a wounded German pilot die, has a luxurious bath and looks 'quite handsome' for the rest of the evening[17] – offended liberal feeling so much that Kipling was effectively banned from the literary canon. But the story is one of great power, and this fate is undeserved. More generally, the view that Nietzsche has of our inner life is overwhelmingly convincing: life *is* less a careful sort of book-keeping than an area beset by insecurity, anxiety and self-doubt, an area in which various passions 'raise their ugly heads' and diminish

80

the role of reason. We *do* learn, moreover, by trauma and not, as empiricist psychology from Hume to Skinner would have us believe, by some complicated grand addition of separate sensations. And I suspect that there are tasks that go beyond reason. It is certainly possible to calculate the choice of a car, or the siting of a factory, on straightforward utilitarian lines; it is much harder, and perhaps not altogether desirable, to treat one's inner life according to such edicts.

Does an awareness of the dark gods of the human soul mean that liberalism has to be abandoned? A negative response can be offered with some confidence. We can begin by noting that the Nietzschean position is not without a terrible problem of its own. It poses as a *description* of what we actually want, but this makes the unmistakably moral fervour of the message rather odd. If we really want power, then why do we need to be reminded about it? The question suggests that Nietzsche's naturalism suffers from the contradiction that became apparent when discussing Hume: if naturalism is true, why do we read books about it, that is, why do we need to be *persuaded* of its worth? The same point can be put in another and more pointed way: if moralities, especially those inspired by Christianity, make us deny our nature, how was it possible for us ever to have been attracted to them? Perhaps moralism has a definite appeal to us! All-in-all, we are offered an incomplete but nevertheless realistic description which is then covertly turned into a *prescription*. Liberalism would be very mistaken not to take the former seriously, and it is indeed bad news to discover the strength of various passions; liberal society can probably cope fairly easily with sex on tap, indeed it seems to thrive on it, but the notion of an instinctive desire to dominate others is a real threat to the very idea of soft political rule. But there is no reason, in so far as we have any reason at all, to identify with these dark forces; and given the repulsive consequences of Nietzschean politics, there is much to be said in favour of not basing our normative life upon such drives. Realistic appreciation of human psychology should only really make the liberal prescription the more important, at once more difficult to achieve and more necessary. This was certainly the position of Maynard Keynes. His endorsement of the idea of balancing the passions has a great pathos to it, coming as it did at a time when Nietzschean drives – the force of which Keynes explicitly, and in distinction both to his Bloomsbury friends and to the whole British traditional view of human nature, recognized[18] – were plain for all to see. The notion of playing off interest against passion is made more, rather than less, suggestive by the events of twentieth-century history.

A further consideration is still more important. If we can admire Nietzsche's own attempt to find his own individuality, we cannot but loathe the contemptuous elitist scorn that he, and more particularly his followers, showed towards the 'masses'. For why should we accept the view that the lives of most normal people are worthless? The Kantian and empiricist baseline of taking everyone seriously gains in appeal in the light of attempts to exterminate whole peoples. The moral basis of liberalism has most definitely not lost its crucial importance.

Let us turn from the dark forces of the soul to the contention that the individual is not the pillar of strength that liberalism had once believed. The origin of this criticism goes back to the conservative reaction to the French Revolution. The fear that unabated individualism could lead to chaos has been much reinforced by the obvious consequences of Nietzschean romanticism; both Bell and Dunn have been affected by this body of thought. This criticism of liberalism is clearly aware that the individual needs social support; at its most striking it doubts the existence of a real self altogether. What are we to make of the questioning of the solidity of the self? There is obvious and absolute truth to the insistence that 'no man is an island'. However, dangerous prescriptions can follow from this descriptive point. At its worst the demand for social integration can *join* with the demand for authenticity to create those highly questionable political practices that have been examined. This is not, let me repeat, to say that Durkheim, a liberal despite having been influenced by conservative thinkers, was himself in favour of this particular type of social ritual. But the claim that the individual suffers when alone and needs integration can all too easily lead to the demand for some new shared ideology, the worth of which may well be questionable.

There are good reasons for downplaying the call for social integration. A measure of anomie is probably preferable, in the abstract and for most actors, to any version of enthusiastic communalism. Much more importantly, there are strong empirical reasons for suggesting that people continue to belong to groups, families and associations, and that they gain both meaning and solidarity from this. The most elegant way in which this point has been made, however, is in the early work of the late Erving Goffman, most notably in his remarkable *The Presentation of Self in Everyday Life*. This book investigated the ways in which the self is created and presented according to circumstances. An obvious point that follows is that individuals have different selves – or masks – according to different audiences, and that freedom in large part consists in the ability to change from one to another. But Goffman makes more striking points. He notes that people are keen to help each other protect their masks or 'fronts' and that they will engage in 'face work' to maintain all sorts of illusions:

Much of the activity occurring during an encounter can be understood as an effort on everyone's part to get through the occasion and all the unanticipated and unintentional events that can cast participants in an undesirable light, without disrupting the relationships of the participants. And if relationships are in the process of change, the object will be to bring the encounter to a satisfactory close without altering the expected course of development.[19]

Goffman asks the interesting question why people are so kind and supportive in encounters, and he finds the nub of his answer in Durkheim. Although the great French sociologist was an opponent of Robinson Crusoe-style individualism pioneered by classical liberalism, he felt that a version of individualism – one which gave the individual social support and which created social obligations quite as much as rights – was the 'normal' ideology for a complex and socially mobile industrial society; it is this part of Durkheim's work that makes it necessary to insist that he himself was not close to reactionary modernism. Goffman's work begins where Durkheim's ends; he accepts Durkheim's view of individualism but he actually demonstrates how the sacred quality of the individual is created and maintained in everyday life. The social practices Goffman describes demonstrate that the individual is *not* made to feel like an island in modern industrial society. The detailed practices which are involved in this – particularly the ritual displays of deference and demeanour[20] – do not concern us here. But two general points deserve highlighting. First, he suggests that the study of small-scale interaction in society is important because it is there that the larger moral order is affirmed. This stands in marked contrast to thinkers like Rousseau and Sartre who wished to have the values of society affirmed in public and on a large scale – by various carnivals of the republic! However, a large and complex modern society is unlikely to indulge in frequent self-endorsements of this type. Hence the rituals of daily life – in which the moral value of the larger society, namely respect for the individual, is affirmed – become extremely important for the ordering and symbolic integration of society.[21] Secondly, he insists that the practices involved in social interaction are social, and that they have little to do with any sense of personal individuality: 'It may be true that the individual has a unique self all his own,' he notes disarmingly, but 'evidence [of such a unique self] is thoroughly a product of joint ceremonial labour.'[22]

84

That such a sentence is possible shows how far we have come from the picture of the individual standing alone, master of his own fate and destiny. However, Goffman's work seems at times to veer to the other extreme: it looks as if there may be all too much integration, and that conformity may pose a greater problem. Is there some way in which Durkheimian awareness of the need for social support can be combined with a genuine sense of self? A positive answer to this question can be provided by examining in some detail different conceptions of the self in Goffman's work.

In Praise of Masks

The best way to set the scene for this analysis is by recalling that critics of romantic/existentialist persuasion endlessly criticized Goffman. It is worth pausing a moment to spell out what is meant by this label. Such critics were deeply impressed by the need to establish an authentic self. Although the source of many of their ideas is Nietzsche, their immediate indebtedness was to Jean-Paul Sartre, a thinker who made much of being a man of the left. What was important in Sartre was his attack on 'bad faith', i.e. the attack on the practice of sloughing off the 'burden of freedom' by pretending not to have choices at every moment of life. Several of Goffman's critics sought to add to Sartre's general ethic the more historical perspective that they discovered in David Riesman's *The Lonely Crowd.*[23] Riesman argued that there had been a change in character type in modern American life, and that this boded ill for the moral life of the individual. The typical early American had been 'inner-directed', that is, had a strong conception of self, born out of conflict with firm family rules, and was accordingly capable of acting decisively. The American of consumer capitalist society was seen as altogether a weaker and lesser affair: 'other-directed', bereft of much sense of self at all, a hollow shell tugged this way and that by the latest fad and fashion. Delicious ironies could develop out

of Riesman's position. Lionel Trilling favoured the deep
instincts described by Freud as an ultimate redoubt of the
self and a safeguard against social pressure and condition-
ing; this put him at odds with Sartre who had argued that
the very recognition of such instincts amounted to a sophisticated version of bad faith.[24] Daniel Bell's friendship with
Trilling has not prevented him from taking exactly the
opposite tack: deep instincts are indeed there, but they are
powerful and perverse and desperately need to be controlled.[25] Many further examples of such cultural criticism
could be furnished, but what matters for our purposes is
the claim that derived from this approach. The practices of
impression management and interaction continuity that
Goffman described were seen, not as necessary *per se*, but
as the results of a social pathology.[26] In contrast, such
critics recommend that we learn to trust each other, to
become sincere and authentic; in so far as Goffman supports 'ground rules' of public order he is seen as being 'on
the side of the system'.[27]

We can began by saying that there are two conceptions
of the self to which Goffman pays attention. We have
already noted his description of social practices showing
respect for and in fact constructing the self. But some
conception of the personal self can be derived from his work
in contrast to what can usefully be termed the social self.
We can see this personal self at work in Goffman's descrip-
tions of those occasions in which various social rules of
interaction concern themselves less with giving ritual back-
ing to the sacred quality of the self and more with enabling
the individual to get through his daily round with the
minimum of interference and trouble. This is especially
true of relations in the large American city; here individuals
seek to appear non-threatening to each other so that the
vulnerabilities they are exposed to by the city do not
become all-engrossing.[28] The same point is made negatively
in *Asylums*. 'Total institutions' are able to destroy the two
facts which give the individual a meaningful sense of

freedom: his ability to control information about himself and his right to choose to separate the audiences before whom he can play separate roles.[29] In both these cases, Goffman seems to be pointing to some sort of volition lying behind different fronts. He was notoriously unwilling, however, to produce any systematic theory of the self, and we must search elsewhere for this.

Marcel, the hero of Proust's *A la Recherche du temps perdu*, lives in a world with an extraordinary resemblance to that described by Erving Goffman. He finds it exceptionally hard to discover his own identity and those of people around him. On the one hand he romanticizes, from a distance, love and 'society', but finds that real acquaintanceship brings disillusion; on the other hand, he finds it almost impossible to know when people are telling him lies. The novel is, somewhat surprisingly, a success story in that Marcel does, in old age and after a great deal of personal suffering, *establish* an identity. Whereas before he suffered from 'the intermittences of the heart' – has been, in other words, a succession of roles and experiences without a firm integrating identity – he now manages to build up a personal self by means of which experience makes sense. His self is not given, but made.

This conception of the personal self stands in diametric opposition to the 'ontological' self, always available, always crystal-clear, that is, in the last analysis, apparent in the work of Sartre. In my opinion, the viewpoint shared by Goffman and Proust, that is, that we have to work hard at understanding ourselves and harder still at constructing a firm identity, corresponds far more accurately to our condition than Sartre's facile insistence that we carry a true self with us at all times. The central argument of this section can now be made by means of six interrelated points. What is important for liberalism is the relationship between the 'civility' of those practices involved in supporting the social self and the creation of a personal self; it will be argued that the civility of the social self is not an affront to authenticity but a necessary condition without which identity cannot be achieved. This obviously places liberalism in opposition to existentialism and romanticism. What is being offered can be summed up by saying that a defence is being offered for the paradox that lies at the heart of Proust's novel: that *because* the self is usually intermittent, moral ground rules are the more necessary.

1. The first argument favouring civility above authenticity is scarcely likely to convince an existentialist. It is an argument in favour of laziness. Sartre was exceptionally puritanical in demanding that we never for a moment relinquish the burden of consciousness. Proust's attitude is that habit, i.e. 'bad faith' in Sartrean terms, is a human comfort; though he thinks that artists should escape from habit sometimes, he does not suggest that they do so all the time. Secondly, Proust constantly notes that knowledge of one's self and of one's art comes when one is not prepared for it, and that such knowledge cannot be ordered at will.

2. A second set of arguments, directed against the view that Goffman somehow adulated the status quo of American society, may go no further in convincing an existentialist.

We can note to begin with that the accusation in question is one of guilt by association. The fact that Goffman favoured a set of rules is unfairly used to suggest that he is in favour of the rules presently operating in American society. This ignores Goffman's own assertion that 'mutual dealings . . . could probably be sustained with fewer rules or different ones'.[30] Furthermore, the charge of conservatism ignores the fact that *Asylums* is best read as an appeal for 'the people' against a practice of industrial society; and surely it is a novel and powerful appeal since it suggests not the fashionable case that we do not need ground rules, but that it is inhumane to deprive anyone of the benefits (notably rights to privacy and control of information about the self) provided by such rules. Finally, it is worth noting how extraordinary is the attack on social rules as being in themselves repressive of individuality. Goffman argues against this, that 'persons *can* come together and voluntarily agree to abide by certain ground rules . . . the better to free attention from unimportant matters and get on with the business at hand'.[31] This argument is Durkheimian in its conception of society as enabling, and that without it we would be incapable of communicating at all. Moreover, the belief that the absence of such ground rules would encourage us to approach each other with warmth and spontaneity is illusory. Goffman is surely right to note the distrust and fear that uncertainty of response breeds.

3. Goffman once defended his work from the charge of being politically suspect on the grounds that 'he who would combat false consciousness and awaken people to their true interest has much to do, because the sleep is very deep'.[32] One example of such sleep may be drawn from *Stigma*, where Goffman comments directly on existentialism.

The thesis of *Stigma* is straightforward. Goffman pictures the stigmatized person occupying an invidious position, full of personal strain; such a person considers himself normal yet knows that 'the normals' are uneasy in his presence. Goffman reviews the advice given to the stigmatized, and notes that one school of advice descends in all its essentials from Sartre's *Anti-Semite and Jew*. That advice is to 'be authentic'. Goffman's unsettling intelligence shows how unhelpful such advice is for the stigmatized. The one thing that, say, a disabled person does not wish to be told is to be authentic since this means recognizing oneself as less than normal. He notes rather acidly that: 'the shrewdest position for him to take is . . . one which has a false bottom; for in many cases the degree to which normals accept the stigmatized person can be maximized by his acting with full spontaneity and naturalness as if the conditional acceptance of him, which he is careful not to overreach, is full acceptance.'[33]

4. The fourth point concerns matters directly political. One of Goffman's critics, Christopher Bryant, considers the

world he describes as unhealthy since it exalts the private above the public virtues in a manner interestingly condemned by Ralf Dahrendorf in his analysis of the social roots of Nazism.[34] Liberalism *does* face a problem of balancing privacy with political participation, but this is not at all to say that a model of participation should somehow be grounded on the search for authenticity. Dahrendorf most certainly does not wish to do this, and Bryant is therefore misusing Dahrendorf's points. Dahrendorf distinguishes between public virtues as a 'model of general intercourse between men' and private virtues 'which provide the individual with standards for his own perfection, which is conceived as being devoid of society'.[35] He suggests that the motto of the former might be 'keep smiling' and of the latter 'be truthful'. What this amounts to is quite clear: Dahrendorf, a thinker clearly aware of the dangers to liberalism of political passivity, is in favour of politics being based on civility rather than a concern with authenticity.

There are a number of reasons why the search for authenticity should be kept out of politics, why politics should not be personalized. The most famous example of a politician of this century basing his legitimacy on a claim to personal authenticity is, of course, Hitler.[36] All-in-all, there is much to be said for Dahrendorf's comment that:

Men who are trying to get on with one another are probably spared the extreme evilness that makes it possible simply to rule some people out of the world of men in order to expedite them out of it afterwards.[37]

Of course, the romantic/existentialist critics would clearly deny any necessary link between the search for authenticity and political repression. But we can begin to question this by thinking again of Sartre. It is too often forgotten that the early *Being and Nothingness* is a deeply pessimistic book. The real problem of being is other people *per se*; they witness and thereby expose attempts to give one's existence an air of settled stability. In marvellous passages on sadism and masochism, Sartre paints a picture of Hobbesian intensity in which each individual tries, but inevitably fails, to turn the other person into an object. In the later *Critique of Dialectical Reason*, Sartre sought to solve what had seemed to be a problem of human nature by making the individual stick to his authenticity. There is nothing unique about this attempt to solve the problem of being in political terms: in a certain sense, Sartre is the descendant of Rousseau. Both thinkers believe that individuality is weak, whether as the result of being prone to fashion or to bad faith, and both insist that a political system must bind the individual to his true and authentic 'best' self. Rousseau seems to do this through the General Will, while a similar moment occurs for Sartre when the alienated 'series' becomes a 'group-in-fusion' in which all are joined in a common purpose. How these moments occur – how the social contract can be formed without the presence of the new men it is supposed to create – is something of a mystery. But there is no doubt of the consequence of this strategy. An authentic group is held together by a vow according to which anyone who abandons this very strenuous view of authenticity should be killed. The search for authenticity leads here to an illiberalism of the left.

5. The two remaining points deal with the paradox of Proust's work already noted, that is, that he saw the intermittence of human experience and yet called for the preservation of a moral order. The first argument that can be given in support of this position is negative. Proust's novel is famous for the opening scene in which the young Marcel is able to get his way, and thereby has his mother come and read to him in his room. The narrator returns to this scene on a number of occasions, and ends up concluding that the father was irresponsible in that he merely gave way on arbitrary grounds; he is contrasted with Marcel's mother and grandmother who stick to principles even

though they find at times that this causes them pain.[38] But this position is upheld, and the father condemned; for the novel suggests that the absence of standards in his early life has made it all the harder for Marcel to develop the will power that he needs to become an artist and to arrest the confusion of his life. This argument may be neatly summed up thus: 'Not to know who you are is as bad as not knowing what you are.'[39] In other words, a child needs a set of rules against which to react if he is ever to be anything.

6. A second argument concerns the functional nature of masks and fronts. On one occasion Goffman noted that 'a disguise may function not so much as a way of concealing something as a way of revealing as much of it as can be tolerated in an encounter'.[40] Related closely to this is the more general point that masks are often enabling devices in other ways. If one is unsure of a situation, then playing a role may be reassuring.[41] More importantly, it is through and behind masks that people have the freedom to investigate and to find an identity. As Proust made clear, this freedom is all too often not pleasant; it is not a question of choosing roles at random, as some existentialists have argued, but of learning how to control and understand the roles that we have been, and continue to be, forced to play.

With this in mind it becomes possible to explain why the politics of authenticity are *bound* to become authoritarian. The personal self described above suggests that people do not have a real self, always available at the slightest touch of introspection; on the contrary they can establish something like this, an integrating identity for the intermittences of life, through time and effort and with luck. Hence any political theory that tries to anchor human personality at one particular point and prevents people, for example, from making mistakes and learning from them is bound to end up coercing them into one particular mould.

Recapitulation
This has been a long discussion of a complex matter. The central moral to be drawn from the discussion of Goffman

can therefore usefully be underlined. A good way of doing this is to recall an essay by Raymond Aron comparing the conceptions of political liberty of Montesquieu and Rousseau.[42] Where Montesquieu emphasized the absence of arbitrariness, Rousseau stressed the need for autonomy. Aron detected totalitarian designs in Rousseau's General Will, and therefore favoured the civility proposed by Montesquieu. But Aron was careful to warn that mere civility could be conservative; in our private lives we should indeed try and develop autonomous moral wills. This has been, by process of analogy, precisely my case. It was a blow to the hopes of classic liberalism to discover that the individual was by no means the captain of his own soul. But this discovery ought not to rule out traditional liberal aims, most notably those concerning privacy and respect for others. They are the more necessary as without them we may never be promoted to captains at all. All this can be put in a slightly different way. Liberalism does not base itself on romanticism's view of the self since that can lead to the denial of basic respect for the equal worth of all human beings. Respect for others must mean respect for their privacy, for the masks without which more development is not possible. Finally, it can be noted that this stance rests on *confidence*. It is those who need totalizing ideologies whose lives are fundamentally poverty-stricken, not those who are involved in the myriad complexities of mundane existence.

If all this is to maintain a Kantian residue, two final points can be made to diminish any air of romanticism about the argument; both stress that the residue is restricted. First, it is worth repeating that the attempt to build up a sense of identity through trying on several 'masks' is unlikely to be an easy or automatically successful task. Proust's work testifies to this, and similar arguments have recently been made by Colin Campbell.[43] Secondly, Goffman's view of society is, to use a Weberian expression, extremely disenchanted. Goffman sees the minutiae of social life as being subject to social patterning; he is thus one of the few sociologists who study small-scale interaction who do not seek thereby massively to enhance a sense of human creativity as a result. This is an important point to make since his work has often been used by those who wish to counter social determinism. At the conclusion of a celebrated essay on 'Role Distance', Goffman explicitly notes that this phenomenon is 'almost as much subject to role analysis as the core tasks of roles themselves'.[44] This is particularly striking when it is realized that it is this essay which is cited by those who see an escape from the cage of social determinism in his work.[45]

The Betrayal of the Intellectuals

The thesis of this final section is contained in its title, namely that our judgement about the mood of pessimism to which liberals became prone in the nineteenth century represented a betrayal on the part of a sizeable number of intellectuals of the liberal inheritance. Betrayal is a harsh and ugly word, and it is used here deliberately. Intellectuals have a duty not to write their own hopes and fears into their visions of society, as seems to have happened all too frequently in the modern era.

A representative example of the pessimistic fears of liberals was Hobson's already mentioned *The Psychology of Jingoism*. How justified were Hobson's fears? Did rioting on the night that the relief of Mafeking became known really evidence bestial passions on the part of the people? R. W. Price's *An Imperial War and the British Working Class* allows us to reject Hobson's view with finality. Meetings tended to be broken up by middle-class jingoes, and working-class participation was for entirely different reasons – as an excuse to get drunk, or as a means of getting a cheap passage to South Africa. Price's judgement is clear:

His book ... was a moralistic account coloured by a failure to observe society at any deeper level than those of events like Mafeking Night.

It merely revealed Hobson's low opinion of the 'brutal' and 'credulous' working class. Hobson . . . was duped by the seeming mass excitement caused by war into believing that this was a new feature peculiar to the new age.[46]

Moreover, Hobson's accusation that the workers had betrayed the intellectuals and reformers opposed to the war falls down on the simple fact that the anti-war movement was poorly led and elitist in conception. Hobson's book concerns not so much the facts as 'a series of logical conclusions which are frequently based on a series of false premises of their own intellectualized conceptions of the issue and what is involved'.[47]

It would be neither sensible nor justified to relapse into a populistic belief that the people are always right on the basis of this evidence. Nevertheless, the stupidities of the intellectuals can be further seen by considering modernism, that is, nothing less than the characteristic world view of the intellectuals of life in the modern era, perhaps most notably of the period from 1870 to 1930. On reflection, it is noticeable that modernist art and sociology are at one in the portrait they give of life in modern society.[48] Our lives are seen as being alienated, anomic and disenchanted; we are told that we are 'hollow men' living in a 'wasteland', that our lives make no sense and that our very condition is one of absurdity. Lukács was surely correct in arguing that something of the logical extreme of this viewpoint has been reached in the work of Samuel Beckett.[49]

What are we to make of this? Should we follow our artists and accept that this is indeed our condition? The largest part of the answer to these questions must be negative. Lionel Trilling once observed that it is exceptionally hard for us, given the aura enjoyed by high culture, to accept the notion that art does not always tell the truth, and can accustom us to falsehood.[50] Though striking, this formulation is an unhappy one. Art always tells us something about society, provided that we decode its message.[51] Thus it would be a great mistake, as G. K. Chesterton realized long ago, to take slum novels as an accurate account of the lives of the poor and of the working class as a whole. Chesterton argued that novels such as Maugham's *Liza of Lambeth* were sensationalist because they saw events from the outside: the interior of a pub may seem squalid and lurid to a middle-class observer and yet be a haven of warmth and cosiness to others after hard work. But such books do tell us something:

In short, these books are not a record of the psychology of poverty. They are a record of the psychology of wealth and culture when brought into contact with poverty.[52]

When we use this methodological insight to consider modernist art, it becomes obvious that the misery the intellectuals ascribe to the lives of every member of modern society in fact reflects their own position, deprived of any recognized patronage and having to exist in the interstices of the market. But if the status of humanist intellectuals has fallen in the modern world, and if their art is often pessimistic and bad-tempered because of this, then there is everything to be said for not taking their edicts as a serious guide to larger social reality. For a moment's thought must make us realize that for most human beings in industrial society, life is no longer nasty, brutish and short but pleasant, and reasonably well furnished with conveniences. It may be the case that the intellectual ferment of Weimar Berlin or *fin-de-siècle* Vienna is missing, but who would seriously favour such places, filled with poverty and anti-Semitism, at the expense of the duller but wealthier cities of the post-war world? It may, to take a different example, be the case that the political suppression of Eastern Europe has occasioned great art in the last three decades. It would be a stupidity to create societies of this sort simply *'pour encourager les artistes'*.

It is as well to own up in conclusion to the nature of the attitude to intellectuals adopted here. On the one hand, the cultural pessimism of intellectuals has been considered silly; the charge has been that it reflects the position of intellectuals themselves rather than that of most members of industrial society. Such intellectuals are seen, in this perspective, as irrelevant to more basic social processes. On the other hand, however, much has been made of the danger implicit in various intellectual strategies, above all in those concerned to solve the problem of being through politics. There is a danger that intellectuals may be judged unfairly, damned whatever they do. However, it is not really unfair to bear both these points in mind. In normal circumstances, that is, when industrial societies work without drama by means of established cultures, the dreams of cultural pessimists do not have much appeal. When history is on the move, that is, when social structures break down and cultural patterns accordingly lose their authority, matters can be entirely different.

NOTES

1. E. Gellner, *The Psychoanalytic Movement, or, The Cunning of Unreason* (London: Paladin, 1985), pp.14–15.
2. M. Ignatieff, *The Needs of Strangers* (London: Hogarth Press, 1984), chapter 3.
3. F. W. Nietzsche. *A Nietzsche Reader*, selected and translated by R. J. Hollingdale (Harmondsworth: Penguin, 1978), pp.186–7.
4. Ibid., p.158–9.
5. J. Dunn, *Western Political Theory in the Face of the Future* (Cambridge: Cambridge University Press, 1979), p.28.
6. Gellner, op. cit., chapter 1.
7. This point has been made repeatedly by Ernest Gellner. For a particularly clear statement see his *Thought and Change* (London: Weidenfeld and Nicolson, 1964).
8. Cf. I. Watt, *Conrad in the Nineteenth Century* (Berkeley: University of California Press, 1978).
9. M. Tournier, *Friday or the Other Island* (Harmondsworth:

Penguin, 1974). Cf. J. M. Coetzee, *Foe* (New York: Viking, 1987).

10. E. Durkheim, *The Elementary Forms of Religious Life* (London: George Allen and Unwin, 1915).

11. For a discussion of Marcuse in this light, see J. A. Hall, *Diagnoses of Our Time* (London: Heinemann Educational, 1981).

12. G. Steiner, *Heidegger* (London: Fontana, 1978).

13. Interesting comments on the nature of such philosophies can be found in J. Mendilow, 'The Political Philosophy of Thomas Carlyle (1795–1881): Towards a Theory of Catch-All Extremism', in J. A. Hall (ed.), *Rediscoveries* (Oxford: Oxford University Press, 1986).

14. E. Junger, 'Nationalismus und modernes Leben', (1927), cited in J. Herf, *Reactionary Modernism. Technology, Culture and Politics in Weimar and the Third Reich* (Cambridge: Cambridge University Press, 1984), p.83. Emphasis added by Herf.

15. Herf, op. cit., pp. 226–7.

16. This comment is reported in S. Lukes, *Emile Durkheim* (Harmondsworth: Penguin, 1975), p.339.

17. R. Kipling, 'Mary Postgate', in *Short Stories, Volume 2: Friendly Brook and Other Stories* (Harmondsworth: Penguin, 1971).

18. J. M. Keynes, 'My Early Beliefs', in *Two Memoirs* (London: Rupert Hart-Davis, 1949).

19. E. Goffman, 'On Face Work', in his *Interaction Ritual* (Harmondsworth: Penguin, 1972), p.41.

20. E. Goffman, 'The Nature of Deference and Demeanour', in his *Interaction Ritual*, op. cit.

21. Ibid., p.90.

22. Ibid., p.85.

23. D. Riesman et al., *The Lonely Crowd* (New Haven: Yale University Press, 1950).

24. L. Trilling, *Sincerity and Authenticity* (Oxford: Oxford University Press, 1974).

25. D. Bell, *The Cultural Contradictions of Capitalism* (London: Heinemann Educational, 1976). For a critical commentary on Bell's theory see my *Diagnoses of Our Time*, op. cit., chapter 4.

26. Many thinkers have argued along these lines: A. Gouldner, *The Coming Crisis of Western Sociology* (New York: Basic Books, 1970); R. Sennett, 'Two on the Aisle', *New York Review of Books*, 1 November 1971; J. O'Neill, *Sociology as a Skin Trade* (London: Heinemann Educational, 1972); I. Craib, *Existentialism and Sociology* (Cambridge: Cambridge University Press, 1976); and A. Dawe, 'The Underworld-view of Erving Goffman', *British Journal of Sociology*, 24 (1973).

27. Dawe, op. cit., p.251.
28. E. Goffman, *Relations in Public* (Harmondsworth: Penguin, 1972), pp.121–2.
29. E. Goffman, 'On the Characteristics of Total Institutions', in his *Asylums* (Harmondsworth: Penguin, 1968).
30. Goffman, *Relations in Public*, op. cit., p.xiii.
31. Ibid., p.xiv.
32. E. Goffman, *Frame Analysis* (Harmondsworth: Penguin, 1975), p.14.
33. E. Goffman, *Stigma* (Harmondsworth: Penguin, 1968), chapter 3, especially p.148.
34. C. G. A. Bryant, 'Privacy, Privatization and Self-determination', in J. B. Young (ed.), *Privacy* (Chichester and New York: John Wiley, 1978).
35. R. Dahrendorf, *Society and Democracy in Germany* (New York: Anchor Books, 1969), p.286.
36. J. P. Stern, *Hitler, the Führer and the People* (London: Fontana, 1974).
37. Dahrendorf, op. cit., p.295.
38. R. Shattuck, *Proust* (London: Fontana, 1974), p.17.
39. D. Martin, *Two Critiques of Spontaneity* (London: London School of Economics, 1974), p.16.
40. E. Goffman, *Encounters* (Indianapolis: Bobbs Merrill, 1961), p.77–8.
41. Martin, op. cit., p.25.
42. R. Aron, 'De la Liberté politique: Montesquieu et Jean-Jacques Rousseau', *La France Libre*, 3 (1942).
43. C. Campbell, *The Romantic Ethic and the Spirit of Modern Consumerism* (Oxford: Basil Blackwell, 1987).
44. E. Goffman, 'Role Distance', in *Encounters*, op. cit., p.152.
45. The sociologist I have in mind who uses this essay to escape social determinism is Peter Berger in his *Invitation to Sociology* (New York: Anchor Books, 1963), pp.135–6.
46. R. W. Price, *An Imperial War and the British Working Class* (London: Routledge and Kegan Paul, 1972), pp.175–6.
47. Ibid., p.242.
48. M. Mann, 'On the Ideology of Intellectuals and Other People in the Development of Capitalism', in L. N. Lindberg (ed.), *Stress and Contradiction in Modern Capitalism* (Lexington: Lexington Books, 1975); J. A. Hall, 'The Intellectuals as a New Class. Reflections on Britain', *New Universities Quarterly*, 34 (1985).
49. G. Lukács, *The Meaning of Contemporary Realism* (London: Merlin Press, 1963); and *Studies in European Realism* (London: Hillway Press, 1950).

50. L. Trilling, *Beyond Culture* (Harmondsworth: Penguin, 1967).
51. J. A. Hall, *The Sociology of Literature* (Harlow: Longman, 1979), chapter 2.
52. G. K. Chesterton, *Heretics* (London: Watts, 1905), p.281.

4
WORKERS, STATES AND CAPITALISTS

At first sight, there is something inherently offensive to liberalism in any attack on democracy. For if the individual is to be sovereign, is it not then proper that the people should rule? Regrettably, matters are more complex than this. In *Democracy in America*, Tocqueville claimed that the movement to democracy is the key and inevitable social process of modernity. However, it is well known that Tocqueville operated with two conceptions of democracy. On the one hand, he insisted that an equalization of social conditions *was* part of the spirit of the age. But, on the other hand, he concerned himself with the question of political liberty, and sought to ask whether the equalization of conditions would secure or undermine liberty. To ask this question was to suggest that there was no cast-iron guarantee why a democratic age need necessarily be a liberal one. It was analytically possible in Tocqueville's eyes that there could be a tyranny of the majority which would democratically oppress some minority and create a foul sort of society; it was equally the case that the majority might freely elect some sort of Caesarist ruler rather than choose to continue to live in liberty. Tocqueville's logical case is unquestionable: for what is democracy, in the last analysis, but the rule of the majority, and why should not such a majority choose at any particular time to overturn any constraints that have been placed upon it? The core of liberal political rule resides in the absence of arbitrariness rather than in mere numbers.

Tocqueville expressed himself dramatically by talking

about the dangers of a 'tyranny of the majority'. There are examples of cases in which minorities have been – indeed continue to be – suppressed legally, by majorities working through the ballot box; there have also been occasions, although there are not many of them, when Caesarist rulers have received, at least initially, popular support. Tocqueville's analysis of the accession to power of Napoleon III is perhaps the most brilliant account of the latter.[1] We need to bear in mind the question of whether the people were a threat to the established order. Did the behaviour of the people represent a threat to the social cohesion of liberal democracy? However, it is very important to note that Tocqueville's social thought does *not* tend to make the behaviour of the people the 'independent variable' of central importance. The people accept or acclaim a despot in societies where political despotism has already been present. The evil of despotism is that it separates social groups and classes from each other, and thereby takes away from them the capacity of co-operating so as to help the common weal. Tocqueville's thought suggests that a liberal society will be one in which social groups are both strong and autonomous, that is, one with a strong civil society. This an an insight to which we can add during the course of this chapter. My argument as a whole will be that it is despotic tendencies on the part of a state which are responsible for creating political consciousness on the part of a working class. This raises a key problem: can we talk about the state as an actor with its own will? Is it not rather the case that the state is controlled by capitalists? The answer to this question will have a considerable impact upon the way in which the relation between liberalism and capitalism is judged. In this chapter, some evidence on the relationship of capitalists to the internal actions of states is presented, with particular reference to Europe before 1914; in the next chapter, that story is continued and systematic attention given to the relations between capitalists and the external actions of states.

Class Capacities

What baseline generalizations can be made about the capacities of different social classes to create revolutions, given our position in the late twentieth century? Certain statements carry general weight and deserve consideration immediately. The purpose of much of the rest of this chapter will be to complicate matters; that is, to introduce various qualifications necessitated by historical variation.

There can be no doubt, to begin with, that certain classes have been striking and effective historical agents. One such class comes to mind as soon as we think of the great revolutions of the modern world, those of France, Russia and China. Each of these depended crucially upon the peasants taking the law into their own hands, killing aristocrats and seizing land.[2] Interestingly, the revolutionary capacity of peasants was not appreciated or anticipated by Karl Marx. He considered that peasants shared a class situation but, like potatoes in a sack, did not possess the capacity to organize and link themselves laterally.[3] This is quite wrong. Peasants and farmers have in fact shown astonishing capacities for communication and organization. Peasant mobilization has been particularly strong when the landlords have been absent, something in itself which causes resentment and allows revolution,[4] and when they have had historic organizations of their own, notably the Russian *Mir*, to fall back upon. But underlying all of this is, I suspect, something much more basic. Peasants are like the bourgeoisie in actually knowing how to operate particular economic institutions; when they seize land, they can then farm it. In contrast, and in opposition to Karl Marx, the working class brings with it no really new organizational capacity. If a working class seizes, say, an unprofitable car factory, heavily involved in the international division of labour, what then can actually be done with it?

A large amount of effort in the social sciences has been spent in explaining away, by the classification of special factors, why the working class has not so far been revolutionary. For no advanced capitalist country has suffered revolution at the hands of an industrial working class, something which can now stand as a refutation of Marx's views. Some conservative writers, convinced of the loyalty of working classes to their nations, have long been aware of this; but their testimony may not, on account of its bias, sway judgement. What is far more impressive, however, is that the same conclusion has been reached by authors on the left. Lenin's *What is to be Done?* is the most high-powered and historically significant statement of this theme.[5] Lenin's conclusions about class consciousness were hugely destructive of revolutionary hopes. He argued that labour naturally tended to be 'economistic' in concentrating its demands on better conditions of work and higher wages. His contention was that political consciousness had to be imported from the outside, by professional revolutionary intellectuals such as himself. We shall later have a fundamental reservation to make about Lenin's sociology of the working class, namely that it misses out the importance of state behaviour – and thereby misleads us about the nature of the Russian Revolution! However, there is everything to be said for Lenin's basic argument: left to themselves, workers are most unlikely to disturb the social order.

Two recent works from the left have reached very similar conclusions. Michael Mann's analysis of *Consciousness and Action among the Western Working Class* is a book of exceptional pathos in that its author's hopes are dashed, so to speak, in front of his eyes by the evidence he presents. This is broadly of the type that the productivity of capitalism has so entrenched the working class inside the capitalist system that it is incapable of acting even when, as in France in 1968, potentially revolutionary situations occur.[6] A rather similar air hangs over Barrington Moore's unduly neglected *Injustice*, the central part of which is an extended analysis of why the German working class did not become revolutionary. Moore does not allow us to believe that this was simply because of any natural urge to harmony, and he cites many ways in which co-operation occurred only as the result of heavy background coercion.[7] Nevertheless, what matters is the end result: workers went to war for their nations.

There is one particularly clear way to drive home the point at issue. It is very noticeable that both Mann and Moore discuss national working classes. In itself this amounts to a refutation of Karl Marx. For the German revolutionary thinker had believed that the key classes of the modern age, that is, capitalists and workers, would be transnational. The extent to which capitalists inhabit a society larger than that of any single state in the modern world is a vexed one, to be discussed below. The situation of the working class, in contrast, is extremely clear. In 1914, Lenin and other members of the Second International did not expect European working classes to fight in what they considered to be a capitalist war. Their expectations were shattered. Workers fought for their nations, and thereby showed that nation is nearly always a more powerful form of identity than class. This is one of the two or three key events in the history of Marxism, very largely because it allowed for geopolitics to play, as we shall see in the next chapter, the major role in social change during the twentieth century. Probably the degree of the loyalty of workers to their states should not be exaggerated. Workers were sometimes genuinely loyal, but in other cases they had their own conception of what the nation should be – a conception not often shared with the elites controlling the national state. Perhaps what matters most is the structural fact that states controlled resources so that class conflict had to take place within national boundaries. But the brute fact remains that political elites could rely on workers to take part in modern war.

Class Loyalty in Britain

Adam Smith and David Hume claimed that there was an elective affinity between commerce and liberty, and the second chapter of this book argued that they were correct

105

to do so. This is so remarkable, nay miraculous, that it is worth characterizing the whole process in more aseptic, sociological terms. The crux of the European combination of commerce and freedom was the pluralism characteristic of European social structure: there were several sources of power, no one of which was able to dominate but all of which were prepared to co-operate with the others. The development of commercial society did not destroy pluralism for the banal reason that this development was not planned, as is typical in countries seeking to force their development in order to catch up with the advanced societies. Such planning was not possible because there was no model which could be imitated. This point can be put in rather different terms. What is at issue is *time*. Consider the peasantry. All roads to modernity require solving the peasant problem, that is, ways must be found to encourage the peasants to move from the land to industrial employment.[8] Any sudden solution to the problem is bound to disrupt society from top to bottom, and is almost only ever imaginable when handled under the aegis of authoritarian government. In the English case the peasantry was dispossessed via enclosure from the sixteenth century in a process that took over three centuries to complete. One must not be too romantic about this process, as are those who praise the virtues of English gradualness. The British solution to the peasant problem was achieved under the aegis of something that, at least in peasant eyes, must have felt like a despotic centralized authority, namely the united landlord class working through Parliament. Yet this does not detract from the fact that it was the slowness of the process that allowed pluralism and rights to opposition, the very bases of liberalism, to survive intact.

The Scottish moralists, believing that hierarchy was a natural condition, theorized a world in which hierarchy and capitalism went snugly hand in hand. This combination was put into question by the French Revolution. A consequence of this was that it thereafter became vital to

106

consider how capitalism could function with the presence of organized working classes which had their own goals. How was it possible in these new circumstances to preserve the commerce *plus* liberty equation so beloved of the Scottish moralists?

The first thing to note is that this beneficent situation nearly went to the wall. Fear of revolution among the ruling classes occasioned the creation of an authoritarian state, armed with Combination Acts and Stamp Acts, that sought to stamp out political dissent altogether. Interestingly, this repressive drive did not last for very long in Britain; the Combination Acts were repealed in 1824, with the first extension of the franchise coming in 1832. There are fundamental reasons of historical patterning that largely explain the situation, and they have been neatly captured by Barrington Moore:

England's whole previous history, her reliance on a navy instead of on an army, on unpaid justices of the peace instead of royal officials, had put in the hands of the central government a repressive apparatus weaker than that possessed by the strong continental monarchies . . . The push towards industrialism had begun much earlier in England and was to render unnecessary for the English bourgeoisie any great dependence on the crown and the landed aristocracy. Finally, the landed upper classes themselves did not need to repress the peasants. Mainly they wanted to get them out of the way in order to go over to commercial farming; by and large, economic measures would be enough to provide the labour force they needed. Succeeding economically in this particular fashion, they had little need to resort to repressive political measures to continue their leadership.[9]

The fact of liberal political rule is of exceptional importance. However, *the* general mechanism upon which attention needs to be focused if we are to understand different types of industrial political economies is slightly different:

[T]he major determinant of the forms of political action adopted by the different national labour movements was the role of the state and of the social groups it claimed to represent; for at the level of industrial action clear similarities existed between similar occupations in different countries. Furthermore, it remains true that certain kinds of governmental interference in industrial relations did transform what began as economic protest into political action.[10]

Let us first examine the British case to see how this variable has operated in practice.

The presence of a liberal state in Britain, that is, a state not deliberately seeking to repress working-class organizations, made it rational for workers to concentrate their struggles, once Combination laws *had* been repealed, inside the workplace rather than against the state itself. Perhaps a certain softness to the British system resulted from it being the first industrial nation; it was not necessary to push conflicts to any absolute extreme since there was enough money in the system to buy off discontent. Probably crucial, however, was what we might describe as a virtuous and self-reinforcing cycle. Liberal politics bred industrial conflict rather than no-holds-barred political struggle. Yet it was perhaps the very absence of political struggle that encouraged the retention of liberal politics in the first place. How can this cycle be broken into? A key variable concerns the franchise. As late as 1914, Britain was not a democratic society in the sense that the suffrage had not been extended very far – certainly nothing like enough to equal the male suffrage of France, Germany and the United States, and significantly less than that enjoyed in Imperial Germany. This was important. On the one hand, it limited the fears of the middle classes: they might have to face industrial militancy but they did not lie awake at nights thinking that a working class could actually seize power and create a new form of society – something working classes suffering under political repression *did* claim as their goal. On the other hand, it created a sense of loyalty among the working class. They had to fight for citizenship rights, and the fact that these were not refused did not prevent them thereby gaining some sense of identity. But that sense of identity became political only when the state for once did become repressive; the Labour Party benefited from it when the Taff Vale court decision brought state power, albeit only temporarily, into action against trade unions.

These observations about the British case can be drawn together by considering Arthur Henderson and the Labour Party he did so much to shape. The distinguished historian of British labour, Ross McKibbin, has noted that Henderson was (indirectly) a founder of Newcastle Football Club, a leading Methodist lay preacher, a prominent figure in lawn bowls – all in addition to his role as organizer of the Labour Party.[11] This neatly captures the strong and entirely autonomous associations of British labour; it had its own life and was not that much bothered with politics. It fought loyally in the war, and there is not much sign that significant sections of the working class harboured notions of the nation of very great distinctiveness. During the war, the trade unions became very embittered by those middle-class socialist pacifists who criticized a conflict in which they were dying. Thus when the Labour Party finally gained a constitution and became capable of gaining political power, it was no accident that the unions ensured, through instituting the block vote of unions at party conferences, that they, rather than the middle classes or the socialist societies, would control the ultimate destiny of their party. This control has never been released, and the Labour Party has remained true to its name.[12]

Class Consciousness in Germany
British experience of commerce with liberty provided a model of development which had remarkable power over the modern imagination. We can see this very clearly in a book such as Ralf Dahrendorf's *Society and Democracy in Germany*, which considers it a 'problem' that Germany 'failed' to become democratic.[13] This formulation must be rejected. Once we remember that the very first emergence of capitalism and industrial capitalism took place in an

unplanned way over a very long period of time, we can then see how historically *normal* is the German route of forced development.

German development broke altogether with the British pattern. The earliest period of industrialization took place behind tariff walls. Friedrich List provided the justification for this. An open international market favoured, in his view, highly developed British industry; the infant industries of Germany needed protection. List justified this by arguing that there was nothing particularly just about the workings of that market; rather, its boundaries had been established as the result of geopolitical success. In the middle of the nineteenth century, however, Germany slowly abandoned its tariffs, and it seemed as if the tenets of British liberalism would carry the day throughout Europe. But the depression that began in the early 1870s was countered by Britain and Germany in very different ways. Where Britain remained open to the world market, Germany chose to retreat once again behind agricultural and industrial tariffs; this decision was clearly demanded by special interests, but it was also desired by the traditional geopolitical elite of Germany which preferred to retain, even at a considerable cost, sectors of the economy vital to war rather than to risk the uncertainties of the world market.[14] In this period, the state played a central role, in conjunction with banks, in shaping the economy, not least in encouraging the growth of industrial cartels. In the next chapter, the character and importance of the German mercantilist/protectionist geo-economic strategy will be examined; focus here needs to be on the consequences of state formation for relations with the working class.

German development saw the combination of authoritarianism with capitalism. There can be no doubt that this combination suited leading social classes. The grain-exporting, highly militaristic Junkers could assert their interests because of their over-representation that the estates system of Prussia – without whose co-operation Imperial Germany would neither have been born nor maintained – gave them. This power enabled them to demand agricultural protection. This situation was the exact opposite to that of England: there the aristocracy had less entrenched power and, anyway, being already heavily involved in commerce, had much less to lose. The German bourgeoisie also differed from its British counterpart in becoming fundamentally loyal to an authoritarian state. Such loyalty is not hard to explain. Prussia had united Germany; this appealed to the bourgeoisie both for nationalistic and for economic reasons, that is, all business interests benefited from the creation of national markets while the heavy industrialists did particularly well out of tariff protection. Equally importantly, the state provided the legal infrastructure on which capitalism depended, and was generally solicitous of its needs and interests. This is not to say that the bourgeoisie did not try in any way to create a liberal political system. However, the attempts which were made foundered because it was always possible for the state elite to divide liberal alliances by playing upon either nationalistic or religious sentiments.[15] It is worth highlighting what is implicit in this last sentence. The autonomy of the state was limited by the power of Junkers and, to a lesser extent, of heavy industrialists. This is not to say that it had no room for manoeuvre at all. Bismarck was fabulously adept at gaining some state autonomy by a complicated, and ever-changing, balancing between regions, classes and religious groups. However, we must note that the creator of the marriage of iron and rye was a politician. While it is certainly true that the policy in question suited and was asked for by Junkers and heavy industrialists, it would be a mistake to assume thereby that the state had no autonomy whatever from these social classes. Bismarck was adept at making all sorts of alliances, a significant number of which were based upon organizing hatred, either of foreigners or of the working class. A large

111

part of the tragedy of German politics consists in the fact that where Bismarck could escape commitments made for convenience, as on the famous occasion when he back-tracked on an early move towards social imperialism, other politicians tended to trap themselves, largely because they believed their own rhetoric.[16]

In Imperial Germany a vicious cycle to the relations of state and society existed which contrasts very neatly with the British situation. The Wilhelmine state tried to co-opt the working class with the carrot of the franchise and with welfare legislation, and to scare it by means of various sticks, the most important of which were the anti-socialist laws of 1878–90. It was the latter which proved to be crucial. The working class was forced into political conflict against the state which was preventing it from prospering on the purely industrial front. A consequence of the attraction of the German working class to socialist political consciousness was that large segments of the middle class developed a bunker-type mentality; they felt so threatened that they embraced the authoritarian state with fervour. It is very important to realize that their fears were realistic since mass suffrage characterized the political system. The results of all this in the workplace in Germany, as compared to Great Britain, were very striking:

[G]erman employers and especially those in the heavy industrial sector revealed an almost total hostility to independent working-class organization (although many were prepared to establish dependent company unions, the so-called 'yellow' unions) until the political pressures of government in the course of the First World War and above all in the wake of the revolution of 1918. This is clear if one compares the figures concerning the number of workers covered by collective agreements in Britain and Germany before 1914. In Britain in 1910 no fewer than 900,000 miners, 500,000 railway workers, 460,000 textile workers and 230,000 metalworkers benefited from such agreements, whereas in Germany three years later the equivalent figures related to only 16,000 textile operatives, 1,376 metalworkers, and a miserly 82 miners![17]

The key consequence of this social formation is quite clear. Political repression was a dangerous route to follow. Experience of prison, rather than of low wages, gave bitterness to social action while the presence of a repressive state necessitated action taking a political form. Thus by the end of the nineteenth century an authoritarian state had bred the largest and best-organized politicized labour movement in Europe.

Recent revisionist German historians have claimed that domestic fear of the working classes encouraged the state elite to gain national unity by engaging in aggressive external policy.[18] Some politicians did use language which suggested such fears, and there is an element of truth to this position. But these revisionists have themselves been revised. There is evidence to show that some of this fear was for public benefit only; and it was often designed for domestic rather than external use, as in 1912 when a socialist scare proved useful against the right. In private, different sentiments were often expressed: Bethmann Hollweg, for example, was certain that war would not avoid but rather *cause* social revolution.[19] In general, however, labour could be relied upon as far as foreign policy-making was concerned, and the test of war showed that it was prepared to defend its nation. However, there was no sign that the working class shared a conception of the nation with its rulers, and a great deal of insistence that it was fighting a defensive war against autocratic Tsarist Russia. But this reservation did not ultimately matter.

The comparative typology of working-class movements will allow us to understand the German situation rather better. However, this is a good place to stress an analytic point very firmly. German social evolution demonstrates that the equation between commerce and liberty was contingent rather than necessary. The middle classes of this society had no compunction about supporting an authoritarian political order provided that it was sympathetic to their needs, most importantly that of national unification.

Nevertheless, the fact that the new capitalist elite lent support to a traditional regime should not facilely be interpreted as proving that this new elite controlled the state, or that this state 'did their work'.

A Typology of Class Feeling

There is a considerable diversity to the industrial politics of contemporary capitalist states, and the range of variation in the period before 1914 was markedly greater. There are a number of variables which explain such variation.[20] The style of working-class politics will vary according to patterns of industrialization, with working classes that have been created during industrialization, for example that of Sweden, proving to be good material for a corporatist style of political economy. Equally important is whether different conflicts are 'superimposed' on top of each other.[21] A striking example of this is the superimposition of religious and class conflict in late-nineteenth-century France; this situation made it necessary for a man of the left to be at once secular *and* socialist. This naturally exacerbated the intensity of political conflict. It stands in decided contrast to the British case, where a religion was available for workers, with the consequence that the intensity of class conflict was thereby much muted.

However, it is a third variable, that of the attitude of the state towards its working class, that is the most important. This variable has already been illustrated through analysing the British and German cases. However, if we are to assess with real thoroughness the fears that liberals had of labour, then it is necessary to offer a more complete typology of the variations of relations between states and workers before 1914. The polar points of this typology are not represented by Britain and Germany, but we can understand these cases better by placing them within a general scheme.

At one pole of the typology stands the United States. Obviously there has been no large-scale organized socialism in the United States, and three peculiarities of the American situation explain why this is so. First, the country was so diverse socially that it was, and is, very hard, perhaps impossible, for any one cause completely to dominate it. This was true not just for the workers, but also for the political elite. Certainly America did not boast any kind of authoritarian state, not least because, having no feudal past, it had no 'old regime' in the first place. Secondly, class struggles took place only in the industrial arena because the state was not systematically opposed to the working class. The American revolution had been made by small farmers and artisans quite as much as by landowners and merchants. In consequence, white adult males quickly gained citizenship rights:

By the early 1830s all of them, in all states, possessed the vote – fifty years earlier than anywhere else, fifty years before the emergence of a powerful labour movement. Thus the political demands of labour could be gradually expressed *within* an existing political constitution and party system.[22]

These citizenship rights were much extended as the result of the mass participation in the armies of the Civil War.[23] The peculiarity of the American situation is that a labour movement was never involved in seeking citizenship rights; these were either enshrined in the very idea of America, or achieved early on as the result of conscription warfare. This is important since the salience of a working class is likely to depend upon the extent to which it was involved in the struggle for citizenship. Thirdly, endless waves of immigration, to the land of the free, diluted the concentration of labour.

It is worth pausing for a moment to assess this polar position. Following the spirit of the nineteenth century, let us call it that of pure liberalism – but with a warning that the nature of liberal citizenship will be redefined in Chapter 7. European historians and social scientists for the last fifty years have investigated the question 'why is there no socialism in the United States?' – the title of a striking book on the topic by Werner Sombart.[24] Now this phrasing suggests that the United States is peculiar, a deviation from the norm, best understood with reference to Marxism, in which a more and more organized working class girds up its loins in order to join battle with capitalism and thus to achieve socialism. This way of putting the matter may be entirely wrong. If there is a 'natural' norm, perhaps it is that of the United States.[25] For what is implied in this chapter is that it is the presence of repressive elites, and not capitalism per se, which is responsible for the emergence of class conflict.

The British case stands fairly close to this polar position. We have seen that the British state was generally liberal. But the fact that workers had to fight for citizenship gave them a feeling of class loyalty. In a fundamental sense class did and does not exist in the United States, whereas it clearly does in Britain. The British working class became an estate of society rather than simply being citizens in society. This position has usually accorded with relatively peaceful, even passive political conflict; but great militancy can result when the liberties of the estate are threatened.

At this point, let me jump towards the other pole since this will then make it easier to place German bureaucratic-authoritarianism within the scheme. The other pole is that provided by late-nineteenth- and early-twentieth-century Russia. It is certainly the case that the peasant seizure of land in 1917 was a vital factor making revolution possible, not least because it thereby made it impossible for reactionary forces to be recruited in the countryside to put down the social experiments in St Petersburg and Moscow. It is equally true that defeat in war debilitated the establishment.[26] Nevertheless, there were genuinely revolutionary pressures for many years before this, and they originated from the working class of St Petersburg and Moscow. Interestingly, the workers involved were for once far more radical than their leaders, and at crucial moments even the

Bolshevik Party was following rather than leading its workers. This is ironical given Lenin's analysis of economism in *What is to be Done?*, although it is always important to remember that Lenin's intellectual work was subsumed by his career as a revolutionary: by 1917 he no longer subscribed to his earlier pamphlet. Workers made a vital contribution to revolution: the Russian Revolution probably deserves to be called the only working-class revolution in world history, although honourable mentions in the despatches of the left should be accorded to the German working class's attempted revolution of 1919.

It is possible to gain a much better understanding of the Russian Revolution as the result of Tim McDaniel's meticulously researched *Autocracy, Capitalism and Revolution in Russia.*[27] Autocratic government was different from the bureaucratic-authoritarianism of Imperial Germany. The Tsarist government sought to be the father of all the people. A consequence of this was that it was suspicious of every intermediary organization and grouping that stood between it and the people. This political culture provided very poor soil for capitalism. There was no tradition of private property, a limited legal tradition and none of that contractualistic tradition that had characterized feudal Europe.

At the end of the nineteenth century, a furious debate took place between those who wished to westernize Russia and those who wished to remain loyal to native traditions. Neither side definitively won this debate, and the Russian state consequently prevaricated between two options: in so doing, as is so often the case, it managed to get the worst of both worlds. The westernizers introduced capitalism, but were unable, despite several government reports, to introduce the basic union organization that might have limited class conflict to the workplace. A vital point about such limitation is that it would have co-opted the workers into a routinized existence, and thereby made them visible and accountable. On the occasions when this policy was tried, most notably immediately after the 1905 Revolution, it

117

seemed as if it was likely to prove successful.[28] However, the policy was not consistently maintained. The traditionalists tried to integrate the workers directly into the state, as in the Zubatov movement. One important consequence of the failure of this movement was that the workers, whose hopes had been raised by the state, blamed the state rather than employers or the market. This was one factor that explains why the autocracy eventually moved towards a policy of total repression. It was that policy which produced workers with revolutionary political consciousness. Such workers had little choice; they had to destroy the autocracy before anything else would be possible.

The bureaucratic-authoritarianism of Imperial Germany was quite different from this. The German state never tried to undermine the hierarchical principle upon which capitalism depended; it had none of that monarchist populism which so raised the expectations of Russian workers. It could therefore afford, after the experiment with anti-socialist laws, to take the state out of industrial relations, that is, to hand them back to the capitalist class. A consequence of this was that the German working class, politically aware though it was, did not really develop the revolutionary consciousness that once seemed a possibility.

This is a good moment at which to highlight the variables at work in the typology; this can be done by recalling Tocqueville. The liberal end of the typology is one in which full political and social pluralism is permitted; the autocratic pole seeks to destroy both of these qualities. It is worth noting immediately an absolutely vital issue that follows from this typology. Michael Mann has very specifically argued that the combination of capital with authority was widely admired in 1914, and that there is every chance that it would have had continued success but for its accidental destruction in war[29]. This is a vital matter in any study of liberalism. There is no doubt that capitalists did ally themselves with authoritarian regimes. However, there are some good reasons, to be examined in Chapter 7, for believing that the 'logic' of the scientific-industrial complex may move societies towards a recognition of civil society, and thereby towards softer political rule. This is not to say for a moment that this is inevitable. If Tsarist Russia faced working-class revolution because of its repressive apparatus, it behoves us to remember that Marxist autocracy under Stalin found a way completely to squash political and social pluralism, although the long-term cost of that option may yet cause it to be re-examined.[30]

This typology invites use. One usage that suggests itself is that of seeing how different types of development present different class feelings which have to be dealt with by a modernizing elite. Nicos Mouzelis's *The Politics of the Semi-Periphery* is an example of this approach: it describes the very particular problems that faced those countries which had early democracy and late industrialization.[31] However, it is enough for the purposes of this book simply to fit one or two other societies into the typology. Modern Mexico would stand between the British and German cases examined here because social pluralism is respected; there are, within unspecified limits, different parties, even though the chances of victory are not, to put it mildly, in any way fair. Very interestingly, some societies can move around in this typology. Until even the late 1930s Argentina would have been very close to the British case, not surprisingly as it sought to adopt something like the Westminster model.[32] At that time, there was a clear understanding on the part of a basically liberal elite that the working class could slowly be integrated into society, and that there was no fundamental need to fear organized socialism. Perhaps one reason for this optimism was that much of the working class, being largely comprised of new immigrants who were not allowed to vote, had a small electoral presence. But whatever the basis of this optimism, this policy worked, and it seemed for a full decade as if Argentina's path to development was assured. However, this liberal elite lost control of the state, very largely because of the sustained consequences of the creation of trading blocs in the inter-war years. In a situation of social stalemate, Juan Peron gave Argentina an entirely new direction. Peron was trained in Mussolini's Italy, and he copied the fascistic measures of Italy and Spain. He introduced protectionist measures and sought to establish corporatism; that is, he sought to involve the organized working class, as had never been done, in the state and not in the workplace. These policies proved disastrous. They increased the intensity of class conflict very markedly, especially as protectionism ruined the competitive capacity of Argentinian industry. It is entirely proper to see Raul Alfonsin's liberalizing Argentina as the restoration to power of a wiser, more liberal elite.[33]

Conclusion: A Ruling Class?

Let us return to the general question. Were liberals right to fear the working classes? Was the activity of the working class such as to undermine the social cohesion of various national societies? The evidence overwhelmingly points to a negative answer. Working classes left to themselves, i.e. allowed to organize and to make demands at the industrial level, are not revolutionary. Working-class revolutionaries are the result of authoritarian state behaviour. This is an aseptic, sociological answer, the purpose of which is to show that the drift to illiberalism was a mistake which was not logically necessary. There is no reason to believe that this facet of capitalism must destroy liberal societies; capitalists can learn that their interests are best served by accommodation rather than by repression.

It is at this point that genuine purchase can be gained on a topic that has not been openly confronted to this point. Throughout this chapter, and especially in its closing stages, I have distinguished between 'elite' and 'class'. No Marxist will be happy with this distinction since it does, and is designed to, suggest something more than that a class as such cannot rule for logistical reasons. My contention is rather that state elites can have autonomy from social classes. It would be extremely silly to claim that such autonomy is always available. There are striking cases when it is clearly not present at all.[34] Was it present in the late nineteenth and early twentieth centuries in the nation-states of the advanced capitalist world? This is a vital question: for it would not make any ultimate sense to talk of the state creating class consciousness if the states in question were in the pockets of the capitalist class.

The evidence suggests that the decisions taken with regard to the working class at key junctures were taken in most states by elites for their own reasons, and in substantial autonomy from leading capitalists. The most striking example is that of Tsarist Russia. The autocracy hated capitalists, and sought to undermine the very principle of hierarchy on which they might have been able to establish a new order. Similarly, Peron's rule systematically went against the knowledge of those liberal capitalists, previously influential in the state, that a working class left alone will pose no problem. The situation in Imperial Germany was more complex. The autonomy of the state was certainly limited by societal pressure, especially that applied by the Junkers. Furthermore, the bourgeoisie clearly went along with authoritarianism: although this was comprehensible, it is worth noting that the bourgeoisie failed, as it seems to with what both liberals and Marxists must think of as a regrettable regularity, to recognize its very best interests. In so far as such capitalists played a part in the functioning of vicious regimes, they have, of course, blood on their hands. But something of the dynamism of the German state resulted from the autonomous actions of the traditional and authoritarian elite.

There is no reason in principle, as is proven by the history of Great Britain and the United States, to believe that capitalism cannot ally itself with a liberal political regime. However, the behaviour of capitalists in the past is such that we can say that capitalism will not bring freedom by itself.

NOTES

1. A. de Tocqueville, *The Old Regime and the French Revolution* (New York: Anchor Books, 1955).
2. Cf. T. Skocpol, *States and Social Revolutions* (Cambridge: Cambridge University Press, 1979).
3. K. Marx, 'The Eighteenth Brumaire of Louis Bonaparte', in *Surveys from Exile* (Harmondsworth: Penguin, 1973), pp.238–9.
4. This point was first made by Tocqueville in *The Old Regime and the French Revolution*, op. cit.; it has been taken up by Skocpol in *States and Social Revolutions*, op. cit.
5. V. I. Lenin, *What is to be Done? Burning Questions of Our Movement* (first published 1902), in *Collected Works*, Vol. 5 (London: Lawrence and Wishart, 1961).
6. M. Mann, *Consciousness and Action among the Western Working Class* (London: Macmillan, 1973).
7. B. Moore, *Injustice: The Social Bases of Obedience and Revolt* (New York: M. E. Sharpe, 1978).
8. This is a principal thesis of Barrington Moore's *Social Origins of Dictatorship and Democracy* (Harmondsworth: Penguin, 1969).
9. Ibid., p.444.
10. D. Geary, *European Labour Protest 1848–1945* (London: Methuen, 1984), p.60.
11. R. McKibbin, 'Why was there no Marxism in Great Britain', *English Historical Review*, 99 (1984). McKibbin's case is amplified in 'Work and Hobbies in Britain, 1880–1950', in J. Winter (ed.), *The Working Class in Modern British History* (Cambridge: Cambridge University Press, 1983) and in 'Working Class Gambling in Britain, 1880–1939', *Past and Present*, 82 (1979).
12. R. McKibbin, *The Evolution of the Labour Party, 1910–24* (Oxford: Oxford University Press, 1974).
13. R. Dahrendorf, *Society and Democracy in Germany* (New York: Anchor Books, 1969). Cf. my discussion of Dahrendorf's work in *Diagnoses of Our Time* (London: Heinemann Educational, 1981).
14. P. Kennedy, *The Rise of the Anglo German Antagonism, 1860–1914* (London: George Allen and Unwin, 1980); P. Gourevitch, *Politics in Hard Times: Comparative Responses to International*

Economic Crisis (Ithaca, NY: Cornell University Press, 1986). These are stimulating books, but I find both slightly economistic.

15. D. Blackbourn and G. Eley, *The Peculiarities of German History: Bourgeois Society and Politics in Nineteenth Century Germany* (Oxford: Oxford University Press, 1984).

16. H. Kissinger, 'The White Revolutionary: Reflections on Bismarck', *Daedalus* (Summer 1968); A. J. P. Taylor, *Bismarck* (New York: Vintage Books, 1967).

17. Geary, op. cit., pp.56–7.

18 H. U. Wehler, *The German Empire, 1871–1918* (Leamington Spa: Berg, 1983).

19. R. Kaiser, 'Germany and the Origins of the First World War', *Journal of Modern History*, 55 (1983).

20. I am indebted here to discussion with Nicos Mouzelis, Michael Mann, Colin Crouch, Tim McDaniel and Carlos Waisman. Key works by all these authors, with the exception of Crouch, are cited immediately below. The essay of Crouch's that has proved most helpful is 'Sharing Public Space: States and Organised Interests in Western Europe', in J. A. Hall (ed.), *States in History* (Oxford: Basil Blackwell, 1986).

21. R. Dahrendorf, *Class and Class Conflict in Industrial Society* (London: Routledge and Kegan Paul, 1959).

22. M. Mann, 'Citizenship and Ruling Class Strategies', *Sociology*, 21 (1987).

23. T. Skocpol and J. Ikenberry, 'The Political Formation of the American Welfare State in Historical and Comparative Perspective', *Comparative Social Research*, 6 (1983).

24. W. Sombart, *Why is there no Socialism in the United States?* (ed. C. Husbands) (London: Macmillan, 1976).

25. Considering America as 'normal' goes against the grain of most theorizing, and it is a mark of Michael Mann's originality to have been, to my knowledge, the first person to make this point. His preliminary statement on the matter is contained in 'Citizenship and Ruling Class Strategies', op. cit.

26. Skocpol, *States and Social Revolutions*, op. cit.

27. T. McDaniel, *Autocracy, Capitalism and Revolution in Russia* (Berkeley: University of California Press, 1987).

28. V. Bonnell, *Roots of Rebellion: Workers' Politics and Organisations in St Petersburg and Moscow, 1900–14* (Berkeley: University of California Press, 1983).

29. Mann, op. cit.

30. The idea that Stalinism represents a (successful) continuance of the Russian autocratic tradition was suggested to me in conversation by Tim McDaniel.

31. N. Mouzelis, *The Politics of the Semi-Periphery* (London: Macmillan, 1986).

32. The problem of the reversal of development is treated by Carlos Waisman in The Reversal of Development in Argentina (Princeton: Princeton University Press, 1987).

33. This is a good moment to point to a weakness of my typology – which I would have corrected in the text had my concern been to understand working-class action *in toto* rather than simply to investigate whether liberals were justified in fearing the working class. The weakness is that the scale suggests that authoritarianism will tend to exclude participation. While it is true that Tsarist Russia and Imperial Germany sought to control and exclude, it is important to note that fascism, especially in its Latin American variants, sought both to mobilize the masses and to have authoritarian rule. The key example of such politics is Peronism. I am indebted to Carlos Waisman for this point. See his *Modernisation and the Working Class* (Austin: University of Texas, 1982) for a positive abundance of variables.

34. L. Zamosc, *The Agrarian Question and the Peasant Movement in Colombia* (New York: Cambridge University Press, 1986). This is an interesting book from the perspective of this chapter since it suggests that the Colombian peasant movement was created, at least in part, because of the way in which the state treated the peasants. I suspect that this is generally less true of peasant movements than it is of working-class movements, but the whole matter needs investigation.

5
STATES, WARS AND
CAPITALISTS

Mainstream liberalism's striking theory of the incidence of war and peace was discredited by the onset of the Second World War – which is not to say that it is without influence on our preconceptions even today. The theory in question is economistic; amusingly, it is, once again, the mirror-image of Marxism. Where Marxism argued that capitalism spread war, liberalism's hope was that the spread of capitalism would usher in a reign of peace. My argument will be that wars are at least sometimes, and in my opinion often, the result of autonomous geopolitical processes, i.e. that no general *social* theory of war and peace is available or indeed possible. However, the wars that have taken place in the modern industrial era have naturally tended to be justified on economic grounds, and it will prove hard, but possible, to separate economic and political factors when discussing the Peloponnesian wars of twentieth-century Europe. It is worth highlighting an implication of the position to be taken about the autonomy of geopolitics immediately. To say that geopolitics is autonomous is to deny that capitalists, at least on some key occasions, control states, a judgement which has significant consequences for political practice.

Geopolitical events have, to use the words of that unorthodox Marxist Leon Trotsky, been 'the locomotive of history' in the twentieth century. One purpose of this chapter is to state clearly those inadequacies of mainstream liberalism's understanding of geopolitics that played some small but revealing part in actually allowing the geopolitical disaster that struck Europe. The fact that this was so does *not* mean that the general ethic of liberalism should be considered worthless in consequence.

Dreams and Nightmares

Liberal theory, at least from the time of Erasmus, has been exceptionally hostile to war. It has tended to see it as bestial folly, the sign of ancient and atavistic forces, and it has consequently sought to reorder social relationships so that war might be avoided. Liberalism sought to make a world modelled after its own predilections: cosmopolitan, peaceful and rational. This part of liberal theory has noble intent, and it is certainly much neglected in recent general discussions of the nature of liberalism. This is inexcusable given the presence of two fine treatments of 'the liberal conscience', namely A. J. P. Taylor's *The Trouble Makers* and Michael Howard's *War and the Liberal Conscience*; these stand behind my account of this aspect of liberalism.[1]

There were several strands that made up the liberal dream, albeit they were often interlinked. First, the liberal conscience argued that wars were the result of dynastic politics. They were caused by a feudal class who gained profit and status in their pursuit. Not surprisingly, this view was propagated at the time of the French Revolution by a host of thinkers, perhaps most notably by Tom Paine. The solution to this social cause of war was democracy, and, in particular, the creation of open decision-making; this led to the cry for 'no secret treaties' in foreign policy. For the people were held to be naturally pacific since it was they, after all, who were killed in wars; the more they influenced policy, the greater would be the chances of the reign of peace.

Although liberalism never turned its back on this view, a second analysis gained favour during the nineteenth century which was subtly different: feudal militarism was still seen as a cause of war, but a different analysis of it was offered and in consequence an entirely different solution proposed. War was considered by some who held this theory, notably by Auguste Comte (by no means a liberal in every respect), Herbert Spencer and Thorstein Veblen in his classic *Imperial Germany and the Industrial Revolution*, as relatively rational in periods of scarcity when a fight for a fixed amount of resources could very definitely increase one's own wealth; but the age of industry was held to have changed this, and to have finally made war quite irrational. Somewhat in contrast, Richard Cobden, the clearest exponent of the Manchester School of political economy, considered that war between nations always diminished the size of the total economic product. Where the former tended to stress the importance of having men of industry in key positions inside a nation-state, the latter tended to stress the benefits of unconstrained free trade between nations. The hopes of the latter were marvellously captured by Cobden in his parliamentary speech on the Don Pacifico debate in 1850:

The progress of freedom depends more upon the maintenance of peace, the spread of commerce, and the diffusion of education, than upon the labours of cabinets and foreign offices ... [There should be] as little intercourse as possible between Governments; as much connexion as possible between the nations of the world.[2]

Lest it be thought that these remarks are merely historical, it is as well to insist that they are part of current parlance, a sign of how deeply liberalism has affected the terms within which we live our lives. For are we not all against war, convinced that other people push us into conflict? Are we not tempted to believe that industrialization and material prosperity, as in the détente policy of Nixon and Kissinger, will integrate the Soviet Union into the world polity?

There were tensions inside the liberal conscience as it unfolded during the course of the nineteenth century, and two of these, again interrelated, can be identified. The first

127

can be dramatized by recalling the conflict between the high priests of the Manchester School, namely Cobden and his friend John Bright, and Gladstone, the leader of the Liberal Party for most of the latter part of the nineteenth century. Cobden and Bright were against all interference whatever, with the favourite toast of the former being 'No foreign politics!' This did not mean that they did not care about liberal goals. Rather they believed that any injustice in the international polity would right itself as naturally as the hidden hand ironed out irregularities in economic life. Ascetic and this-worldly Protestant activism could not endorse such a passive view. Gladstone, in particular, was far too much a moral crusader to accept this, despite his deep allegiance to certain Manchester School presuppositions, most notably the need for retrenchment and free trade. The difference came to a head in the late 1870s and early 1880s. Gladstone, 'the people's William', led the famous agitation against 'the Bulgarian Horrors', i.e. the massacre of Bulgarians by Turks in the 1870s. Gladstone opposed the foreign policy of Disraeli, which supported Turkey against Russia for 'balance-of-power' reasons, with arguments drawn from universal morality. It was in this context, during one of his Midlothian speeches, that he distinguished his interventionist demands from the absolute non-interventionism of the Manchester School:

What is called the Manchester School has never ruled the foreign policy of this country – never during a Conservative Government, and never especially during a Liberal Government . . . It is not only a respectable, it is even a noble error . . . But however deplorable wars may be, they are among the necessities of our condition; and there are times when justice, when faith, when the failure of mankind, require a man not to shrink from the responsibility of undertaking them.[3]

Gladstone justified intervention on the grounds of 'the public law of Europe', something which did not actually exist but which corresponded to our highest sentiments.

This represents a third, analytically distinct strand to liberal conscience, and we shall hear more of such crusading views later, for Gladstone's views were influential in the United States, particularly on Woodrow Wilson. The really decisive break between the two approaches came when Gladstone annexed Egypt. This was too much for Bright, who resigned from Gladstone's cabinet. What seemed like a straightforward denial of public law was, however, capable, in Gladstone's eyes, of being defended. Public law applied to the advanced European nations, but those nations, provided that they shouldered the full burden involved, were justified, on account of their greater level of civilization, of intervening in non-European areas in order to bring them higher up on the ladder of civilization. However, to everyone else it looked as if Gladstone was a moralist in opposition, but that his foreign policy in office ran according to traditional balance-of-power principles.

A second reason for going beyond the negative injunctions of Manchester was provided by nationalism. Giuseppe Mazzini explicitly criticized the conservatism of the Manchester position; it had, in his eyes, no conception of the need for people first to establish their nations *before* the beneficent and felicific economic calculus could come into being at all. Mazzini preached the necessity for war so that various peoples could become free. This whole matter was one on which some liberals prevaricated quite desperately. The Manchester School was, however, unequivocal:

In 1856 Cobden denounced the various nationalist groups in England: 'They have *their* scheme of foreign intervention, the wildest and most anarchical of all, for it sets aside the allegiance to treaties and international obligations and would set up a universal propaganda of insurrection and rebellion'. While in 1864 his friend and colleague Henry Richard, who devoted his life to the running of the British Peace Society, declared that 'this idea of nationality is a poor, low, selfish, unchristian idea, at variance with the very principle of an advanced civilisation'.[4]

John Stuart Mill was sufficiently imbued with this position to note with distaste in 1849 that 'in the backward parts of Europe and even . . . in Germany, the sentiment of nationality so far outweighs the love of liberty that the people are willing to abet their rulers in crushing the liberty and independence of any people not of their race and language'.[5] Nevertheless, Mill insisted that the right to self-determination was central to liberalism. In 1874 he published his 'A few Words on Non-Intervention', in which he allowed intervention if it could help the peoples of Europe become free.[6] Of course, *the* great moment of liberalism's championing of the rights of subjected peoples came in the Versailles Treaty of 1919, largely at the behest of Woodrow Wilson. It was noticeable, however, that a certain gap had opened up between the American and European liberals. In 1917 H. N. Brailsford had begun to argue against any extension of the principle of nationality since each new state, possessed of its own minorities, would 'reproduce in little the hatreds and confusions of Europe'.[7] Michael Howard's comment on this tortuous development of an already much troubled position is worth recording:

Ironically therefore, as Allied war aims hardened in favour of the destruction of the German and Austrian political systems in the name of democracy and of national self-determination, the voice of the liberal opposition was heard defending the preservation of the power of Germany and the structure of the Austrian Empire in order to maintain a viable state-system in Europe; something not far removed indeed from a balance of power. By the end of the war . . . the radicals were urging something very much like a restoration of the *status quo* of 1914.[8]

Let us now turn attention away from the dream of a world made peaceful by free trade, and examine the explanation that liberals offered for the wars which nevertheless took place in the nineteenth and early twentieth centuries. The best way in which light can be cast upon their nightmare is to scrutinize the thought of John A.

Hobson, whose *Imperialism* remarkably influenced both Keynes and Lenin.

It would be a great mistake to suggest that Hobson was in any way at odds with the dream which has been outlined. Interestingly, nearly a full decade after the publication of *Imperialism*, he argued the standard Cobdenite case in *An Economic Interpretation of Investment*:

As the area of investment widens for any class or nation of investors, their interests and sympathies expand, and the influence they exert through public opinion or politics upon the conduct of affairs in the places where they have invested becomes a factor of growing importance. Regarded merely as an educational influence, this expansion of the area of investment is of considerable efficacy. A man whose business interests are confined within his parish is parochial in his sympathies and outlook. If, on the other hand, his trade brings him into touch with businessmen in many other towns in his native country, his country means more to him – he is a better citizen. Still more is this the case where trading interest is supplemented by investment and a businessman has a 'stake' in a number of industries in various places.[9]

Hobson is usually seen as the critic of imperialism, but when we unpack his thesis on imperialism it becomes apparent that there is much less of a contradiction in his position than there would seem to be at first glance. After 1895, imperialism set the mood for British political debate, and Hobson was representative of liberals in responding on several occasions. In an interesting article in 1898 he opposed the extension of Western influence in China on the grounds that it was *not* necessarily true that 'trade followed the flag';[10] he argued that we might acquire expensive possessions around the world, the maintenance of which would encourage sacrifice and autocracy at home, and discover that our trade remained with advanced nations. The trouble with this rationalist argument against imperialism is that it failed to explain the popularity of the South African War, a popularity shared in business circles, which began in 1899. If imperialism was economically irrational, did this not mean that social actors in this case were being utterly irrational, incapable of calculating their own interests? If this were true, did it not signal the end of all liberal hopes?

Imperialism found a way round this difficulty. In the second and third chapters, Hobson reiterated the argument made in connection with China, namely that most British capitalists did not benefit in terms of raw materials, investment, markets or trade from the South African connection. Nevertheless, it was possible to explain the war in rational terms; what was not rational for the nation and the business community as a whole *was* in the interests of a particular section of the business community:

The only possible answer is that the business interests of the nation as a whole are subordinated to those of certain sectional interests that usurp control of the national resources and use them for private gain.[11]

These private interests were those of international Jewish finance capital, about which Hobson wrote in blatantly anti-Semitic terms.

What is interesting in this is the desire to provide a social, or rather economic, interpretation of war. Hobson's hopes had been that economics could remove war, and he never doubted but that a properly organized home economy – one without that under-consumption by the masses which gave excessive profits to financiers which were then used in imperialist ventures – would allow such dreams to come true. But his fears are the neat inverse of his general case. There is little to be said in favour of Hobson's general account of the social origins of war, and even less to be said about his specific explanation for the Boer War. This has not stopped his negative case becoming extremely influential. In so far as Marxism has an explanation for war, it tends – as is so often the case with Marxism – to be in complete opposition to liberal hopes with which it thereby continues to share a frame of reference. Marxists have tended to drop the liberal dream altogether, and simply to explain war in terms of the needs of capitalism. The pioneer work of this type was Lenin's *Imperialism, the Highest Stage of Capitalism*, and Marxist theory has not gone far beyond the terms of this key work ever since. Lenin believed that the First World War was explicable in terms of the fight between capitalist states for markets; for a while this conflict took place in the colonies, but it eventually re-emerged in the European sphere. This is clearly consistent with Marxist economic premises, and similar theories have been offered to explain the involvement of the United States in Vietnam.[12]

These dreams and nightmares can be assessed in two stages. In the next section an alternative explanation of war and peace between nations is offered. Analysis of the wars of twentieth-century Europe will enable us then to establish in which ways these two theories, that is, liberalism/Marxism and that of the autonomy of geopolitics, help us to make sense of what happened – a careful formulation made necessary by the fact that both theories have elements of truth, not surprisingly since class and geopolitics do interact with each other.

The Sociology of War

In the first chapter of this book a distinction was drawn between the sophisticated liberalism of Adam Smith and the naïve economistic liberalism, which proved to have great influence on some of Marx's key presuppositions, and which came to dominate neo-classical economics; the former had a real appreciation of the autonomy of political power, while the latter tended to see it as the mere reflection of economic processes. The liberal conscience is excessively economistic in a wholly similar manner. Following Howard and Taylor, what has been referred to here as *the* liberal view is the dissenting, rationalist, economistic and puritanical view which sees war as unnatural and removable, and, when it does occur, as the consequence of special interests –

capitalists, arms manufacturers and salesmen, or militaristic politicians hiding behind secret treaties. It is only fair to add that there have been thinkers who have wished to remain loyal to the liberal tradition but who have rejected the dictates of the liberal conscience as unsound. I have in mind here Machiavelli, Montesquieu, Kant and, more recently, Elie Halévy and Raymond Aron. Analysis of their view of the nature of war is appropriate here for the simplest of reasons: liberalism can only survive if it takes geopolitics seriously. Where appreciation of the dangers of political power always remained more or less central to liberalism, proper geopolitical understanding has proved rare.

There is no need, on most occasions, to seek for any reductionist explanation, either social or economic, for the occurrence of war. International society differs from that of a national society in being bereft of any central government. In these circumstances it is natural that states seek to guard their independence and security. This is the traditional wisdom of those who have thought most deeply and realistically about war down the ages, from Thucydides to Machiavelli, and from Hobbes to Clausewitz. Hobbes's comment neatly sums up their general position:

[Y]et in all time Kings, and Persons of Soveraign authority, because of their independency, are in continuable jealousies, and are in the state and posture of Gladiators; having their weapons pointing, and their eyes fixed on one another; that is, their Forts, Garrisons, and Guns, upon the Frontiers of their Kingdoms; and continuable spyes upon their neighbours; which is a posture of war.[13]

In a world of essential indeterminacy, state actors sometimes prefer, as Raymond Aron realized, to take risks than to act conservatively:

Even the desire for revenge is not more irrational than the will to power. Political units are in competition: the satisfactions of *amour propre*, victory or prestige, are no less real than the so-called material satisfactions, such as the gain of a province or a population.

Not only are the historical objectives of political units not deducible from the relations of forces, but the ultimate objectives of such units are legitimately equivocal. Security, power, glory, idea are essentially heterogeneous objectives which can be reduced to a single term only by distorting the human meaning of diplomatic-strategic action. If the rivalry of states is comparable to a game, what is 'at stake' cannot be designated by a single concept, valid for all civilisations at all periods. Diplomacy is a game in which the players sometimes risk losing their lives, sometimes prefer victory itself to the advantages that would result from it.[14]

Such thinkers do not adulate struggle in some sort of Nietzschean and Social Darwinist manner. Their general position simply leads them to reject the liberal conscience as mistaken. However, these thinkers are not without moral views of their own, that is, they insist that we can respond with judgement to a state of affairs that must first be recognized and understood. Thus Aron puts as the legend to his great treatise *Peace and War* the thoroughly Kantian sentiment of Montesquieu that:

International law is based by nature upon this principle: that the various nations ought to do, in peace, the most good to each other and, in war, the least harm possible, without detriment to their genuine interests.[15]

It seems paradoxical that a 'realist' should endorse such a statement; the matter needs investigation.

The thinkers being discussed would all agree that observation of this maxim is, in fact, in the long-term interest of states themselves. Aron makes the point especially clearly in his demonstration that Clausewitz was forced to move progressively away from his initial enthusiasm for total, Napoleonic-type war. This change in his thought was necessitated by observing how Napoleon's blind ascension to extremes created a great coalition that destroyed him; in contrast, Frederick the Great's limited and more finely judged wars, which Clausewitz came to admire more and more, achieved the objectives they set themselves without incurring disaster. It was this experience which necessitated the great German theorist revising his initial definition of war as 'the continuation of politics by other means'. His final, complete definition has been neatly summarized thus:

War, considered in its concrete totality, is composed of a strange trinity: the *original violence* of its element, the hatred and hostility that must be considered as a blind natural tendency; *the play of probabilities and chance* which make it a free activity of the soul; and the subordinate nature of a *political instrument* by which it belongs purely to the *understanding*. The first of these terms is related mainly to the people; the second, to the military commander (*Feldherr*) and the third to the *government*.[16]

Clausewitz's thought centres on the need for states to calculate the intentions of their adversaries. For this to be possible, political leaders must be cool, wise and rational. They must not be swayed by the demands of the military, nor must they give in to popular passion.[17] This last point shows how far Clausewitz is from the liberal conscience: he does not accept that the entry of the people on to the political stage would ensure a reign of peace. The historical record does not show, as Michael Howard has demonstrated on many occasions, that there is in fact an *automatic* correlation between the coming of mass democracy and the establishment of an era of peace; sometimes the people, especially if passionate hatreds are encouraged by misguided elites, can be more militaristic than soldiers and politicians.[18] I would not want this point to be misunderstood. A central tenet of liberalism is that of the need to control power, and this applies to those who exercise foreign policy.

It is easy to summarize the arguments of this section by making three general points. First, let us recall that European capitalist society has never been ruled over by a single state, and that a state system in Europe pre-dated the emergence of *industrial* capitalism. All that is really being claimed is that this state system continued to be able to generate social conflict in its own right.[19] Secondly, thinkers with a genuine grasp of geopolitics have not been surprised at the occurrence, *pace* Marx, of rivalry between states inside socialist society, as in the Sino–Soviet conflict, nor that rivalries in South-East Asia have resulted in outright war. This is history as normal. The final point is the most general, the most important and the most contentious. The thesis of this section amounts to saying that a liberal view of geopolitics should seek, given the costs of war, to preserve the balance of power between states. Perhaps this thesis does not apply to all of human history, but it does, as we shall see, make a great deal of sense in modern social conditions, not least because of the creation of nuclear weapons.

Wars in Chain Reaction

We can move away from these abstract considerations and justify the contentions made about the autonomy of geopolitics by considering the relationship between capitalism and war in the twentieth century. The most important single problem that confronts us is that of describing the origins of the First World War. What truth is there to the contention of Lenin – a contention, it should be underlined, which would make capitalism a clear and present danger to liberalism – that this war had its origin in the nature of capitalism?

Capitalist society was larger than any single state in 1914, as it is today. If the workings of that larger society depended upon international exchange, then it would seem on *a priori* grounds extremely unlikely that capitalists would favour war. This case was argued by Norman Angell in *The Great Illusion* in 1909. He insisted that war would bring economic disaster to those who won as much as to those who lost, and that 'the capitalist has no country, and he

137

knows, if he be of the modern type, that arms and conquests and jugglery with frontiers serves no ends of his, and may very well defeat them'.[20] There is some evidence to back up this argument. Arms manufacturers gained most of their profits from sales outside their own nations, and their interest lay in an arms race rather than in actual war.[21] More importantly, international bankers were well aware of how much they benefited from the free flow of trade. This led the head of the London Rothschilds to try and persuade *The Times* not to encourage British support for France and Russia during the July crisis of 1914.[22] Furthermore, industrialists stood to lose from war: ironically, in the decade before 1914, Britain became Germany's best customer and Germany the second best market for British goods.[23] These are examples of international capitalist logic being opposed to war. If only that logic had been obeyed, and the liberal dream fulfilled! However, it is quite obvious that this logic was not very powerful. Capitalists might inhabit a larger society, but they had no real capacity to control the behaviour of states within it. This point can be put in a slightly different way. The majority of capitalists were, in crucial respects, members of their particular nation-states.

The fact that capitalists compete via nations is by no means inevitable; it is a reflection of the fact that capitalism has no single state, that this mode of production developed inside a state system. But if we forget this problem, so fundamental for Marxism, it remains possible to assess whether capitalism caused war in 1914 in a different way: were European states driven by the needs of their capitalists into a foreign policy that resulted in war? This is a Marxist theory in two obvious senses. On the one hand, it is loyal to that part of Marxism which stresses that the problems of capitalism result from its anarchic character. On the other hand, it presumes that states have to serve the needs of their capitalists. It is very important to note that two rather different theories lurk behind this simple statement. The first suggests that the state is controlled, in more or less complicated ways, by capitalists; this tradition does not allow any ultimate autonomy for state behaviour. The second theory sees the state as being in control, with the waxing of economic power, to be achieved by various geo-economic strategies, as its main task. This second theory is Marxist only so long as the state seeks to help capitalists; when the state has its own economic objectives, its behaviour cannot be understood in Marxist terms at all. While all modern states are concerned about the wealth of their societies, it will also be necessary to insist that the calculation of economic advantage is not necessarily the main task that foreign policy-making elites set themselves at all times.

The most important version of the theory that competition between capitalist states causes wars is that which centres on the view of imperialism as necessary for national capitalisms and hence as the 'hidden agenda' of conflict that led to the First World War. This cannot be true in any simple sense. The scramble for Africa had been at its peak in the 1880s, and it had certainly not occasioned war between France and Britain; very much to the contrary, the imperial rivalries of these countries had been solved amicably. Furthermore, imperialism held little economic attraction for most members of the bourgeoisie – which is not to deny that a few profited, although this section by no means had control of the state. French colonies were not necessary to French capitalists either on grounds of the search for new markets or as the result of a need to find new investment opportunities. What is most striking about the majority of French capitalists at the turn of the century is that they were unwilling to invest in the colonies; certainly these colonies, given their poverty, presented few opportunities for trade. French capitalists preferred to invest in Russia since development there was capable of realizing large profits.[24] The conclusion to be drawn from this is banal but clear. French imperialism was not 'caused' by the objective needs of capitalists themselves. The German situation is similar. German economic success arose from trading in advanced markets. Certainly German capitalism was not about to perish for lack of the Belgian Congo, the prize most sought by German imperialistic statesmen! Even the British situation was not much different. Lower economic returns came from the colonies, including India, than from investments in, for example, Argentina; and in the long run, trading in an underdeveloped market proved disastrous for the British economy, allowing it to stagnate in technological terms.[25] The surest way in which Germany could have ensured the loss of British ascendancy was to have waited for it to exhaust itself by means of increased colonial expenditure; this would surely have happened quickly had Chamberlain's catastrophic plan for Imperial Preference been adopted.

It would, however, be unsatisfactory to leave matters at this point. Sociologists have rightly made much of the fact that what is believed to be real is real in its consequences. By process of analogy, it can be argued that in economics what matters more than 'the facts' is what people *believe* to be the facts. As it happens, I do not believe that it is idle to distinguish between 'causes' and 'reasons', not least because it is important, perhaps especially for liberalism, to ask about social conditions which encourage belief to be firmly grounded in reality. But let us delay discussion of this normative issue, and continue to inquire about the nature of the relationship between economics and politics at the turn of this century. Two particular geo-economic strategies can be distinguished. The British strategy favoured open world markets – including open access to its imperial possessions – on the Smithian grounds that increasing specialization and interdependence would bring prosperity to all and diminish the risks of war. In contrast, Germany chose to react to the economic depression that began in the 1870s by means of tariff protection on the grounds that key sectors of the economy, notably agriculture and heavy industry, were necessary for any advanced state for strategic reasons: if there were to be war, a state without these industries, unless it had protection equivalent to that provided by the British navy, would surely go down to defeat. There is nothing inevitable that makes a protectionist country militarily aggressive. But the combination of powerful industrial development and a protectionist mentality can, and in Germany did, encourage the view that the possession of colonies was necessary for market purposes, to ensure that markets would be available since Britain might eventually deny access to its empire. This line of reasoning was much in evidence from 1897, the year in which Tirpitz's plans for a naval race with Britain were accepted – a move that more than any other factor led to war. All this can be put in a nutshell: the German strategy based itself on the argument that it was necessary to challenge British hegemony.

Let us examine the inner workings of the German strategy in more detail. Were German policies adopted because of capitalist pressure, or were they automatically chosen by the state? Did domestic politics dictate geopolitics, that is, was *Aussenpolitik* merely a reflex of *Innenpolitik*? No simple answer can be given to this question. Certainly the alliance of Junkers and heavy industrialists limited state autonomy, most obviously in undermining the relatively liberal regime of Caprivi in 1894. On the other hand, the strategy of *Weltpolitik* was partly adopted by the state for its own reasons: the state had gained at least a measure of autonomy by balancing between different groups, and this strategy proved particularly helpful in dealing with the regions – a key matter in a state which was very far from being unitary. What is very striking about the whole situation is the great strength of nationalism within the political culture that developed, fed alike by leading classes and state elites. Nationalism became visceral, powerful and embittered.

There is a very important analytic consideration that deserves to be emphasized at this point. Capitalists like to be left alone so as to make money; they do not normally produce their own geopolitical vision. If *some* capitalists helped create the German geo-economic strategy of *Weltpolitik* because it was in their direct interest to do so, it is very important indeed to remember that many German capitalists who had little to gain economically from empire supported this policy quite as much. Capitalists sometimes accede to the visions propagated by intellectuals and politicians; geopolitical actors can, to adopt a metaphor beloved by Max Weber, sometimes serve as switchmen sending economic interests down one or another track. This is bad news for liberal economism; it is equally worrying for Marxism – we are by now used to hearing about the false consciousness of the working class, but one does not intuitively expect the same from bourgeois actors. The important consequence of this is that states can interfere with the pure logic of larger capitalist society. Imperialism is the classic instance of such interference, but the geo-economic plans that were entertained, before and during the war, by German state leaders is another.[26] Perhaps the whole situation can be described in simpler terms. Nationalism crossed class boundaries; certainly German businessmen were German first, and capitalists second – which is to say that nationalism was defined as part of their 'material interest'.

If this was an aggressive and dangerous political culture, it still remains necessary to isolate the exact decisions that led to war. Bismarck after 1870 and von Bülow throughout his chancellorship were, *and were able to be*, both cautious and pragmatic. Bethmann Hollweg could have behaved with equal caution, and certainly there were no explicit instructions from capitalists telling him what to do; he was not a puppet controlled by economic interests of any sort. It matters greatly that he was both curiously fatalistic and a prisoner to mercantilist/protectionist geo-economic political culture.[27] All this should not be misunderstood. I do not wish to claim that mercantilist pressure can never be so strong as directly to occasion a geo-economic *Weltpolitik*; to the contrary, such pressures probably played a role in Japan's foreign policy in the 1930s.[28] However, in 1914 Germany's demand for world markets had never made less sense: the European economy was booming and no major markets were about to be closed to Germany. Probably increased tariffs would not anyway have made much difference. Protection of Junkers estates had not fundamentally worked, as the figures of rises in imported grain show, and the power of heavy industrialists in the economy was diminishing as diversification took place; both these factors would in the long run have made a new Caprivi-type initiative possible. Crucially, Bethmann Hollweg took a huge risk in pure geopolitical terms. One consequence of Bismarck's linguistic excesses, that is, of his self-professed boasts of Machiavellianism and of admiration for a neo-Nietzschean struggle between states, was that Germany took on three, and eventually four, of the world's major powers in a war on two fronts. In summary, it can be said that Bethmann-Hollweg had sufficient autonomy as a state leader to make it mistaken to speak as if he had to take decisions that led to war; that he did so shows not just that he miscalculated, but that, in a certain sense, he did not think at all.

Perhaps too much effort has been spent analysing the impact of economics on German state behaviour. Geopolitical wisdom would suggest that it was always likely that such a German challenge would arise. It is historically normal for newly powerful states to seek a place in the world. Given this, it is important to stress that the causes of the war should not all be placed in Germany's camp. It is true that German geo-economic thought was mistaken, and that it was geopolitically stupid to fight a war on two fronts against the greatest powers of the age. But Britain, even if it had a greater stake in naval matters, given its need for supplies of food from the Dominions, was equally mistaken not to have made the German access to the status of a major power rather easier. Complaints about German economic success were sometimes unwise; German goods were successful because they were better, and this had little to do with tariffs, as some British commentators, to their credit, realized. More effort should have been made to understand the German desire to protect domestic grain: if a state wishes to pay more for its supplies, there is nothing in liberalism that should rule this out – although it does require economic adjustment on the part of the country with cheap surpluses. Furthermore, it was hypocritical of Britain to boast of its liberalism, even given the free trade status of its empire, when it was securely in possession of an empire; as noted, the possession of an empire was *not* likely to help its economy in the long run, as a more liberal political elite would have realized. However, it is worth repeating that these economic strategies may well have been fairly irrelevant. Even had Germany been more liberal internally and more open to the world market externally, it is still quite likely that war between a fading and a rising power would have taken place.[29]

What this means is that it is almost certainly a mistake on our part to search for some special cause of the war. That we do so reflects upon the character that the war came to exhibit. Perhaps the politicians should have learned the lesson about the impact of industry upon warfare, as this had been plain to see in the American Civil War. As it was, they were taken by surprise and the war quickly ran out of political control. Equally importantly, the politicians might have reflected more about the way in which conscription would affect the character of the war. They were again taken by surprise by the discovery that citizen participation in war tended to bring in its wake demands for general, non-dynastic war aims: in the British case, a war 'for little Belgium' became a war to end wars. But the result was clear. The politicians lost control of the conduct of the war. In 1917 it was clear to liberals like Keynes that the war was no longer truly Clausewitzian, that is, it was no longer a rational venture in any sense at all. But all attempts to call a halt were defeated.

What do the origins of the First World War tell us about liberalism? Most obviously, it is the intelligence and political culture of state leaders that, in the last analysis, really matters in geopolitical affairs. There may be some truth, moreover, to the notion, made much of by British liberals before 1914, that the authoritarianism of the German political system, the fact that it paid so much attention to the wishes of Junkers and heavy industrialists, was partly responsible for its unfortunate political culture. It certainly can be the case that external adventure is attractive to authoritarian regimes faced with internal pressure, and there is everything to be said for the liberal norm of controlling power. In both these cases a dose of liberalism where illiberalism ruled before has much to recommend it. However, it is necessary to conclude this chapter on a much more sombre note. The wars of the twentieth century have occurred in chain reaction, and liberal naïvety played some small part in allowing this to happen.[30] Let us turn to this charge after first assessing the impact of the First World War on the defeated societies of Europe.

The war debilitated economy and society in Europe. Defeat in war encouraged revolutionary turbulence. Defeat of a state tended to lead to a transfer of loyalty from nation to class. In Russia, this meant the final defeat of Tsarism and the ultimate victory of the Bolsheviks. After an initial period of war communism, Lenin introduced a New Economic Policy which sought to combine an element of the market principle with socialism. This might well have produced a slightly more liberal and more successful economy. However, geopolitical pressure, notably the defeat of the Chinese communists in 1927, dictated speeding up industrialization. This gave Stalin his chance. He turned Marxism into a closed system and established a totalitarian tyranny of the left.

Germany came close to a socialist revolution in 1919, but the established forces remained in sufficient array to put

145

this down. It is important to note that it was an SPD government which was responsible for putting down a communist rebellion; this made it impossible for a united left to stand together in Germany as a pillar of Weimar democracy. This was the first of a series of conjunctural factors that eventually led to a revolution of the right. If Hitler gained his troops from ex-servicemen and from 'service class' members particularly opposed to communism – then, it must be recalled, a genuine force for international revolution – it is important to remember that he gained his access to power as the result of the behaviour of established social forces. I do not mean to suggest that fascism was, as Marxism has it, merely the 'agency' for capitalism. This theory is rendered rather ridiculous by the fact that it was the agents which did the bidding; fascism had its own nature, and was a movement in and of itself. Moreover, fascism did not take root in the leading capitalist societies of the United States and Great Britain; but it did take a significant hold in Romania, despite that country being essentially agrarian. Fascism is best seen as a pathology of forced modernization: memories of pre-industrial 'harmony', of '*Kinder, Küche, Kirche*', were revived in an industrial country to create the anti-liberal ideology of reactionary modernism which has been examined already. But if only von Thyssen actively helped the Nazi party from early on, his business colleagues preferring to support the parties of the right, it is extremely noticeable that the capitalist middle classes did not prove themselves friends of Weimar; on the contrary, they gave it no positive support whatever, and showed extreme resentment of a regime that helped raise the wages of the working class.[31] This stands as the greatest single consideration questioning liberalism's tendency to rely on capitalism as a mechanism for decent political rule. There were, of course, other factors at work. The inability of classes to co-operate was partly the legacy of the divide-and-rule policies that authoritarianism had depended upon for so long; this is a world that Tocqueville would have understood. Equally important, however, was the active involvement of sections of the traditional elite, most notably von Papen, in putting Hitler into power.

How did liberals behave in these circumstances? Woodrow Wilson's Gladstonian morality was felt at Versailles in the demand that Germany accept guilt for having started a war. This was surely a highly questionable policy. Germans did not feel guilt for having indulged in what had been the traditional recourse of European states over centuries; they thereby gained a justified sense of resentment upon which Hitler was later successfully to feed. This is not to say that all liberals were behind the Versailles Treaty; very much to the contrary, most liberals condemned the harsh terms imposed on Germany, and felt that core liberal principles had been flouted. The classic statement of this view was Keynes's *The Economic Consequences of the Peace*. This polemic argued, brilliantly and passionately, that the treaty was not just vindictive but also self-defeating: how could the Allies both ruin the German economy – thereby hurting their own export industries – and demand the payment of reparations?[32] There was indeed much to be said for a liberal peace, and this part of Keynes's argument retains force. However, we live in an imperfect world, and have to act in situations which are sullied and impure. In 1919 the fears of the French ruled out of court a generous peace. By and large, liberals failed to realize this. Throughout the inter-war years, everything that was best in their mentality told them that Germany had just claims to make; the liberal conscience, in other words, created a climate in which appeasement flourished.[33] Given that a generous peace treaty was impossible in 1919, there was much to be said for supporting the harsher treaty that did emerge, especially as it was *not* genuinely Carthaginian, and had considerable achievements to its name in the Balkans. As it was, the worst of all possible results was achieved: the creation of a peace treaty which was not respected or enforced. The liberal conscience thus played some part in making the Second World War possible. Norman Angell, one of the exemplars of liberal morality, realized this late in life when he admitted that although 'Balance of Power had a bad smell with nearly all Liberals, including this one . . . later on [they] came to see that power politics were the politics of not being overpowered'.[34]

It is true that some appeasers, caught between the two great power systems of fascism and bolshevism, took the easy way out, giving in and refusing to stand up for liberalism, and that they deserve criticism for this. However, my point is slightly different. Liberal economistic idealism, based on a lack of proper understanding of the occasional autonomy of geopolitical pressures, made for a lack of awareness of what was happening. It would be absurd to argue that liberal failings were anything like the most important factor in causing renewed global conflict; but they played some part.

Conclusion: A Ruling Class?

The wars of twentieth-century Europe have changed history. They resulted in Europe, and in particular Germany, being displaced from its central place in world history. Furthermore, state socialism was helped into power by war, and it was, of course, spread further on the backs of the Red Army. Given that one proper standard of judgement to bring to bear on an ideology is that of the plausibility of its sociological presuppositions, what then can be concluded about liberalism's view of geopolitics? More particularly, is there a relationship between war and capitalism such that liberalism should speedily seek to distance itself from the latter?

Wars have characterized virtually all human societies, and have been a 'normal' characteristic of state systems in which the search for geopolitical security is as basic as, perhaps more basic than, any other. The greatest hope for peace in state systems has rested – and obviously still rests in the case of the 'duel' between the superpowers – upon the intelligence of state leaders. Geopolitical understanding is a type of wisdom in its own right, and it is one that liberalism has occasionally ignored to its own cost. For it was naïve to believe that the coming of modern market-created economic abundance would be such as to supersede the laws of geopolitics, and stupid to ignore key autonomous actions on the part of state elites.

My argument has been that the wars of the modern liberal era have not principally been caused by capitalists; they have resulted from the actions of elites. Obviously, there was some overlap between these two categories. This was especially true in Imperial Germany. But even there the fact that class pressure limited state autonomy by creating protectionist regimes and by helping to form a particular political culture does not in itself account for the decision to go to war. War was the result of Bethmann Hollweg abandoning the rather cautious geopolitical policy of his forebears in a grasp at world power; the societal pressures on the state were not so great as to make this anything other than a misguided and mistaken action of an autonomous elite actor. The more important discovery, however, was that capitalists can be persuaded to seek their interest in ways which are not necessarily objectively the most promising. Thus many more German capitalists accepted the demand for *Weltpolitik* than had direct economic interests, present or potential, in the acquisition of empire. We are forced to repeat the conclusions of the previous chapter: elites matter, and capitalists often do not know their own best interests.

It is quite clear where all this leaves liberalism. Informed judgement dictates two complementary ethics. On the one hand, liberals must remember the occasional autonomy of geopolitics, not least that they may protect their own states. On the other hand, it remains possible to hope that the spread of a liberal vision of interdependence, that is, of the market principle rather than of protectionist/mercantilist geo-economic strategies, may help towards the establishment of peace. Given that there are no necessary economic 'causes' to imperialism/mercantilism, liberals need to work to make the 'reasons' given by statesmen for their actions more aware of the positive sum possibilities of international economic life. For the latter to be achieved, however, it is necessary to make state elites aware of the benefits of the market. While this is far less of a problem in modern circumstances than it was at the end of the nineteenth century, secure adhesion of faith in the market on the part of key elites is likely to depend upon the smooth operations of the international market.

NOTES

1. A. J. P. Taylor, *The Trouble Makers* (London: Panther, 1969); M. Howard, *War and the Liberal Conscience* (Oxford: Oxford University Press, 1978).
2. R. Cobden, *Political Writings*, Volume 2 (1867), cited by Taylor, op. cit., p.49.
3. W. E. Gladstone, *Political Speeches*, Volume 2 (1879), cited by Taylor, op. cit., p.65.
4. J. A. Hobson, *Richard Cobden: the International Man*, (1918), cited by Howard, op. cit., pp50–51.
5. Cited by Howard, op. cit., p.50.
6. Ibid., p.54.
7. H. N. Brailsford, *A League of Nations* (1917) cited by Howard, op. cit., p.79.
8. Howard, op. cit., pp.79–80.
9. J. A. Hobson, *An Economic Interpretation of Investment* (London: Financial Review of Reviews, 1911), p.103.
10. J. A. Hobson, 'Free Trade and Foreign Policy', *Contemporary Review*, 74 (1898).
11. J. A. Hobson, *Imperialism* (London: James Nisbet and Co., 1902), p.51.
12. G. Kolko, *The Roots of American Foreign Policy* (Boston: Beacon Press, 1969); H. Magdoff, *The Age of Imperialism* (New York: Monthly Review Press, 1968).
13. T. Hobbes, *Leviathan*, cited by R. Aron in 'La guerre est une caméléon', *Contrepoint*, 15 (1974).

14. R. Aron, *Peace and War* (London: Weidenfeld and Nicolson, 1966), p.91.

15. Montesquieu, *L'Esprit des Lois*, cited by Aron, *Peace and War*, op. cit., p.vii.

16. R. Aron, 'Reason, Passion and Power in the thought of Clausewitz', *Social Research*, 39 (1972), pp.607–8.

17. I am relying on R. Aron, *Penser la guerre, Clausewitz*, 2 vols (Paris: Gallimard, 1976) for this interpretation of Clausewitz.

18. Howard op. cit.; M. Howard, *War in European History* (Oxford: Oxford University Press, 1976).

19. R. Aron, *War and Industrial Society* (Oxford: Oxford University Press, 1958); M. Mann, 'Capitalism and Militarism', in M. Shaw (ed.), *War, State and Society* (London: Macmillan, 1984).

20. N. Angell, *The Great Illusion* (3rd edition, 1911), cited by J. Joll, *The Origins of the First World War* (Harlow: Longmans, 1984), p.137.

21. Joll, op. cit., pp.126–7.

22. Ibid., p.136.

23. Ibid., p.138.

24. R. Aron, *Imperialism and Colonialism*, Montague Burton Lecture (Leeds: Leeds University Press, 1959).

25. L. E. Davis and R. Huttenback, *Mammon and the Pursuit of Empire* (Cambridge: Cambridge University Press, 1987).

26. I am drawing on several works, although sometimes critically, for the ideas contained in this paragraph: P. Kennedy, *The Rise of the Anglo German Antagonism, 1860–1914* (London: George Allen and Unwin, 1980); H. U. Wehler, *The German Empire, 1871–1918* (Leamington Spa: Berg, 1983); V. Berghahn, *Germany and the Approach of War in 1914* (London: St Martin's Press, 1973); J. A. Nichols, *Germany after Bismarck: The Caprivi Era, 1890–1894* (New York: Norton, 1968); S. Pollard, *Peaceful Conquest: The Industrialisation of Europe, 1760–1970* (Oxford: Oxford University Press, 1970).

27. F. Stern, 'Bethmann Hollweg and the War: The Bounds of Responsibility', in his *The Failure of Illiberalism* (New York: Alfred Knopf, 1972).

28. N. Chomsky, 'The Revolutionary Pacifism of A. J. Muste: on the Background of the Pacific War', in *American Power and the New Mandarins* (New York: Vintage Books, 1969).

29. D. Calleo, *The German Problem Reconsidered: Germany and the World Order, 1870 to the Present* (Cambridge: Cambridge University Press, 1978).

30. The view of these wars as being in chain reaction is derived

from R. Aron, *Les Guerres en chaînes* (Paris: Gallimard, 1951).

31. D. Abraham, *The Collapse of the Weimar Republic* (Princeton: Princeton University Press, 1981); H. A. Turner, *German Big Business and the Rise of Hitler* (New York: Oxford University Press, 1985). Cf. J. Joll, 'Storm over German History: Business as Usual', *New York Review of Books*, 32 (1985).

32. J. M. Keynes, *The Economic Consequences of the Peace* (London: Macmillan, 1919). For an excellent discussion of the formation of Keynes's views on the war and its consequences, see R. Skidelsky, *John Maynard Keynes*, Volume 1 (London: Macmillan, 1983).

33. This is the burden of the argument of Howard, *War and the Liberal Conscience*, op. cit., and Taylor, op. cit.

34. N. Angell, *After All* (1951), p.137, cited by Howard, op. cit., p.107.

REPRISE

By 1945 Europe, the heartland of liberalism, lay in ruins. The chapters that make up Part II of this book have analysed the role that liberalism played in the collapse of Europe; particular attention has been focused on the difficult question of whether various failings of liberalism were so logically central to its vision as to have effectively undermined it. The purpose of this Reprise is less to offer new information or argument than to draw together and to reflect upon the wide-ranging and occasionally complex arguments that have been made.

The question that is being asked may give rise to an evasive response, and it is as well to confront this openly before proceeding further. As Europe fell apart at the hands of illiberalism, surely, by definition, liberalism itself is blameless? Such an argument has some merits which will be touched on soon; but as a type of strategic defence for liberalism it is facile. For there was *movement* from liberalism to illiberalism, and it does not serve liberalism's best interests to deny this. Let us first recall the nature of that movement, and then consider how important it was in allowing the rise of illiberalism inside European civilization.

Was liberalism right to tie its fortunes to capitalism? Fear of the working classes led to political exclusion in several countries, and that policy created a response which seemed to justify fear. The least that can be said is that the bourgeoisie accepted this policy, even though sociological wisdom makes it clear that such a policy was not necessary for the proper functioning of capitalism. This is a blot on the liberalism–capitalism connection. Another blot has a similar nature. Many German capitalists abandoned the liberal ideal of peace through free trade. This was in the direct material interest of some major industrialists, but many others had their interests channelled by geopolitical actors into a mercantilist/protectionist geo-economic strategy that was probably not to their long-term interest. Fear of the working class played some part in the creation of this strategy; certainly it is abundantly clear that the German bourgeoisie did not really even seek to control that geopolitical strategy of the ruling elite which led to the outbreak of war in 1914.

However, these 'blots' pale into insignificance in comparison with the role played by the German bourgeoisie during the Weimar Republic. Although it makes little sense to talk of fascism as the agent of capitalism, there can be no doubt that the German bourgeoisie allowed, by not resisting, the emergence of this force. These were hard and selfish men whose character was superlatively portrayed in the work of George Grosz. They loathed Weimar because social democracy led to an increase in welfare and security for the working class. They were interested only in order. Tocqueville understood what this meant:

When the taste for physical pleasures has grown more rapidly than either education or experience of free institutions, the time comes when men are carried away and lose control of themselves at sight of the new good things they are ready to snatch. Intent only on getting rich, they do not notice the close connection between private fortunes and general prosperity. There is no need to drag their rights away from citizens of this type; they themselves voluntarily let them go. They find it a tiresome inconvenience to exercise political rights which distract them from industry . . . Such folk think they are following the doctrine of self-interest, but they have a very crude idea thereof, and the better to guard their interests, they neglect the chief of them, that is, to remain their own masters.

As those who work are unwilling to attend to public affairs, and the class which might have wished thus to fill its leisure no longer exists, the role of government is left unfulfilled.

If, at this critical moment, an able and ambitious man once gets power, he finds the way open for usurpations of every sort.

So long as he sees to it for a certain time that material interests flourish, he can easily get away with everything else. He must above all guarantee good order. People passionately bent on physical pleasures usually observe how agitation in favour of liberty threatens prosperity before they appreciate how liberty helps to procure the same . . .

I freely agree that public tranquillity is a very good thing. Nevertheless, I do not want to forget that it is through good order that all peoples have reached tyranny. That is certainly no reason for nations to despise public peace, but they should not be satisfied with that alone. A nation which asks nothing from its government beyond the maintenance of order is already a slave in the bottom of its heart. It is a slave to its prosperity, and the road is free for the man to tie the fetters.[1]

All this can be summarized very simply by saying that there is much justice to the argument, made by John Dunn, that liberalism has not been well served by standing so close to a Smithian capitalistic theory which systematically down-plays the importance of moral cohesion. And this is not, we can recall, simply a question of the peculiar character of the German bourgeoisie. In the inter-war years, the desire for order and for peace made it extremely hard to alert European democracies as a whole to the dangers that fascism posed.

But if the link with capitalism helped allow fascism into power, it is worth reiterating that fascism was a force in and of itself. There is a point here to be made against the liberal record in this context which goes beyond the rela-tionship between liberalism and capitalism. Fascist ideol-ogy resulted from what has been termed the betrayal of the intellectuals, that is, the movement of intellectuals away from liberal beliefs to a scorn for the masses. This move-ment is all too comprehensible. It was, in one sense, born from a logical, if unwise, playing out of certain tenets of liberal belief. At a structural level, it clearly represented the material situation of isolated intellectuals who felt bereft of attention. It was disastrous.

Any fully balanced portrait of the drift of Europe into illiberalism must stress that these factors, though weighty, did not stand alone; probably, indeed, they were less significant than others to which we can now turn. The social actors produced by the capitalist mode of production, that is, proletariat and bourgeoisie, were by no means the ones which had determinate impact at key junctures in Europe in this period. Any examination of the historical record cannot help but be struck by the crucial role of elites. This is true of most European countries, especially in geopolitics, and the general point can be stressed by recalling the most striking examples. It was the autocratic elite of Tsarist Russia, and not the bourgeoisie of which it was suspicious, which decided to exclude the new working class from political life. The case of Imperial Germany is somewhat more complex. Certainly the Prussian Junkers had huge importance both in demanding exclusion of the working class from politics and in creating a mercantilist/protectionist political culture. This is to stress that the autonomy of the state was curtailed by the interests of the Junkers and of their allies, the heavy industrialists. However, I have insisted that the state had a measure of autonomy internally and a fair amount in geopolitical affairs, not least in terms of the style in which they were conducted. Much of the disaster that struck Europe in the twentieth century has to be laid at the door of the irresponsible and authoritarian rulers of imperial Germany.

That all this was so amounts to being good news for liberalism for the simplest of reasons: these considerations call for an increase of liberalism. An initial demand is for the behaviour of elites to be subjected to the control of society *as a whole*. At first sight, this demand seems in straightforward contradiction with the arguments made about the *limits* to the autonomy of the state in Imperial Germany. But the contradiction is more apparent than real. The state in Imperial Germany was not *free to* serve the interests of the whole society because it was insufficiently *free from* selected groups, largely on account of the estate basis of the Prussian political system. However, to seek to be able, in the last resort, to control elites, that is, to 'circulate' them at elections, is not to say that liberalism either imagines it possible, or wants, to do without a political elite altogether. At this point a second liberal demand gains relevance: it is that the culture of political elites can benefit from a dose of liberalism. This point deserves illustration. Contemporary elites need to understand that the exclusion of the working class from politics is not only unjust, but also unwise and unnecessary. Similarly, it is important that political elites understand the economic options that face them. It is of course possible that the world polity could be so ordered that mercantilism/protectionism becomes an unavoidably rational strategy, as was *not* the case with Imperial Germany. A final element of a liberal culture for political elites is the most important. Political elites in every age need to learn about the virtue of self-restraint, that is, to become aware that immoderate behaviour is often not forgotten and that short-term advantage can lead to long-term disaster. It is perhaps the case that the virtue of self-restraint has special importance in democratic societies. For while it is possible to combine democratic accountability with the benefits of wise action by political elites, it would be foolish to say that this is easy. A further reason for the loss of autonomy of the Imperial German state was that it became, at least in part, the prisoner of passions which it had itself stirred up. The elites of democratic societies may undermine the autonomy they need if they resort to demagogy. All this can be put in a nutshell: an accountable society will still have a political elite, and its degree of intelligence and wisdom matters.

A second, morally neutral, general cause for Europe's drift to illiberalism should not be forgotten. Even had the elite of Imperial Germany been liberal, events might still have been much the same. Conflict between Germany and Britain was probably likely whatever the nature of their regimes. Certainly, it is only too easy to understand why politicians lost control of an industrial war fought with conscription armies. And it was defeat in war that created the crisis that led to the installation of forces that drove Europe to collapse.

All that has been said to this point can easily be summarized: liberalism's hands are dirty, but not as filthy as those of other actors. This is an appropriate moment to consider Marxism. Could it not be claimed that the adoption of Marxism would have allowed for cleaner hands all round? This question can be formulated differently. Given that the historic evidence lends some credence to Arblaster's case against liberalism, would it not be wise to accept what seem to be his Marxist conclusions? The answer to these questions must be in the negative. One reason for this, not discussed to this point, is academic and philosophical. Marx's work is based on a view of man, a philosophical anthropology, which privileges a certain conception of work. It is this which leads Marx to claim that the liberation of man would consist in a society in which it was possible for the individual to be at once artist, producer and lover. But what Marx took to be a fulfilment of human nature is really but one vision of human ends. I do not find the vision particularly attractive, but the crucial objection to be made against it is rather different. How is it possible to abolish the division of labour *and* to have the benefits of an industrial society? Is it really possible to be Einstein in the morning, Casanova in the afternoon and Picasso at night? However, two forceful sociological reasons for not adopting Marxism are of still greater import. First, Marxism does not take the problem of controlling political power seriously enough; it presumes that the abolition of property relations will also eventually lead to the abolition of the state. Stalinism and indeed the very nature of socialist society make this, to be blunt, a silly position. It remains the case that placing all power in one set of hands all too easily leads to disaster. Secondly, we have seen that the working classes of national societies are not likely, barring political repression, to create a revolution. Marxism fails in practice, whatever its virtues as a theory.

It is now time to turn again to analysis. The geopolitical outcome of the Second World War left two power blocs facing each other, and it was scarcely surprising that hostility developed – even though there was genuine uniqueness to the fact that these enemies soon had a mutual interest, because of the character of nuclear weapons, in preventing any occurrence of open hostility. Social reconstruction in Europe and Japan, influenced both by the physical presence of the United States and historical experience, took the character of an historic class compromise: the extreme parties of left and right disappeared, capitalism was accepted and political citizenship for the working class extended quite generally. Furthermore, international capitalist society possessed a hegemonic power seemingly capable of preventing the protectionism and consequent trade wars that had blighted the atmosphere of international politics in the inter-war years. All this amounts to saying that many of the circumstances that led to the collapse of liberalism have been removed. Is it then possible that some of the lessons concerning the weaknesses of liberalism can be learnt so that history need not repeat itself? Clearly, it remains necessary to analyse the connection between capitalism and liberalism, above all for the brute reason that liberal societies all have capitalist economies. Has capitalism changed, and if so is this change appreciated in the appropriate quarters? Are the states of contemporary liberal societies sufficiently autonomous from the proletariat and/or from the bourgeoisie as to be able to act in the long-term interests of society? All these questions amount to asking whether capitalism can now be a good mechanism for liberalism. *If* capitalism can be made to work relatively smoothly, it would have undoubted advantages for liberalism: economic growth would allow for a certain *douceur des moeurs*; some sort of guarantee of liberal rule might result, moreover, from power being in different sets of hands – in so far, that is, as power is not controlled by capitalists themselves. This raises a further issue of huge importance. Can power in non-democratic societies be controlled, that is, can such societies gain a measure of liberalism, through means alternate to the spread of capitalism? But first let us turn to what is the most difficult question of all. Can liberalism be restated as a morality so that, if various sociological mechanisms again fail, social disintegration need not follow? It is important to remember in this context that the moral 'emptiness' or 'neutrality' characteristic of modern society is not just the result of allowing the doctrines of self-interest such a central role; the corrosive powers of science on totalizing ideologies are at least as important. What sort of morality does science allow us?

NOTES

1. A. de Tocqueville, *Democracy in America* (New York: Anchor Books, 1969), p.540. I owe this reference to A. O. Hirschman, *The Passions and the Interests: Political Arguments for Capitalism before Its Triumph* (Princeton: Princeton University Press, 1977), part III.

III
LIBERALISM SINCE 1945

INTRODUCTION:
AN END TO IDEOLOGY?

John Dunn has recently claimed that liberalism has frag-
mented in such a way that there is no longer any significant
link between its epistemological, moral and social aims.[1]
This argument amounts to saying that there is no general
theory of modern liberalism available. There is a considerable overlap with this view and the insistence of Anthony
Arblaster that modern liberalism is tired out, and, in so far
as it has energy left, a naïve defence for the status quo.[2]
The third part of this book takes issue with this position
and offers, although not with any absolute confidence, a
general theory of liberalism.

It is not, of course, true to say that there have been no
attempts to reconstruct liberalism in the twentieth century.
Before the First World War, both the Progressive thinkers
in America and the New Liberals in the Britain sought to
reconceptualize liberalism, largely in order that it might be
able to deal better with collectivist issues.[3] Despite some
conceptual advances on this point, it is fair to say that these
thinkers did not fundamentally rethink liberalism: rather
they retained naïve views both about epistemology and
geopolitics. A far more serious contender as an innovator
and renovator of liberalism is Maynard Keynes.[4] But the
fact that Keynes, to his credit, was almost completely
absorbed with problems of practice means that his thought
does not serve as a convenient place at which to begin
discussion. In the last analysis, the work of Sir Karl Popper
serves us no better; the suggestive early work on the nature
of an open society seems to have been submerged by the

163

philosophy of science. However, the 'end of ideology' school did offer a general account of liberalism designed to suit modern circumstances, and analysis of their views will allow a specification of the argument to be made here.

An 'end of ideology' was apparently first proclaimed by Edward Shils in Milan in 1955, and the expression then became adopted by Daniel Bell and, with characteristic reservations, by Raymond Aron.[5] Shils's initial proclamation was made at one of a series of Congresses for Cultural Freedom that were held in the 1950s in various European cities, and which were attended by a myriad of celebrated European intellectuals, all of liberal disposition but with political opinions ranging from moderate right to moderate left. The Congresses had initially been set up at a time of show trials in Eastern Europe, and their tenor was often quite aggressively pro-Western. It was later discovered that these conferences, as well as periodicals such as *Preuves* and *Encounter*, had been financed by the CIA, and this, together with the resurgence of student 'ideology' in the 1960s, accounted for the opprobrium heaped upon this school from the 1960s onwards.

Two beliefs were central to the thinkers of this school. Raymond Aron expressed the first with particular force and cogency. He had lived through the 1930s, often in despair, and had written eloquently about fascism and bolshevism, the two great revolutionary forces of the twentieth century.[6] These power systems were based on totalizing ideologies which claimed to be able to analyse the shape of history, and thereby to tell us how we should conduct our social and moral affairs. The great hope of the whole school was that the political economies of the advanced Western societies need no longer be tormented by these extremes. Moreover, this hope seemed to be justified, that is, their argument was that the appeal of the great ideologies reflected particular circumstances, notably unemployment and depression, and that they had, in modern social conditions, lost their force.

The second tenet of belief was closely related. These thinkers welcomed a certain softening of political extremes which was represented, in British politics, by the term 'Butskellism': that is, a political system in which the right, often now of Christian democratic hue, accepted some measure of central planning and of welfare provision while the left reciprocated by allowing some autonomy for the market and formally accepting representative democracy. Underlying this change was a much more ambitious view about the nature of social evolution in general. The key event of the modern age was held to be that of the creation of industrial societies; it was further believed that industrialism had attached to it a certain beneficent logic. If their first hope was the end of circular and self-enclosed political visions, their second was that industrialism carried in its breast a dynamism that would lead to the 'convergence' of social institutions of the great rival political economies of the modern world. Thus the United States would need to allow a greater measure of social justice if it were to gain the trust of its citizens, and the Soviet Union would be forced into accepting not only the market principle but also a dose of democracy, the requisite moral principle of modernity.

The thinkers of this school do not seem to me to be ignoble, and the ease with which they could presume that all this was on the historical agenda should surely evoke generalized envy. How should their assertions be judged?

Although it is still probably unpopular to say so, the basic sociological observation about ideology is well grounded, *especially since it was recognized that ideology within the Third World was likely to gain in power during modernization.* The societies which are industrialized tend to be no longer attracted to all-embracing ideologies, albeit national loyalty retains a measure of legitimating force. Critics of the 'end of ideology' thinkers pointed to the student movements of the 1960s as a refutation of their expectations, but this scarcely convinces. For these movements had a narrow social base, and, in retrospect, produced few general ideas of any significance whatsoever. The demands for a less alienated world, largely left unspecified, were not such as to make the central power structures of industrial societies tremble; indeed, the movement as a whole, although with the honourable exception of the anti-Vietnam movement in the United States, represented nothing so much as a rather self-indulgent protest of the *jeunesse dorée* of the time. Beyond this, however, it is hard to detect any new general ideologies which look as if they will have the capacity to mobilize large sections of society, thereby to transform it. This is not to deny the importance of feminism and of ecological and peace movements; but the social bases of these movements remain narrow, and they retain the character of single-issue movements. Crucially, neither Marxism nor fascism has any fundamental body of support in the advanced societies. If fascism was discredited by the concentration camps, Marxism has suffered as much at the hands of history. The Promethean promise of the Soviet Union has clearly not been fulfilled. There seems now to be almost an inverse relationship between the proletariat and socialism: at least in Britain there was a connection between the spread of Marxist groups and loss of working-class support.

However, the critics of this school were entirely correct to assert that there was something very odd about the defence of liberalism which they offered. That defence rested on the insistence that it was non-ideological; in contrast, all opponents were convicted of the sin of being ideologists. This is a complex matter, but two comments, pointing unhappily in different directions, can be made. First, liberalism is, as argued, most definitely one ideology among others, and it was highly disingenuous to pretend otherwise. Indeed, even harsher judgements may be appropriate: to be blunt, this view discouraged thought, and contributed to the naïve condemnation of the Marxism of the Soviet Union as ideological, without a proper attempt at understanding its physiognomy and social role. I suspect that the failure to think properly about liberalism as a world view derived from the confidence with which it observed the mechanisms of social change in the post-war world. To understand this is not to excuse it: the refusal to spell out the moral basis of liberalism in the past, a consequence of the trust in capitalism's efficacy as a mechanism for liberalism had been a mistake, and these thinkers should not have repeated it. The key point at issue is that there is nothing inherently 'natural' about liberalism; on the contrary, this particular vision and set of institutions is an historical rarity. Equally importantly, it was a great disservice to liberalism not to argue for it openly as an ideology which has a greater claim upon us than does its alternatives. Any defence of this sort, to come to the second comment about the notion of ideology, needs and wants to stress the peculiarity of liberalism as a belief system; it is this special quality which accounts for the claim that it, in comparison, say, with Marxism or fascism, is not an ideology. Those totalizing ideologies 'fill out the world' in that they try to explain where we came from, how we should live and what we may expect. Raymond Aron, bearing these qualities in mind, chose to call such ideologies 'secular religions'; formally they did without God, but at a more subterranean level they sought to furnish a similar degree of certainty. Liberalism offers less, and it is vital to understand this restraint if we are to see if it can be defended. These points can be summarized by saying that there is 'a proper use for ideologies'.[7] But what sort of moral theory can, given the corrosive effects of modern epistemology, be offered?

The more sociological tenet of belief of this school similarly had a positive and a negative side. Although the notion of a genuine convergence between the Soviet Union and the United States was a piece of licentious exaggeration, to which the more sophisticated members of the school did not succumb, there is something to the notion that the scientific-industrial complex may contain within itself seeds for liberalization.[8] Nevertheless, the general sociology of the 'end of ideology' school *was*, except for the honourable exception furnished by Aron, rather complacent and blood-less.[9] One way in which this was true was in the fact that they did not create any systematic understanding of the importance of war, a curious omission given the impact that this force had had on their own times.[10] Furthermore, the force which stalked a large part of their discussions was that of 'industrialism' or, in Daniel Bell's case, 'post-industrialism': it seemed as if capitalism had ceased to exist. This meant that they tended not to address questions concerning the running of the world economy; this proved exceptionally unfortunate given the creation of a genuinely international division of labour after 1945 and of entirely new international money markets after 1973. Further, these thinkers tended to assume that the withering away of Marxist ideology would translate itself into harmonious domestic politics for Western nations. We have already seen that there was little justification for liberal fears that the working classes of the advanced capitalist societies comprised a revolutionary force, but there is little to be said for the view that social harmony has now come to prevail for good. These thinkers tended to think it was easy to combine liberalism with capitalism, and that the ages of travail for democratic societies inside capitalist society were over; life is always harder than that.

NOTES

1. J. Dunn, *Western Political Theory in the Face of the Future* (Cambridge: Cambridge University Press, 1979), chapter 2.
2. A. Arblaster, *The Rise and Decline of Western Liberalism* (Oxford: Basil Blackwell, 1984).
3. M. Freeden, *The New Liberalism* (Oxford: Oxford University Press, 1978).
4. R. Skidelsky, *John Maynard Keynes*, Vol. 1 (London: Macmillan, 1983). I have benefited from hearing various papers by

Robert Skidelsky which hint at the interpretation of Keynes he will offer in the second volume of his biography. Cf. M. Freeden, *Liberalism Divided* (Oxford: Oxford University Press, 1986).

5. No powerful study of the 'end of ideology' school has, regrettably, yet been made. Christopher Lasch has very hostile but interesting comments in *The Agony of the American Left* (New York: Vintage Books, 1969). For an appreciation of Aron's views, and a comparison with those held by other members of the school, see J. A. Hall, *Raymond Aron* (Oxford: Polity Press, forthcoming, 1988). The main arguments of the school, together with the more important criticisms, are available in C. Waxman (ed.), *The End of Ideology Debate* (New York: Funk and Wagnalls, 1968).

6. R. Aron, *L'âge des empires et l'avenir de la France* (Paris: Editions Défense de la France, 1945).

7. The expression is that of Pascal. It was used in an essay by Raymond Aron towards the end of his life in which he regretted the language that had been employed by the 'end of ideology' school. See 'On the Proper Use of Ideologies', in J. Ben-David and T. N. Clark (eds), *Culture and Its Creators* (Chicago: University of Chicago Press, 1977).

8. Raymond Aron's subtler views are contained in his *Democracy and Totalitarianism* (London: Weidenfeld and Nicolson, 1968).

9. Hall, op. cit.

10. We have already seen that Aron is most definitely an exception here. See two of Aron's greatest books, namely *Peace and War* (London: Weidenfeld and Nicolson, 1966) and *Penser la guerre, Clausewitz*, 2 vols, (Paris: Gallimard, 1976). For an appreciation of Aron's position, see J. A. Hall, 'Raymond Aron's Sociology of States', in M. Shaw (ed.), *War, State and Society* (London: Macmillan, 1984).

6

A GENERAL THEORY OF LIBERALISM –
(A) PHILOSOPHICAL FOUNDATIONS

The rise of illiberalism in Europe at the end of the nineteenth century makes it clear that liberalism is but one vision among others. However, the success of the West after 1945 allowed this realization to be down-played, even forgotten. But the realization was *true*, as more serious attention to Marxism would have made clear; thankfully the recent revival of Islam is again making people in the West aware that their world faces competitors. In consequence, it becomes necessary to spell out what it is about liberalism – defined in terms of the moral worth of every individual and of the attractiveness of negative liberty as a consequent social practice – as an ideology that makes it preferable to other alternatives.[1] This chapter begins by considering three pillars, which in part formalize positions already taken, designed to establish a firm and clear foundation for liberalism – or rather for a particular version of liberalism. This version is, in some ways, 'mundane', and this will not please everyone; however, good reasons for excluding more 'generous' views are available and will be noted.

It is as well to highlight the strategy of the argument of this chapter. When reasons for liberalism as an ideology are offered, what precisely is happening? Are we simply trying to give members of liberal societies a better conscience about themselves? This is not an ignoble aim, and there is no reason to repudiate it. However, to stick at that position is to endorse relativism, to accept that liberals are trapped inside a particular world just as others are trapped in theirs. That is not an acceptable resting place; the discussion of rationality and relativism that this entails shows, moreover, that it is not a necessary resting place. The arguments in favour of liberalism are made in the belief that they have the power to sway judgement. It is as well to be absolutely clear that, in a sense, a sleight-of-hand is being performed here. A move is being made from a recognition of the relativity of beliefs to an insistence that liberalism is more universalizable than others; liberalism may recognize itself as one ideology among others, but it treats this simply as a problem to be overcome. This seems, but is not, contradictory. This is not to say that escaping relativism is in any way easy. A safe and secure validation for liberalism cannot be created at a stroke; rather too much for comfort will in consequence rest on the sociological underpinnings to liberalism examined in the next chapter.

As each of the three pillars of liberalism have some relationship to modern science, it is useful at this point to recall an important analytic issue already encountered. This can best be done by considering Popper's philosophy of science. The most obvious merit of Popper's work is that it does not try to refute Hume; on the contrary, it takes Hume's most sceptical thoughts and builds a philosophy on their basis.[2] Popper's key idea is simple, far-reaching and profound. Since knowledge can never, given the possibility of new evidence, be absolutely firm, a scientific attitude is one which allows for theories to be falsified; this attitude will encourage investigation and the growth of knowledge. In contrast, pseudo-scientific theories, notably psychoanalysis, are circular and irrefutable, and therefore block and frustrate empirical research. For the most part Popper sees himself as describing the practice of scientists. However, when confronted with evidence of craven 'scientists' who protect their theories, and probably their tenure at universities, by adding escape clauses to avoid refutation, Popper moves to a prescriptive plain: really good science

171

has been revolutionary, and the protection of tenure will not gain Nobel prizes.[3]

All this is to raise uncertainty to even greater limits than was the case with John Stuart Mill, and it is no surprise to discover that Popper has increasingly defined science simply as the possibility of criticizing. He has himself noted an asymmetry to his thought as a whole: he admires fireworks in science, but advocates piecemeal social engineering in society.[4] There are good reasons, however, for not allowing Popper's acceptance of this disjunction to stand.[5] Modern science is not really revolutionary; on the contrary, the change from Newton to Einstein, of which Popper makes much, is really an example of piecemeal and cumulative change inside modern science, as is suggested by the fact that the conceptual change was not so great as to necessitate destruction and rebuilding of all bridges. Criticism by itself is not enough; what does matter is the acceptance of modern cognitive practices in order that the asking of questions can prove effective. How can you falsify a theory without a background assumption of empiricism? Mechanism and empiricism are necessary to prevent ideologies being judges in their own case and to encourage the search for explanatory structures: the acceptance of such norms does deserve the label revolution.

What has been said about Popper follows from the earlier discussion of science. But to say this is to be reminded of a vital problem. Are cognitive norms shared only by scientists? Is the uncertainty principle restricted by ideologies which consider science merely as technology? Is there a nexus between science and liberalism? These questions need to be kept in mind throughout even though they will begin to be confronted directly only at the end of this chapter.

Negative Utilitarianism
Modern science has produced amazingly high-powered knowledge. This is a satisfaction in its own right. In so far

as such knowledge enables us to control the world effectively, we can at least hope, perhaps even suspect, that we are getting closer to the truth about reality in itself. No proof in this matter is now, or ever will be, available.

However, the fundamental reason for placing science at the heart of liberalism is much simpler. What matters more to the majority of human beings than the pleasure of research is something more straightforward. High-powered modern science plays a vital role in producing the technology necessary for modern, post-scarcity social life. Spencer and Comte were right to insist that war, nastiness and brutishness were generally characteristic of pre-industrial militarist societies; such practices were rational in conditions of scarcity. The scientific/industrial complex at least gives us the possibility of decent behaviour. None of this is to say that modern societies are havens of social justice; but such societies have raised living standards, and they do at least allow for the possibility of non-zero sum political life. This general consideration amounts to an injunction of negative utilitarianism: certain horrors, foremost among them plague, war and famine, from which men and women have suffered can be alleviated, and it behoves us to accept a way of life that allows this.[6] But matters can be put in a more positive light: industrial societies are based upon historically high levels of geographical and social mobility, and these increase the 'life chances' of individuals, allowing for identities to become achieved rather than socially ascribed. Societies which do not have this productive system are now illegitimate in the eyes of their citizens. Equally importantly, such societies find it hard to defend themselves against intervention, and elites of old regimes are clearly aware of this. Bluntly, developing societies are seeking to modernize as fast as possible, and this determination remains crucial to the modern world polity. Even were there not good reasons for adopting the scientific/industrial complex, liberalism would still need to base its thought upon the emergence of industrial society. This is the fundamental benchmark of modern world history. Occasionally, romantic intellectuals lament that the process of modernization destroys community. However, there is no sign whatever in contemporary society that large numbers of people are prepared to do without a standard of living to which they have become, or wish to become, accustomed; to pretend otherwise is a conceit to which intellectuals are, regrettably, all too often prone.[7]

Settle for Less

If science deserves supports, this is not to deny that it has what many consider to be a serious price-tag. A scientific world tends, so to speak, to be morally neutral and empty. This can be explained by means of several related and mutually supporting reasons. The most important consideration is that stressed by Popper: uncertainty is unavoidable. All the research programmes in the world will not make it possible to establish some universal system of knowledge which is guaranteed to be true for ever. In consequence, no totalizing ideology can be true.

The fact that the acceptance of science entails a humbling of the authority on which moralities have characteristically relied can be explained further by noting the consequences of mechanism and empiricism upon moralities. Mechanical, reductive explanation *must be* morally unsettling. Ernest Gellner puts the matter felicitously when suggesting that Noam Chomsky, rather than Sigmund Freud, offers us a realistic view of what is involved in the explanation of human behaviour:

Any explanation of human conduct or competence in terms of a genuine structure is morally offensive – for a genuine structure is an 'it' not an 'I'. Chomskian structures are also known to be, in part, well hidden from consciousness; he himself lays great stress on this. If this be the correct strategy in the study of man, then the *I* is ultimately to be explained by an *it* (alas). The Freudian *id* was beastly, but, when all is said and done, it was cosily human

174

in its un-housetrained way; at worst you could say that it was all too human; it was human nature seen in the image of conscious man, but with gloves off. (Like us, but without the advantages we've had, if you know what I mean.) The explanation of our unthinking, quasi-automatic competence into explanatory schemata, outlining structures which are not normally accessible to us at all, is far more sinister. This kind of *id* is not violent, sexy and murderous, it is just totally indifferent to us.[8]

I am not at all sure that the ability of science to explain our behaviour is yet a clear and present danger. Moreover, there may be an ultimate paradox to the attempt by the constrained to understand the constraints upon them. However, it becomes necessary only in the last analysis to say that there is some ultimate human redoubt that cannot be explained. In the meantime, there is certainly some move towards explaining ever more areas of human life. Perhaps liberalism's respect for science thus subtly undermines its respect for the individual. The situation is no better and much more immediate when we turn to empiricism. The very heart of this cognitive practice is, as noted, its *a priori* atomism, that is, the habit of taking social practices one by one. This serves as a powerful humbler of various totalizing ideologies; only force can save ideologies such as fascism and Marxism from refutation. Empiricism also affects our moral life: we cannot take things on trust and consult experts. All this can be put in a nutshell: mechanism and empiricism *are* reliable tools for increasing knowledge, but their mode of operation makes it hard for us to rely on taken-for-granted moral assumptions. Modern science undermines our day-to-day customary beliefs by providing alternative, more powerful explanations for natural and social phenomena. Traditional wisdoms become attenuated; expertise increases its social role.

The fact that scientific knowledge changes, as Popper insists, makes it impossible to underwrite anything which has the same structure as a traditional moral order. Auguste Comte was wrong to believe that science would first destroy metaphysics and then replace it with morally equivalent secular ethics. The Religion of Humanity still professed in Positivist chapels in various parts of the world was far too bloodless to have general appeal. Another way of putting the same point is to say that the world of liberal ideology is strange because it tries to make a virtue out of doubt. This is a unique cultural experiment, and it is scarcely surprising that it tends to offend against what Durkheim called the 'conscience collective'.

Max Weber was the first major thinker to take note of these issues, and he did so profoundly. It is insufficiently realized how deeply Nietzsche's dictum that 'God is dead' affected Max Weber. This underlay his description of 'the disenchantment of the world', quite as much as did his views about the workings of modern science.[9] The themes of Max Weber's thought have received eloquent, lucid and rigorous treatment from Ernest Gellner, whose concern with the moral effect of mechanism and empiricism has just been examined. Importantly, when Gellner does not directly discuss the disenchantment thesis, he speaks in terms of the modern world being 'cold' or 'empty', and recommends a type of stoicism based on 'ironic cultural nationalism'.[10]

The notion that there is a 'cost' to knowledge should be treated with some care. For there are two positive reasons why liberalism favours the moral universe that is created by science, and the Weber/Gellner characterization of that world helps us to recognize them. The first reason is positive. Communal warmth has its repulsive, conformist side too, and this suggests independent moral reasons for accepting a barer world. Ultimately, all of these boil down to the claim that the desire to become master of one's fate is noble. This ethic has been most fully spelt out by Kant and by Popper. We have already seen that this claim makes little sociological sense, however movingly expressed, when it seeks to deny that the individual is moulded by society, and that much of this moulding is enabling and beneficial.

Moreover, becoming the helmsman of one's craft is, as we have seen, no easy task. Nevertheless, the general claim is by no means silly when it recognizes such limitations, and then encourages the individual to recognize that he is, and may as well recognize that he is, responsible for his own decisions. The attempt to master one's own fate is the only doctrine suited to mankind in an age of maturity.

The second reason for endorsing this moral feel of a scientific world view is, in contrast, purely negative. Liberalism is the least bad social recipe available. A central tenet of Goffman's work was that it is very hard to have large-scale Durkheimian festivals at which social mores could be underwritten, and Goffman therefore spoke, with characteristic ambiguity, about the convenience of having the value of the individual stressed in those interpersonal acts of deference and demeanour that he analysed so well.[11] He has a point. The only occasion on which *positive* re-enchantment (as compared to cultural hangovers/entertainments – the British Coronation, Wembley Stadium, tea at Lord's – which are without much social significance) was tried on a collective basis by a modern industrial society was at the Nuremburg rallies. Uncertainty seems massively attractive in the face of ideocratic dogmatism, just as 'coldness' does when confronted with rabid enthusiastic communalism. It would, of course, be a great mistake to blame thought as being responsible for large-scale social movements of this type; clearly structural problems existed which encouraged large numbers to take the messages of intellectuals seriously. Structural problems even more massive in size exist today for those Third World societies which are seeking to make a speedy transition to the modern world, and it is this which explains the power of ideology in the contemporary Third World. However, it remains true that modern intellectuals have, as a whole, a poor record in relation to such appalling collective fantasies. Liberalism's attractions are vastly enhanced by comparisons with romanticisms which so clearly encourage adoption of dubious utopias.

It is desirable to go some way beyond these bald state-ments by commenting upon the rather unhappy manner in which they have been expressed. Perhaps the best-known part of Weber's sociology is his concern with bureaucracy since it was this that led him to speak about modern man being forced to live in an 'iron cage'. It is appropriate that his work is compared with that of Franz Kafka. Should we accept this characterization as an accurate view of our situation as a whole? There is a good reason for being somewhat suspicious of the air of cultural pessimism that surrounds the disenchantment thesis. Most people were never that 'enchanted' by a world of poverty and disease, and it is entirely proper to say that for them the disenchant-ing effects of modern science are outweighed by the afflu-ence it provides. Sociological studies of the British working class certainly give the impression of a hive of activity on the part of those in work, and this seems far removed from any sort of Kafkaesque scenario.[12] This is not to deny that certain societal spiritual support may be lacking, but it is to suggest that the most appropriate place for seeking solace is private life. The whole point has already been addressed: modern intellectuals, bereft of patronage and deprived, in an age of mass literacy, of the monopoly of literacy that was their greatest claim to public attention, tend to feel that much more alienated than their fellow citizens. The demand for totalizing ideologies that such isolated intellectuals make tends to reflect their own mar-ginality rather than the needs or desires of the majority, at least in settled industrial societies. The point being made can be put in rather different terms. It is tempting to substitute adjectives like cold and empty with alternatives such as lean, spare or fit; but these are not much better since they suggest those endless aerobics classes in which people get in shape – for precisely what? It is tempting to derive an adjective from Samuel Johnson's reply to the observation that he had become a philosopher: 'I have tried too in my time to be a philosopher; but, I don't know how, cheerfulness was always breaking in.'[13] This is reminiscent of David Hume, although it is made the more striking by the fact that Johnson did not have Hume's sunny disposition, and was well aware of the tragic dimension to life. But to talk of cheerfulness is to mock the genuine fear and trembling that can affect human beings and disrupt them from settled routines. The best way to summarize the point is by a recommendation: all things considered, we must and should settle for less. Perhaps even the Scandinavians, for so long experts in the production of anguished souls, have learnt this lesson. In Stockholm, T-shirts are selling well which note that 'Kafka didn't have much fun'.

The whole principle of 'settle for less' stands in contrast to what deserve to be called 'generous liberalisms'. The provision of various generous liberalisms is unquestionably one area of growth in the Western world, although the export potential of this particular industry does not look promising. Let us consider some examples. Michael Sandel has objected to the puritanical, Robinson Crusoe-type flavour that is to be found in the influential American liberal John Rawls, and which he correctly notes derives from the philosophy of Kant.[14] Sandel wishes to replace a concept of the individual which is formal, abstract and asocial with an alternative which is 'richer' and 'warmer', and which pays attention to the capacities of human beings to sustain friendships. Alasdair MacIntyre's *After Virtue* begins with a surgical dissection of the weaknesses of a utilitarian world where self-interest reigns; this is judged in Durkheimian terms as no real society since it is bereft of all trust.[15] We are told that only the creation of some sort of teleological vision, that is, a conception of man with aims to work towards, can solve the void into which modern society and its moral philosophy has fallen. This is to say that disenchantment is a problem from which we can escape. I suspect that this is the single most important driving force in the social philosophy of Jürgen Habermas, the leading representative of the Frankfurt School and a very considerable thinker in his own right.[16] Habermas has

179

complex arguments designed to undermine the disenchant-ing effects of mechanism, and he similarly wishes to play down the moral consequences of empiricism by replacing a correspondence with a consensus theory of truth, that is, by stressing that it is *we* who decide what facts are, and when to consult them. This is necessary philosophical ground-work for his claim that modern societies can achieve a new and rational social identity.[17] In order to do so, it is necessary for every constraint on communication between all members of a society to be removed; when every person feels that they have the continuing right to raise issues or questions, a legitimate order based upon a shared morality will become possible – although such an identity will be subject to revision at any time. Habermas insists that we cannot be told what such an identity will be; the German thinker prefers to withdraw gracefully rather than to be accused of decreeing in advance how others should live.

Generous liberalisms call for a warmer and more com-plete moral universe. They berate the end of ideology school for not realizing that what we need is more ideol-ogy.[18] It is important, however, to note that these thinkers are not modern equivalents of the reactionary modernists. If they want more, they also want a better class of ideology, a little warmth without the nastiness. Interestingly, one best-selling version of generous liberalism, an analysis of the modern American character entitled *Habits of the Heart*, seems to suggest that the best ideology available is that provided by the church, and a rather high church at that![19] Two rather different points must be made against such thinkers. The first is simply to note that such theories are rendered innocuous by having sociologically implausible foundations. How can a complex modern economy be organized on a friendly basis? Should we hug the sellers of socks and software? More importantly, why should we believe that it will be possible to get on with living if everything is negotiable at every instant, as Habermas desires? Furthermore, it is surely relevant to note that

Sandel and MacIntyre do not really tell us what makes up the fuller ideology they have in mind – although MacIntyre hints that he may do so, in his next book! Why should we believe Habermas that a rational social identity will be achieved once various obstacles have been removed? I suspect that the lack of specification derives from the fact that it is impossible to combine rational collective re-enchantment with the characteristic workings of industrial society. It is this that suggests criticism from the opposite angle. Generous liberalisms are not completely innocuous. I do not have in mind here the fact that the proliferation of such views means that other, more urgent problems are ignored; nor is the capacity of these views to raise expectations that cannot be fulfilled what is at issue. It is simply that intellectual disciples are often without much discrimination, as was demonstrated by those who acted in Nietzsche's name. Perhaps this could happen again. It is surely worthwhile exercising self-restraint, and in particular asking carefully about the sociological plausibility of social and political theories, to make sure that it does not happen again. It is useful in this context to recall John Dunn's call for a liberal theory that would be 'generous' enough to be the moral equivalent of a religion.[20] One reason for rejecting this is simply that no such moral equivalent is, or can be made, available; modern cognition rules out all totalizing systems of belief. If any such could, however, be constructed, it is very much an open question whether liberalism's very heart – the sense of openness, contingency and choice – would remain in being. However, an equally important objection is simply that the call for such a belief system may be taken all too seriously, and aid in the creation of another 'secular religion'.

That these comments have been so very negative is, I am afraid, testimony to an allergy on the author's part. Nevertheless, generous liberalisms consistently hint at or imply one point which cannot be ignored. Society does depend upon trust and it cannot be made up simply from a band of

Robinson Crusoes; to put the point differently, Robinson Crusoe cannot exist without social support. Is there a way in which it is possible to pay attention to this single point, and yet to remain suspicious of much of the rest of the ideological baggage of generous liberalism? Can the moral heart of liberalism be stressed without opening a Pandora's box of organized *Gemütlichkeit?* The answer to this question can be positive. There is something to be said for the recent admiration shown to the republican tradition of political theory that stresses the need for public virtue.[21] There are sociological problems to this tradition. Its original incarnation was based on slavery, and it thereafter largely codified the life of small, citizen army communities; the advocacy of spartan virtues in modern circumstances does have an awful air of Baden-Powell and the boy scouts.[22] Nevertheless, the problem that faces liberalism is a real one, and this source of ideas cannot be ignored. To say this is, of course, to admit that to begin discussion of liberalism's social and political theory with the work of Adam Smith, as has been done here, is not entirely happy, satisfactory or justified.

What has tended to happen in modern liberalism is that the notion of negative liberty has been joined to a philosophical tradition which emphasizes the individual's rights against society. Quentin Skinner has demonstrated elegantly that this conjunction, so firmly cemented in our minds, is entirely contingent. One can join together negative liberty with a proper respect for society, and Machiavelli, at least in Skinner's interpretation, managed to do so.[23] This is to emphasize that a shared respect for negative freedom, i.e. a distaste for positive specification of the good, deserves to be defended; to be a part of such an order requires at least something of those public virtues which the theory of republicanism stresses. Liberalism must have some sense of society to protect its minimal vision, otherwise it may be as hard to make contemporary societies cohere in troubled times as it was in the inter-war years. In this context, the description of liberal society as cold, empty or disenchanted is unfortunate. It suggests that liberalism simply has to pour cold water on extravagant schemes so as to retain the status quo. There is much to be said for mocking the attempt to provide new totalizing ideologies, and much to be happy about in a status quo which downplays enthusiastic communalism. But a negative statement is not enough; liberalism can and should be defended in positive terms which allow and sometimes require activity.

A final comment on Skinner's argument will help highlight the issues to be addressed in the next section. On the face of it, there is a terrible danger to Skinner's position. If one abandons a conception of natural rights that the individual can hold against society, then what guarantee is there that local norms will not be repulsive? This is to say that the danger of relativism seems to hang over Skinner's enterprise. The suspicion that this is so is much reinforced by his continual drawing upon the later, and relativistic philosophy of Ludwig Wittgenstein.[24] However, Skinner makes it absolutely clear that he does not wish to accept relativism when he notes that 'one of the subsidiary hopes I entertain for my paper is that it may do something (at least in relation to theories about the social world) to question the thesis of incommensurability itself'.[25] Presumably this means that good reasons can be found for preferring one type of society above another – in this case the society of negative liberty above those that stress various totalizing views. The attempt to find such reasons is precisely the enterprise upon which this chapter is currently engaged. But what does it *mean* to offer universal reasons? How can this conception of rationality be squared with the awareness, which accounts for relativism's appeal, that concepts and ideologies do vary across time and space? Before approaching these tricky matters, we must say something about the third pillar of liberalism

What is Liberty?
This is a huge and extremely complex question; even to ask it makes an author aware of the hubris involved in writing

books of this type. But if a complete answer is impossible, the main lines of the argument made on this point, together with those implied by the first two pillars of liberalism, can at least be summarily stated.

There are three components to liberty. The first component is that of the secure provision of the basic necessities of food and health, the absence of which makes life miserable. To fulfil this element is to satisfy the requirements of negative utilitarianism. Furthermore, liberalism has a positive appreciation for more than a mere sufficiency: a measure of luxury lies behind that spread of fashion which allows a degree of role-playing helpful in the creation of a sense of personal autonomy. In more political terms the desire for autonomy is the second component of liberty, namely that of negative liberty. A desirable society is one in which every person has space in which to develop. There are several interrelated elements at work here, and I shall therefore continue to refer to the omnibus notion of 'soft political rule'. Central to this notion is respect for the absence of arbitrariness/presence of the rule of law. There is a long tradition in European thought, to which Montesquieu, Hume and Smith all belonged, which stresses that it is arbitrariness that makes government insupportable. Tocqueville's insistence that democracy could, in principle, arbitrarily rule some out of society is a part of the same tradition. Its ultimate base is that of a generalized Kantian respect for all persons. But laws may be vicious, and something more is involved in this notion. It implies equality before the law and the right to freedom of opinion. The final component of liberty is, however, that of the right of the people to control political power by democratic means. The attractiveness of this component has grown as the result of the historical disasters of the last hundred years. It is worth noting, however, that in modern circumstances it is only a 'realistic' version of democracy that makes much sense. The complexity of modern society makes it impossible to imagine democracy being of the face-to-face participatory kind favoured by the Greeks, and recommended by Rousseau for small communities. The realistic theory of democracy, in contrast, stresses the benefits of a divided and competing political elite.[26] This view recognizes that modern politics is necessarily oligarchical, but emphasizes none the less that the circulation of elites allows the replacement of incompetent governments as a matter of course.

A coherent liberal view of liberty demands that all three elements be present. What is at issue here is the problem raised by Tocqueville, namely that democracy in and of itself does not guarantee a desirable society. This may seem an abstract point, but it is one of great relevance for the debate concerning the relationship between science and society. Habermas's response to the attempt to keep science as a specialized preserve of scientists has been to demand the democratization of science. In its most sophisticated version, this demand has led to the suggestion that the science/liberalism nexus would be best cemented on the basis of a consensus rather than a correspondence theory of truth.[27] Although this is suggestive and important, it must, in the last analysis, be rejected. Asking for consensus can be illiberal, in the manner of Rousseau's General Will, although Habermas most certainly is not; what matters in epistemology is the second element of liberty, that is, the right to raise questions.

It can be admitted at once that it is by no means easy to combine these three elements. We shall see that forced development makes it unlikely that political liberty is, so to speak, on the agenda of general social evolution. Moreover, regimes which do not grant political liberty may well prove to be stable. This position contrasts with that of Ralf Dahrendorf. It is not distorting the German liberal thinker's social philosophy to say that at its kernel is the belief that the desire for liberty, in the fullest sense of the word, is engraved on every human heart.[28] This may well be true: people throughout the world know what it is to be brutalized by armies and police. With regret, however, it remains necessary to insist that many social orders have been considered legitimate when they have provided for the basic needs of their citizens; the absence of political freedom in, say, the Soviet Union or South Korea is more than compensated for, at least for the majority, by an industrial standard of living. Political liberty and affluence do not go hand in hand. The question then arises as to whether the wide-scale adoption of the scientific-industrial complex will allow a spread of softer political rule.

Rationality and Relativism

It is now time to confront the problem raised by the structure of the argument. Liberalism has consistently been seen here as one ideology among others; nevertheless, a series of related reasons has been offered to suggest that it is the best – or, anyway, the least repulsive – ideology on offer. Now any rigorously sustained relativism would mock such an argumentative strategy as self-contradictory. The point about relativism, it would be maintained, is that concepts and perceptions vary completely by society; truth really is different, as Pascal had it, on the other side of the Pyrenees. The crucial component of this claim is the belief that it is possible to think only through the terms that a particular culture provides. This doctrine has been hugely influential in social science, and indeed in the larger world of political and social theory.[29] The thesis was most eloquently expressed, however, by George Orwell in *Nineteen Eighty-Four*: the power to control the commanding conceptual heights of society are held to be so great that it will become impossible even to *conceptualize* any alternative. If any strong version of relativism of this sort is correct, it becomes, of course, stupid and naïve for liberals to offer reasons in favour of their beliefs. Who do liberals hope to convince?

Relativism has its attraction. It can be an antidote to the soft spinelessness to which liberalism has on occasion been prone; a 'relativistic liberal' would not be bothered trying to convince someone from a different civilization, and might more easily recognize them as an enemy to be fought. Furthermore, relativism seems to be liberal; it is against 'missionary activity', that is, it dislikes interference, especially with other cultures, as classically was the case with imperialism.[30] There is something to be said in favour of giving reasons for liberalism in order that members of the advanced democracies inside the capitalist arena may better understand themselves. Beyond this, however, much of relativism's claim to be liberal is phony. Its ethic suggests that local standards should be accepted. What if such standards are repulsive? No liberal can rest content with a non-universalistic position in the light of the attendant danger. Nevertheless, the question as to how universal standards should be 'applied' in world politics is extremely complex, and it will prove possible to share relativism's distaste for naïve moral crusades, although for sociological rather than philosophical reasons.

Before examining how universal is the appeal of the reasons for liberalism offered above, that is, before assaulting relativism, it is worth stressing that its case is sufficiently cogent to make nonsense of the recent attempt to revive social contract theory in political and social theory. The attempt to discover a just social order on the basis of rational calculation as to what would prove acceptable to people entering into a social contract is surely misguided. This strategy is best represented by the work of the American philosophers John Rawls and Robert Nozick; the dispute between these two thinkers as to the nature of a just social order seems likely to have the status of the celebrated conflict between the ideas of Thomas Hobbes and John Locke.[31] But social contract theories have surely been rendered completely implausible by David Hume's old objections: people do not contract into a society, but are simply born into social orders which they are not usually free thereafter to leave.[32] More importantly, the rational actor in the work of Rawls and Nozick is by no means some neutral construct, as can be seen in the long argument used by the former to lend his actor the characteristic modes of feeling of those of liberal areas of the eastern seaboard of the United States. Such modes of feeling are not universal! If we are to escape relativism, it is necessary to speak to people as they are, in the social orders of which they are a part. Given that modes of thought vary, a more sociologically based strategy suggests itself.

The key part of an assault on relativism must lie in the demonstration that people are not so conceptually imprisoned that they cannot 'see' anything of what is happening in neutral terms. There are two reasons for believing such an attack to be justified. First, philosophers who write about ideologies – and sociologists (who should know better) who follow them – exaggerate their coherence, elegance and internal economy. It is doubtful whether an ideology could be perfected, as is the intention of the rulers of the society depicted in *Nineteen Eighty-Four*, so that it would genuinely become possible to think only in one way; certainly no ideology that is known to me works so smoothly. On the contrary, belief systems are messy affairs, rag-bags full of ideological options that can be pulled out by interested parties as occasion demands. To say this is not to deny that an ideology can have some constraining force, especially when a particular option is missing, and that it can affect the way in which 'interest' is defined; but it does deny that ideology controls. If this consideration limits ideologies by carping at their powers of construction, it is equally important to note that large numbers of people do not believe what they are told.[33] Except in extraordinary cases, people who are starved or beaten know that they are suffering.[34] To say this is, of course, to insist that, in certain basic matters, human beings are the same everywhere, a point which suggests that there may be a measure of descriptive sociological truth to the philosophies of Hume and Kant after all. The second reason is sociological and brutal. Relativism makes little sense in modern circumstances because every national society now recognizes itself to be part of a larger world order, the leading sector of which has huge scientific and industrial power, and whose impact can all too easily be felt through geopolitical conflict. The central contention is that relativism fails since it is possible to see beyond the shackles of ideology. But where does this leave us?

Conclusion

The philosophical foundations for liberalism that have been offered here are banal, spare but, to my mind, none the less plausible. These foundations amount to a restatement of liberalism as a morality. This morality is, thank goodness, distinctive in not seeking to explain and justify everything; liberalism cannot be a totalizing ideology. However, it is a vision which is well worth defending, if need be, and I hope that this specification of its attractions will make citizens of the advanced industrial democracies more self-conscious about themselves.

The larger purpose, however, has been that of trying to establish standards that will be genuinely universal. Universalizability cannot be left as an abstract philosophical matter. It is necessary to ask whether arguments made have the power to convince those who are not already half converted. Will this codification of liberalism make it seem attractive to people who are not already members of liberal societies? What exactly do such people think of us?

Perception is an important phenomenon in the modern world; this makes it vital for liberal societies to put their own house in order. It must be said that those who live outside the heartland of liberalism tend to notice the first rather than the second and third pillars of liberalism, that is, they are attracted less by liberty than by affluence. Uniform pessimism is probably not justified in this matter: there is probably some general awareness of the disasters caused by the totalizing dogmatisms of twentieth-century Europe. Nevertheless, most late developers seek to combine science with traditional belief, that is, to place scientists in a ghetto from which they can create powerful technologies rather than to reform their societies on the basis of the norms of epistemology.

I wish absolutely powerful philosophical foundations for liberalism were available, all of which could be clearly understood by every inhabitant of the planet. That this is not so is a source of profound worry and unhappiness. It is responsible for shifting much of the burden for liberalism's defence to sociological grounds. Can the scientific-industrial complex be placed in a ghetto where it has no impact on social custom *over the long run*?

NOTES

1. That a defence of liberalism should take this form became obvious to me from E. Gellner, 'An Ethic of Cognition', in his *Spectacles and Predicaments* (Cambridge: Cambridge University Press, 1979).

2. K. Popper, *The Logic of Scientific Discovery*, 6th edition (London: Routledge and Kegan Paul, 1972) and *The Open Society and Its Enemies*, 3rd edition (London: Routledge and Kegan Paul, 1957).

3. K. Popper, 'Normal Science and Its Dangers', in I. Lakatos and A. Musgrave (eds), *Criticism and the Growth of Knowledge* (Cambridge: Cambridge University Press, 1970).

4. K. Popper, 'Reason or Revolution?', in T. W. Adorno et al., *The Positivist Dispute in German Sociology* (London: Heinemann Educational, 1976).

5. E. Gellner, *Legitimation of Belief* (Cambridge: Cambridge University Press, 1974), chapter 9.

6. Cf. B. Moore, *Reflections on the Causes of Human Misery and Upon Certain Proposals to Eliminate Them* (Boston: Beacon Press, 1969).

7. One example of this is P. Berger, B. Berger and H. Kellner, *The Homeless Mind* (New York: Vintage Books, 1974).

8. Gellner, *Legitimation of Belief* op. cit., p.99.

9. On this point see the forthcoming book of Ralf Schroeder.

10. Gellner, *Legitimation of Belief* op. cit., chapter 9.

11. E. Goffman, 'The Nature of Deference and Demeanour,' in his *Interaction Ritual* (Harmondsworth: Penguin, 1972). Cf. Chapter 3 of this book.

12. For example, R. Pahl, *Divisions of Labour* (Oxford: Basil Blackwell, 1984).

13. This remark was made on 17 April 1778 according to J. Boswell, *Life of Johnson* (Oxford: Oxford University Press, 1980), p.957.

14. M. Sandel, *Liberalism and the Limits of Justice* (Cambridge: Cambridge University Press, 1982).

15. A. MacIntyre, *After Virtue* (London: Duckworth, 1981).

16. Habermas is a prolific and complex thinker, and is best approached through T. McCarthy, *The Critical Theory of Jürgen Habermas* (Oxford: Polity Press, 1984). Cf. J. A. Hall, *Diagnoses of Our Time* (London: Heinemann Educational, 1981), chapter 3.

17. J. Habermas, 'On Social Identity', *Telos*, 19 (1974).

18. Cf. A. Gouldner, *The Dialectics of Ideology and Technology* (New York: Seabury Press, 1976).

19. R. Bellah, R. Madsen, W. Sullivan, A. Swidler and S. Tipton, *Habits of the Heart* (New York: Harper and Row, 1985).

20. J. Dunn, 'From Applied Theology to Social Analysis: the Break between John Locke and the Scottish Enlightenment', in I. Hont and M. Ignatieff (eds), *Wealth and Virtue* (Cambridge: Cambridge University Press, 1983).

21. The key work in this revival is J. Pocock, *The Machiavellian Moment* (Princeton: Princeton University Press, 1975).

22. A sustained attempt to discuss what might be involved in translating such ideas into practice has been made by Morris Janowitz in *The Reconstruction of Patriotism* (Chicago: Chicago University Press, 1983).

23. Q. Skinner, 'The Idea of Negative Liberty: Philosophical and Historical Perspectives', in R. Rorty, J. B. Schneewind and Q. Skinner (eds), *Philosophy in History. Essays on the Historiography of Philosophy* (Cambridge: Cambridge University Press, 1984).

24. Ibid., p.198. Cf. Q. Skinner, 'Meaning and Understanding in the History of Ideas', *History and Theory*, 8 (1969).

25. Ibid., p.193.

26. J. Schumpeter, *Capitalism, Socialism and Democracy* (London: Allen and Unwin, 1981), part IV.

27. Habermas, op. cit.; McCarthy, op. cit.

28. I discuss Dahrendorf's social philosophy in *Diagnoses of Our Time* (London: Heinemann Educational, 1981), chapter 5.

29. J. A. Hall, 'Theory', in M. Haralambos (ed.), *Developments in*

Sociology, vol. 2 (Ormskirk: Causeway Press, 1986).

30. I am thinking here of the views of P. Winch, most importantly in *The Idea of a Social Science and Its Relationship to Philosophy* (London: Routledge and Kegan Paul, 1958). Cf. B. Wilson (ed.), *Rationality* (Oxford: Basil Blackwell, 1970) and E. Gellner, 'The New Idealism – Cause and Meaning in the Social Sciences', in his *Cause and Meaning in the Social Sciences* (London: Routledge and Kegan Paul, 1973).

31. J. Rawls, *A Theory of Justice* (Oxford: Oxford University Press, 1973); R. Nozick, *Anarchy, State and Utopia* (Oxford: Basil Blackwell, 1975). Cf. J. Gray, 'Social Contract, Community, and Ideology', in P. Birnbaum, J. Lively and G. Parry, (eds), *Democracy, Consensus and Contract* (London: Sage, 1978); N. Daniels (ed.), *Reading Rawls* (New York: Basic Books, 1974); B. Barry, *The Liberal Theory of Justice* (Oxford: Oxford University Press, 1973).

32. D. Hume, 'Of the Original Contract', in his *Essays, Literary, Moral and Political* (Chicago: Henry Regnery, 1965).

33. N. Abercrombie, S. Hill and B. Turner, *The Dominant Ideology Thesis* (London: George Allen and Unwin, 1980).

34. B. Moore, *Injustice: The Social Bases of Obedience and Revolt* (New York: M. E. Sharpe, 1978).

A GENERAL THEORY OF LIBERALISM –
(B) SOCIOLOGICAL FOUNDATIONS

This chapter begins with consideration of the most terrible problem that has faced liberalism since 1945. The desire for affluence has particular social consequences which are deeply unsettling for liberalism. However, it is possible that the 'logic' of the scientific-industrial complex may be such as to diminish initial fears; considerable attention is paid to the exposition of that logic. For hope to be realized, intelligent action is required on the part of state elites, particularly in America. This may, or may not, be forthcoming.

The Great Fear
This central problem that faces liberalism in modern circumstances is simple and straightforward. Adam Smith was right to note that the emergence of capitalism and liberal rule were connected. The natural and organic emergence of industrial society was unique; all industrialization thereafter was, by definition, imitative. However, the directive – no lesser word will do – of modern history is that of speeding up industrialization. In these circumstances, the equation of commerce *and* liberty no longer holds. The generalization to be made about this whole situation is quite horrible: *forced development is socially brutal.*[1] Such development cannot be achieved under the aegis of soft political rule and this means that the chances of a transition to democracy are correspondingly at a discount. We must begin by spelling out why this is so, before considering

those facets of the scientific-industrial complex that may diminish the harshness of this formulation.

A brief look at the nature of the social engineering involved in rapid modernization will explain the harsh formula under consideration. Let us look at two of the principal 'functional prerequisites' of the modern industrial era.

1. *Sectoral change.* Most agrarian societies require something like 90 per cent of the workforce to act as agricultural producers in order that a very small elite may be supported. In contrast, most advanced societies now have in primary sectors under 10 per cent of the workforce, with several advanced capitalist societies having less than 5 per cent so engaged. While it was never the case that a majority of the workforce in industrial societies was engaged in the secondary industrial sector, this is not to down-play the fundamental insight of Barrington Moore's great *Social Origins of Dictatorship and Democracy* that modernization, under whatever political aegis, involves at least disciplining the peasantry and at most forcibly removing it from the land.[2]

2. *Nation-building.* The difficulties involved in nation-building can be best appreciated by considering the situation of states that are entirely new. The citizens of industrial society must have the capacity to communicate with each other at an abstract level, preferably in a single language. This necessitates all states, including those of the old heartland of north-west Europe, creating schooling systems which both mobilize the people and give them the skills to participate in a literate and technical society. New states, however, must do more than simply establish educational systems. In addition, they face such tasks as the removal of tribalism, the destruction of rival cultures, the creation of a lingua franca and the establishment of national bureaucracies.[3]

These are but two of the preconditions of industrial society, but they clearly justify the contention that forced

194

development is socially brutalizing. Successful modernization requires massive social engineering. Peasants are
pushed from their land, customary practices of all sorts
disrupted and new human material created. Interestingly,
some of the earliest attempts to imitate the West, notably
that of the Young Turks, were based on the belief that
modernization would be best achieved by the creation of
secular societies ruled over by parliaments modelled on
that of Westminster. Third World countries have learnt
with time that successful modernization is impeded by
democracy. For people do not easily accept the loss of their
land and of their customary ways of life: this requires force.
It also virtually requires the use of a totalizing ideology.
Nationalism is one such ideology, and it is given obeisance
virtually everywhere. Marxism has considerable appeal in
developing countries, even though the extent of its appeal
is customarily much exaggerated. Perhaps the most powerful ideology in modern circumstances is that of Islam, since
it is uniquely adaptable to modern circumstances. This
may lend great force to Islamic societies because they can
use the culture they possess in order to develop.

It behoves liberals to think very carefully as to the
judgement they should place upon the savageries of modernization. I shall argue that the premise that must guide
us is clear. Popper has claimed that social engineering
makes sense only when done in a piecemeal fashion; in
other words, that revolutions, which he so welcomes in
science, are always disastrous in social life.[4] This is a silly
notion. Some old regimes defeat piecemeal attempts at
improvement, and they *can only* be changed in a root and
branch manner – a generalization that applies to Tsarist
Russia and late imperial China.[5] Total social engineering is
indeed savage, and it should not be romanticized. But *in so
far as such engineering successfully achieves the transition to industrial society*, it must be accepted by liberals on negative
utilitarian grounds.

Hope Regained

It is not necessary to leave things at this point. The forced transition to modernity splits the innermost desires of liberals: they must endorse the change, while being horror-struck at its effects. The sociological question to which we can now turn naturally suggests itself: once the forced transition has been made, is there any chance that, even in the absence of democracy, a measure of softness may come to characterize social and political relations? The particular question I have in mind here is whether widespread adoption of the scientific-industrial complex will have consequences for social evolution. In order to answer this question, we need first to examine the two principal versions of forced development seen in the modern world, that is, state socialism and authoritarian capitalism.

The Soviet model of industrialization is well known; it neatly fits the generalization of forced development requiring dictatorship. This strategy is comprised of complete central planning, the relative suppression of classes and the dominance of a single party, armed with a totalizing, Promethean ideology which it uses to transform society. Adoption of this model in Russia allowed for a forcible solution to the peasant problem, and for massive investment in heavy industry. Consumer preferences would rather have done without this investment; it was made possible only by the fact that the Soviet model was a power system.[6]

What judgements should we make about this model? Its greatest weakness was surely exposed by Stalinism: when power is concentrated without any attempt to control it, it is always possible that a single person, increasingly told by acolytes only what they wish to hear, can cause havoc. A further problem is that automatic adoption of the model in different social circumstances can cause widespread suffering, as was demonstrated by the great Chinese famine of 1958. There is, of course, much debate as to whether the Soviet model was successful, and much has been made of

Bukharin's more sensitive approach to the peasants. It is certainly true that Bukharin had a far better appreciation of Russian economic problems, and that his economic strategy, based upon allowing consumer production so as to encourage the peasants to produce for the market, also held out the possibility of a liberal socialist route to modernity.[7] However, the evidence does not suggest that Bukharin's route really stood much chance. Grain deliveries were falling before Stalin's drives into the countryside and, in any case, were insufficient at a time when external pressure, in the form of the destruction of the Chinese communists, made it vital to speed up industrialization if the Soviet state was to survive at all. Bukharin in any case slavishly endorsed the view that the party had to play the 'leading role', and co-operated with Stalin in hounding Trotsky and Kamenev from public life in 1927. This is not to say that Bukharin was not often right in his views on the peasantry. Stalin's drives resulted not only in the death of perhaps five million peasants, but also in widespread famine, partly caused by peasants destroying their own cattle. The grain harvest of 1933 was five million tons less than that of 1928. But this did not matter, for *the share of the state had doubled*. It was this doubling that allowed for the massive industrialization of the 1930s. So our final judgement must be that the Soviet model was successful, and that modernization could not have been achieved without something like this sort of centralization of political power.

State socialist society has not remained static. What is at issue here is more than the reaction, proclaimed by Khrushchev, against the Stalinist 'cult of personality'. Structural problems dog the Soviet model over time, and three of these can usefully be identified. Most embarrassingly but probably least importantly, the openness of which socialist society loved to boast is being eroded. Peasant social mobility was caused by destruction of traditional elites and, crucially, by the fact that industrialization changed the occupational structure and hence increased the number of white-collar jobs. The rigidity in social stratification that results can, literally, be seen in the public images of Mrs Khrushchev and Mrs Gorbachov: the former looked as if she had just descended from a tractor, a place, one suspects, which is not familiar territory to the latter. Secondly, central planning seems to be much more efficacious at boosting early industrialization, required in the Soviet Union for geopolitical reasons, than it is at managing a complex late industrial economy, as is evident in the slowing of socialist growth rates and in the fact that the exports of the Soviet Union largely consist, as do those of many Third World countries, of non-manufactured goods. Thirdly, it is absolutely clear that the parties of all advanced state socialist societies face problems of legitimation. All Bolshevik parties are now schizophrenic. Where one wing wishes to continue to claim legitimacy by reference to Marxism-Leninism, another, aware that ideological enthusiasm is hard to sustain, argues that social cohesion can be brought by technocratic management resulting in Keynesian-style economic growth.

It is by no means clear what the future evolution of state socialism will be, but there is something to be said for a rather optimistic scenario.[8] It seems likely that late industrial society depends heavily upon scientific knowledge and upon willing participation of middle-class skill in every section of the economy. The 'logic' of late industrialism thus increases the institutional importance of that sector of society with technical rather than ideological competence, and whose way of life benefits from freedom of movement and information. If this argument is correct, then a Hungarian solution to the problems of state socialism, that is, a combination of economic growth with a diminution of ideological intensity, may well become generally available. It is, of course, true that various attempts at liberalization have been put down by the Soviet Union. However, it is equally important to remember that the liberalization of Hungary, managed with skill because it outflanked and did not seek to dismantle the party, took place in the wake of such a defeat. Nevertheless, the fate of liberalization in Eastern Europe as a whole depends upon the evolution of the Soviet Union. At the moment, the forces demanding change seem as insistent inside that society as in others in Eastern Europe. In the final analysis, the success of liberalization in the Soviet Union probably depends upon what happens in the sphere of state competition. The Soviet Union may no longer be able to afford its historic inefficiencies if it has to compete with the advanced technology produced by the core of capitalist society.

It is useful to pause for a moment in order to highlight the claim being made. What exactly is involved in claiming that the scientific-industrial complex may effect social evolution? Most obviously, the desire to have increased living standards makes it increasingly difficult to keep scientists, and the norms on which they depend, in some sort of ghetto apart from larger social processes; it may be possible to pioneer nuclear weapons research in this way, but late industrial society depends on diffusing high-powered knowledge through society. This means that the corrosive effects of science are likely slowly to challenge the truth status of the totalizing ideology on which society runs. The change in the occupational structure of late industrial society, that is, the fact that employment opportunities depend increasingly upon higher education, adds massive pressure for a move towards more technical, regularized and softer political rule. All this can be summed up by saying that increased pluralism plus time make it harder for ideocracies to function as they might like. If these are objective social pressures, it is important to remember that their implementation may or may not be successful. If the entrenched political elite thinks that a demand for softer political rule will spill over into a demand for outright democracy, it will squash liberalization movements. The subtlety demanded of those applying pressure from below will need to be matched by skill on the part of elites, that is, to strike a balance between giving too much and too little, if liberalization in state socialism is to succeed.

Let us turn to the second type of imitative developmental strategy. It is scarcely surprising that various dominant classes and ruling elites, keen to cement themselves in power by controlling the process of modernization, sought by means of 'revolutions from above' to combine capitalism with authoritarianism. Imperial Germany and Imperial Japan showed how economically successful this route to modernity could be, although the traditional elites of China and Russia proved incapable of imitating these examples.

Barrington Moore has suggested that the combination of capitalism with hierarchy is inherently unstable: that, in other words, it is impossible to conserve a social order by allying oneself to a force as rational and dynamic as capitalism.

As they proceeded with conservative modernisation, these semi-parliamentary governments tried to preserve as much of the original social structure as they could, fitting large sections into the new building wherever possible. The results had some resemblance to present-day Victorian houses with modern electrical kitchens but insufficient bathrooms and leaky pipes hidden decorously behind newly plastered walls. Ultimately the makeshifts collapsed.[9]

This view is not accepted by every major historical sociologist, and one of them, Michael Mann, has suggested that the stability of the capitalism *plus* hierarchy political economy would be obvious but for the accident of defeat in war.[10] The fact of war *does* make it exceedingly hard to cast light upon Moore's contention, but several considerations suggest that liberalization may be forced on authoritarian capitalist regimes. The pressures at work have just been mentioned; they place me in opposition to Mann. He is right to dismiss the radical potential of the working classes, but wrong not to realize that a functionally more central middle class comprised of educated labour may yet induce changes inside authoritarian capitalism. One may hope that the adoption of the scientific-industrial complex in authoritarian states within capitalist society may eventually allow for a softening of political rule. It is worth noting that some of these states are less ideocratic than are those of the Soviet bloc, and this may make demands for liberalization that much stronger. Although this is in itself positive, liberalization in this world is as perilous and complicated as it is in the Soviet bloc: if demands are too insistent, state elites can be scared and the introduction of softer political rule delayed. And that liberalization of such regimes depends at least as much upon the skill shown by elites seems clear from the most comprehensive set of studies on the subject.[11]

If evidence is not available from Imperial Germany and Imperial Japan, it is sensible to turn to other societies of this type. The combination of hierarchy with capitalism seemed assured in Francoist Spain. However, the more the Spanish economy advanced, and thereby crucially came to depend on educated labour, the more the pressures on authoritarianism mounted. Very interestingly, Spanish capitalists welcomed such liberalization:

There is no natural, 'ideal' fit between a given social structure and a political constitution. If anything, we have shown that the bourgeoisie may opt for forms of autocratic and anti-parliamentary rule as the most adequate solution to its continued hegemony. Yet it seems clear that at certain stages of economic development it may choose the vast negotiating process entailed by the liberal political framework as the best way for furthering its interests. In this context, it is interesting to note that in Spain, still without having switched their allegiance to a representative multi-party system, the members of the industrial bourgeoisie were already moving towards unofficial collective bargaining and negotiation with the clandestine unions at a very early stage, bypassing the official channels. This started to happen as soon as wage settlements through peaceful means began to look more attractive than outright repression, from the late fifties onwards.[12]

Spanish capitalists had come to realize that accommodation is cheaper than repression. Special circumstances, notably the attractions of the European Community, pollute the Spanish evidence, but it is very striking that newly industrializing countries like Brazil and Argentina are involved in processes of liberalization that seem to be aided by the stage of economic development at which they have now arrived: the supporters of liberalization in Brazil, for example, include the newer middle-class elements of educated labour whose position in the economy is coming to outweigh the influence of old plantation capitalists.[13] South Korea, too, is witnessing attacks on its highly repressive authoritarianism; interestingly, these come from student populations whose importance for the future of society is unquestioned. There may yet, in other words, be something in some societies – most notably, however, those with a tradition of parliamentary rule[14] – which will mean that Adam Smith's equation of commerce and liberty gains a new lease of life. There may even be something to be said for applying these notions to South Africa. Here the historic collusion of capitalism with repression is overwhelmingly obvious. Nevertheless, the dynamic of industrial development, depending ever more on educated labour, raised expectations and helped create a revolutionary situation. As Tocqueville realized, a rise in expectations is related to revolution, a process aided by attempts by the old regime to reform itself; it is not surprising, in light of this, to discover that Soweto has, in comparative terms, relatively high levels of education.[15] In so far as capitalism, through the need to spread education as its manpower needs change, raises expectations, one may argue that it is incompatible in the long run with apartheid. In this context, it is highly significant that capitalists are now seeking to talk with the African National Congress; they are effectively considering abandoning apartheid because it has become too expensive.

This is a convenient point at which to summarize the

argument. Liberalism needs to understand the processes involved in modernization. It can scarcely be happy to discover that forced modernization rules out democracy, but it should nevertheless welcome such development. There are two reasons for a positive endorsement for what is an historical inevitability in any case. The first is the brutal one that industrialization raises living standards. The second argument is by no means definitive: it is that the logic of industrial society may be such as to allow for a softening of political rule in the long run. This is because the standards of modern science may become more important, not least as the functional importance of educated labour increases. All this amounts to a qualification of the initial generalization that forced development entails social brutalization. While it would be vain to expect the emergence of full-scale parliamentary systems in the Soviet Union or in South Korea, it is possible to hope that softer and more regularized behaviour may yet be on the cards.

Modern Man and the State

Towards the end of his life, Herbert Spencer, as much an advocate as was Marx of 'the withering away of the state', wrote despairingly in *The Man Versus the State* of a revival of statism which was, in his eyes, threatening liberalism.[16] This is a convenient moment to assess this theory since it will help underline the argument being made.

Let us recall the fact, represented in the diagram in Chapter 1, that state power has both despotic and infrastructural dimensions. This distinction allows me to warn against one mistake that might otherwise be made in interpreting the argument of this section. Obviously, I have no positive liking of despotism, and would be delighted if India could, in the slightly loose terms of this diagram, move from its feudal status, evident in the inability of the state to establish land reforms and to destroy caste, to becoming a bureaucratic state.[17] Despotism is negatively endorsed here only *in order that decent infrastructural conditions*

may be established, as in the Soviet Union and South Korea.
But it would be a great mistake to assert, and I am not so
doing, that despotism is, *by itself*, enough to ensure development. Examples in both socialist and capitalist arenas –
the Cambodia of Pol Pot and the Haiti of the Duvaliers
spring readily to mind – suggest that despotic powers may
not actually be used to establish a modern society. All this
can be put in a nutshell: development requires strong
states, and mere tyrannies do not deserve that appellation.
It is quite possible that modernization will proceed faster
in Iran under the Ayatollah Khomeini, since he can
mobilize the people, than it did under the late Shah, whose
government was an excrescence on, rather than an expression of, society. One of the great issues of the age is, of
course, whether Islamic *ulama* have the capacity to run a
modern state. I suspect that they do but, equally, on the
basis of what has been said, predict that the spread of the
scientific-industrial complex will eventually undermine
theocracy.

All this amounts to saying that a vital foundation of
liberalism in the modern world is that of successful nationalism. A consequence of this is that of being very wary
indeed of interventionism; virtually any state is better than
none, and interventionism can only be justified when it is
clear in advance that it will succeed, a condition which it is
almost impossible to satisfy. Although I have the situation
of the contemporary Third World most in mind, the point
being made is not without relevance for the European
experience. Was it really wise to intervene morally in
Germany after the First World War by insisting that guilt
be accepted?[18]

As this defence of the state goes against many traditional
preconceptions, however, it is as well to take the argument
a little further. The rise of the West was not 'stateless', and
it is hypocritical of us to expect developing societies to
manage without the benefit of strong states, even though,
let it be stressed again, that strength needs to be of the
right type. The policy implication of this point – that the

advanced societies should encourage state- and nation-building in the Third World – gains much support from another consideration. States swim in the larger sea of the international market, a generalization that increasingly applies even to state socialist societies. In recent years Marxists have claimed that economic development is held back by the workings of international capital.[19] This view of the advanced world needing to exploit the Third World tends to be belied by trade figures showing that most of the Third World has no importance for the international market as it is constituted at present.[20] What is particularly important about this theory here, however, is its suggestion that state power has little autonomous impact in the international market. There are overwhelming reasons for rejecting this theory. The next section argues that the stronger the infrastructural strength of states inside the advanced core of capitalism, the better they seem to prosper. There is a relationship, in other words, between the strength of a state and the ability to compete success-fully in international capitalist society. This makes it vital to try and understand what features comprise the strength of a state in the advanced core of capitalism, a discussion which returns us to the 'needs' of the scientific-industrial complex. Furthermore, it has proved possible for the strong states of the Third World, notably those of SE Asia but including others in the Newly Industrializing Country category, to prosper inside the international market. That this is so means that it is not true to say that the advanced core of capitalist society uniformly exploits the Third World and prevents it developing. None the less, not very many countries deserve to be classified as successful Newly Indus-trialized Countries. Does participation in the world market, of great importance to many third world countries even though it has little salience to the core capitalist states, make it harder to build strong states in the Third World? This brings to the fore again the vexed question of the relations between liberalism and capitalism. Are calls for openness in the world economy genuinely 'liberal' in spirit? Should we – can we – vary the terms on which the international market works so as to favour liberal political goals?

Welfare with Corporatism

The characteristic political economy of advanced societies inside the capitalist arena combines corporatism with welfare. Before justifying this claim, it is as well to distance myself from the belief, recently popular, that capitalist structures of privilege have lost their power in the societies in question. Those who claimed that this was so had three key social changes in mind:[21]

1. Capitalism is held to have changed its character. Entrepreneurial family capitalism has been overtaken by larger corporations in which real power lies in the hands of professional managers. These managers are believed to be more concerned with stability and harmony than with profits.

2. Social mobility is held to have increased, and the solidity of social classes to have been thereby diminished.

3. Such mobility results from the extension of social citizenship rights, notably rights to education. This was held to have undermined privilege. Equality of opportunity was held to have arrived.

In summary, Western societies were seen to be 'post-capitalist'.

This position has been persuasively and extensively criticized, largely by thinkers of Marxist persuasion. Studies of managers, shareholders and directors have shown that the profit motive retains its central place in industry.[22] Furthermore, studies of social mobility have demonstrated that the core societies of capitalism have by no means become fully open: life chances in health, education and employment continue to be heavily determined by class advantage.[23] Privilege offends against the spirit of liberalism, and there is no doubt that liberal standards of social justice have not yet been fully realized. In these circumstances, it is tempting to construct abstract alternative utopias. This tack is not adopted here, largely because the attractiveness of such utopias usually stands in inverse relation to the chances of achieving them. Instead, I have real cases in mind when asking about the extent to which liberals should be opposed to capitalism. My argument will be highly critical, *for pragmatic and sociological reasons*, of those who have recently insisted that liberalism requires a complete advocacy of 'the market'. This is not to say that the market principle of exchange is thereby dismissed.

It is sensible to contrast two phases of the post-war world. The first phase went on until the late 1960s. It witnessed fabulous economic growth; the productive energies of capitalism allowed a dramatic rise in the standard of living. Furthermore, social citizenship rights were extended: they provided a systematic cushioning to capitalist society and some increase in opportunities for the underprivileged. These were years of social peace. Some thinkers maintained that social cohesion was achieved because the working class had been brainwashed through consumerism or through indoctrination by an education system, but this was highly doubtful. Most working people never actually believed in the virtues of the capitalist ethic; acceptance was pragmatic, being based essentially on the capacity of this political economy to provide an ever-expanding supply of benefits.[24] These years have often been called the Keynesian years, in large part because they witnessed capitalism replacing its stick of unemployment with a carrot of growth. Interestingly, Keynes took for granted, much as had Adam Smith and David Hume, that the working class would accept the decisions taken by a liberal and rational elite in order to iron out the troughs and peaks of capitalist development. When growth became harder to achieve from the 1960s, both left and right came to accept – probably, as we shall see, mistakenly – that organized groups, notably the working class, freed by citizenship rights from all kinds of deferential behaviour, had become so aggressive that an 'overloaded' state faced a 'rationality crisis' because it had no room to 'steer the system'.[25] Let us consider the strategies of right and left in turn; assessment of each will make it easier to lay bare the 'proper' political economy for the advanced societies of the West.

The reaction to the view that society had become ungovernable which matters most in the context of this book was what can best be described as the turning away from social Keynes to social Darwin. A radical right, represented most clearly by Margaret Thatcher, tried to dismantle many citizenship rights and to reintroduce social discipline, largely and probably consciously through extending unemployment. Such measures did not represent an attack on formal democracy, but they did make many question the 'softness' of the societies of advanced capitalism. The intellectual justification for this programme was proclaimed to be *liberal*. There were two reasons for this. First, it was claimed that this programme was necessary to make capitalism work; it is vital to see if there is any truth to this. Secondly, radical 'liberal' ideologies insisted that the individual had a right to whatever he created, and we need to cast light upon this claim as well.

Several considerations lead to extreme suspicion of the claim of the radical right to be the real liberals of the contemporary world. Although we do not yet have proper economic histories of the recent past, there are good reasons for believing that much working-class behaviour, especially in Great Britain, was reactive to economic failure which had rather different causes, most importantly the decision, taken for prestige reasons by an autonomous political elite, to keep sterling as an international currency.[26] I suspect, in other words, that working-class action had no more salience for the British elite than it customarily did in the nineteenth century. This is an important point with application well beyond Great Britain. Scepticism should be shown to those theorists who stress the problem of order that liberalism faces. They exaggerate, and push a false conservatism in consequence. However, in so far as the creation of a stable workforce is important, it by no means follows that the policies of the radical right have much to be said in their favour. Comparative sociology seems to suggest that the co-operation of labour in most European countries is achieved by some form of corporatism, that is, some arrangement whereby industrial conflict is diminished by integrating the working class, together with major capitalists, in a national economic plan. Corporatism can be more or less restricted, that is, it can apply to some or all of the workforce: the former policy is adopted by Japan and Germany, which integrate workers in large firms but have a vicious labour market for the rest, while the latter is more characteristic of Scandinavia.[27] But in whichever form, it stands in contrast to the practice of unrestrained collective bargaining which encourages inflation when the economy hits troubled water and which causes economic problems based on resentment of 'them' as against 'us' when radical right policies are adopted.

This point can be taken a good deal further by reflecting about the type of workforce needed by late industrial society. The disciplining of a workforce by unemployment may produce something like a nineteenth-century situation: rather unskilled but obedient labour may become available. However, it is surely extremely doubtful whether such labour is the stuff on which late industrialism depends. What is noticeable about Scandinavian social corporatism *and* the micro-corporatism of Germany and Japan is that the state plays an ever more important role in providing the infrastructure to the economy. One obvious way in which this is true is in the exceptional importance accorded to educational services, the provision of which makes the individualistic tenets of the radical right fantastical. Equally remarkable is the manner in which successful states manage the market in an entirely pragmatic way. In Germany the state provided seedcorn money to encourage several computer firms, and then allowed the market to decide which was the best: interestingly, this was the exact opposite of the inept way in which the British state handled its computer industry. Similarly, Italian small business was created by the Christian Democratic state through a generous loans policy.[28] The manner in which the Japanese state helps its corporations in research and marketing is, of course, now legendary.

Modern political economies cannot be 'left to the market', as the radical 'liberal' right believes. Most obviously, the ability to participate in the market depends upon the provision of a strong social infrastructure. This is a good point at which to recall that Adam Smith believed that the market had had such beneficial effects in early European history *because* there was a 'general diffusion of wealth among the lower orders of men'.[29] It seems, in other words, as if the success of a national economy depends upon a strong state providing a high level of social skill. Participation in the market requires social rights or entitlements without which national success is impossible. The most successful states have found ways in which laissez-faire is curbed internally, so that the unit as a whole can act effectively in the international market. A brilliant treatment of Austria, Switzerland and Sweden has demonstrated that a high level of skill and social infrastructure has recently proved its worth in allowing very fast adaptation to changes in world market conditions.[30] This whole argument can be put neatly by remembering the position of Adam Smith. He realized that new nations would threaten the wealth of established economic leaders, but he was not terrified by this. Economic leaders should abandon old industries to new countries, and adopt new techniques; their future lay in a high wage, high productivity economy – and certainly not in the cutting of wages.[31]

The general contention being made is that radical 'liberal' policies are not just unpleasant but utterly misconceived: they have not worked, are unlikely to do so and ought to be resisted by those who are genuinely liberal in spirit. The very fact that a properly functioning capitalist economy inside a democratic society is possible – that, in other words, British decline is no indication of the fortunes of industrial capitalism as a whole – should warm liberal hearts since it suggests that capitalism allows for politics of a non-zero sum type; the capitalist mechanism in these ways once again has the capacity to fulfil liberal aims. In a nutshell, the successful functioning of capitalism in the stable democracies seems to entail at least some measure of citizenship rights. This is the appropriate point to note a fundamental change in liberalism. In the nineteenth-century constitutional state, represented best by the United States, the working class was thoroughly integrated by means of political citizenship. So much was this so, indeed, that workers did not, at first glance, achieve much in the way of welfare. First glances are, however, deceptive, and it always behoves British academics, prone to boast of their state's welfare achievements, to remember that private education has far less importance in the United States than it does in Britain. Nevertheless, there is a fundamental sea-change between the nineteenth-century constitutional state and the modern welfare state which needs to be emphasized. Modern citizenship depends upon massive social infrastructure, and it seems as if those states which were less constitutionalist in the nineteenth century have historic traditions that make it natural for them to provide it. It is worth stating again that 'first glances' concerning welfare states can mislead. It is by no means certain, for example, that Britain produced the best institutional package. The fundamental problem with British welfare provision is, of course, that less money is spent on it than in any other country of the European Community. But two particular defects deserve to be noted. First, the British system concentrated almost exclusively on the creation of a safety net, and had very little to say about industrial policy. The Swedish situation was hugely different, largely because the working class, having gained self-consciousness, in contrast to the historically antique British working class, at the time of industrialization, was always interested in economic policy. A particular policy of great importance was the provision of mobility allowances in Sweden; this cut labour costs, helped control inflation and thereby enabled Sweden to prosper economically – no small matter since the general prosperity of the country gives more welfare than do the specialized services.[32] Secondly, it is beginning to seem to be the case that the British principle of universalism, absolutely indispensable though that is, was not by itself enough to provide adequate underpinning to a welfare state. It is not yet quite clear, for example, that a flat-rate pension contribution system was wise. It may be that it was too much for the poor to pay *and* less than the more wealthy wanted to pay; perhaps a graded universalistic system would have been more successful, not least in gaining the loyalty of the populace. It can be said in summary that the issue of exactly what comprises welfare in modern circumstances is now absolutely open; the whole question is conceptually difficult, socially important and intellectually exciting.

Nevertheless, within the broad boundaries of conditions that have been identified, there are some policies that liberals will wish to fight for in preference to others. The United States of America has a notoriously inadequate minimal safety net for the unemployed, single parents and the sick, and this cannot but offend the requirements of liberalism for basic social justice. Not enough is known about Japan, and very few indications are available as to the likely social development of that state. It may be that the anti-individualistic ethic of that culture may not be undermined by capitalism, that traditional values are so deeply engrained that no 'end of ideology' will take place there; alternatively, social cohesion in Japan may depend less upon the presence of traditional values and more upon sheer economic success. Whatever the case may prove to be, liberals would wish for an extension of individualism, even if that undermines the success of Japanese capitalism. In general, liberals should have a divided mind about Japan. On the one hand, Japanese ideology shares something even today with the *Volksgemeinschaft* view of reactionary modernism. On the other hand, however, Japan stands as an example to the advanced societies precisely because its political economy is based on a high degree of entitlement, a factor which accounts for its ability to respond flexibly in the world market.[33]

It is worth highlighting the fact that 'success' in the international economy has been taken to mean success of a national *society*. This means that the wealth gained by those working in the City of London, or by those in Third World countries who work in socially insulated areas of high technology, is not in itself considered economic success. One obvious justification for this is simply that liberalism's essential egalitarianism finds a felicific calculus, which ignores large numbers of people, repulsive. But the central thesis is that strong national societies can compete in the world economy. Contention surrounds this assertion. The claim of the left in many advanced capitalist countries has been that international capitalism controls everything, that its operations prevent, for example, the extension of socialism in any single country; a corollary of this argument is often the demand that a particular state should exit from the capitalist system. It is important to draw distinctions here. International capitalist society certainly *constrains* what happens in societies belonging to the world market, but it does not *control* all that happens. We can justify this remark in two ways. On the one hand, the failures of the Labour government in Britain in the late 1970s are less to be blamed on the machinations of international bankers than the unfortunate fact that the party had a poor economic policy, and had no clear idea as to how to finance its social experiments. On the other hand, international capital still invests in Sweden, despite the *extension* of

citizenship rights. All in all, it seems as if the best combination for economic success is that of corporatism with
welfare *and* openness to the world market. In contrast,
openness to the world economy without corporatism plus
welfare makes it impossible to compete. Finally, corporatism plus welfare without openness to the world market is
a recipe for sectoral distortion and, eventually, a poor
standard of living.[34]

The argument as a whole can be summarized very
simply: liberalism in the advanced and democratic societies
of the West *is* social democracy. In order for social democracy to work, intelligent state behaviour is needed, not least
so that the 'logic' of the scientific-industrial complex can be
recognized and realized. It is appropriate at this point to
comment on the thesis that the state does not have sufficient
automony to act any longer in the interests of long-term
societal needs. One version of this thesis stresses that the
working classes of the advanced societies have become so
powerful that there is a problem of 'ungovernability'.
Certainly, there are some limits to state autonomy of this
type. Britain's economic problems can be dated a long way
back, and many of them have not been caused by the
working class. Nevertheless, an entrenched and conservative working class made it hard to solve those problems.
The inability of a central trade union body to control a
huge number of small unions makes it, for example, hard
to institutionalize corporatist policies. Nevertheless, any
increase in organizational capacity among workers is being
undermined by their diminishing share of the total workforce. In general, the evidence suggests that state elites can
gain sufficient room to 'steer the system', and that the best
way of gaining such room is to be found via corporatist co-
optation. The second version of the thesis is that the state
does not have sufficient autonomy from capitalists to be
able even to plan what is in the long-term interests of
capitalists themselves, let alone ensure that capitalism
serves liberal ends. Is it the case, in other words, that

capitalist muscle is being flexed as it was in Weimar against citizenship rights? This is a very large question, but my answer to it has tended to be in the negative. This is not to deny that capitalists are selfish and may want to act in their short-term interests. But the need for skilled labour is sufficiently clear for states to have the capacity to persuade capitalists of the need for social infrastructure. That such infrastructures are being cut in Britain represents a triumph of rhetoric: these actions are those of Margaret Thatcher and her government rather than of capitalism per se. Autonomy from capitalists may be hard to achieve, and results similarly from negotiation; but it is in general possible to achieve a sufficient measure to allow the aims of liberalism to be fulfilled.

A Liberal World Order?

Analysis of the current workings of the international politi-cal economy can benefit from consideration of the striking claim that modern capitalist society needs a hegemonic power if it is to operate successfully. Capitalist society is held to have been stable when certain functional needs – the provision of an international currency, the outflow of capital for development and the ability to absorb exports from developing states – are met by a leading power. If there is no such power, protectionism, trade war and geopolitical conflict are likely to follow. This school of thought believes that Britain once provided hegemonic services, and that the miraculous boom of the Keynesian years is ascribable to American hegemony. However, it is extremely important, for political quite as much as for conceptual reasons, to note that this school is terrified by current conditions. 'Hegemonic stability theory', as this approach likes, perhaps too grandly, to be known, has a technical component which asserts that hegemonic leader-ship is self-liquidating. The provision of collective goods for the system as a whole inevitably undermines the economic strength of the hegemon: small states are 'free riders' failing to contribute their share of the costs, while the export of capital encourages industrialization elsewhere. This school of thought is predominantly American, and it currently argues that the United States has lost its economic leadership: in consequence, the world economy is likely to suffer, in large part because demands for protectionism will take over from demands for open markets as the competitive edge of American industry is lost.[35]

This theory is intellectually ambitious and politically important. It deserves consideration here for obvious reasons. The rise of the West occurred very much as the result of open economic competition occurring within a normative framework provided by the church. Is a similar combination necessary in modern circumstances, and, if so, can it only be provided by a hegemonic power? My argument will be that the theory in question – to which there are several strands, often in open competition with each other – is useful but limited; complementing its weaknesses will allow us to assess the extent to which the ordering of the contemporary world economy serves the goals of liberalism.

Scepticism should be shown to the rhetoric that surrounds some versions of this theory. Some American thinkers have been keen to portray the United States as a Durkheimian norm-giver, precisely in the manner of the Latin Christian Church in the early Middle Ages, stabilizing the system in an entirely neutral manner. Only a cynic would deny that occasionally idealism matters in world politics, but a moment's thought must make us doubt this as a picture of the characteristic behaviour of the United States. Very much to the contrary, at Bretton Woods the United States refused to accept a system of world order, designed by Maynard Keynes, which would have provided rules to discipline strong as well as weak states. America preferred to establish a system based on its own primacy since this gave it greater freedom of action. This is to say that the workings of the international political economy have been designed to suit America. The American state believed that open markets would be good for everyone, and it is entirely proper to see such agencies as the International Monetary Fund, GATT and the World Bank as arms of the American state.[36] This position was accepted by American industrialists who appreciated the opportunities for expansion, and by the allies who did not want the leading capitalist power to revert to isolationism. The presence of American state interests beneath international norms became clear when America used its position to break the rules which it enforced on other states by running, from the mid-1950s, an ever-increasing budget deficit. It is important to note *why* the allies of the United States allowed it to break these rules. The position established by the United States in 1945 was unique because it was based on economic and military dominance. To say this is already to hint at the main criticism to be made here: that hegemony is a political as well as an economic concept.

Nevertheless, it is not easy to get to grips with this harder American-interest-centred version of hegemonic stability theory. In one sense, it is tautologous: you have hegemony when you have a hegemon, and you do not have it when you do not have a hegemon. Much more worrying, to my mind, is the resolutely economistic bias to the theory: it suggests that a leading state, either because it *is* its capitalists in action or because, as an autonomous agent, its main interest is in economic strength, will impose a liberal world order when its industries are powerful, and seek to destroy it in tandem with economic decline. Examination of the British period of ascendancy does not lend much support to these contentions. Britain did not push hard for openness in the world economy during its period of greatest strength, nor did it make significant moves towards protectionism before 1914; scepticism should be directed at the claim that British economic decline was occasioned by the 'services' it provided for capitalist society as a whole.[37] It is very important to stress this. Hegemonic stability theory's economism comes out most strongly in its presumption that the condition of capitalist competition causes wars. We have seen that distinctions need to be drawn here. German policy was often justified in terms of a need to challenge Britain's hegemony; as the international economy before 1914 did not work according to zero-sum principles, that justification was badly grounded. Moreover, change was possible. From 1912, the United States abandoned some of its protective tariffs to ensure that the markets controlled by Britain remained open.[38] This is an important change since it showed that it was logically possible to move from a world order based on hegemony to one based on co-operation of leading economic powers; that is, there is nothing in 'collective goods theory', on which hegemonic stability theory rests, to say that hegemonic leadership is the only way of achieving world order. It would have been harder for Germany to have taken this route, but not impossible; certainly the gamble taken in 1914 owed quite as much to geopolitics as to the condition of international economics. In contrast, the fact that the international economy in the inter-war years *was* run as a zero-sum affair both caused and contributed, and in an ever more vicious cycle, to international political rivalry. This in itself makes it worth thinking again about the relationship between capitalism and liberalism. Perhaps it is no accident that this theory is popular in the United States. Maybe the theory in its most economistic form *does* apply to America either because there society is stronger than the state or because that state systematically devotes itself to the advancement of the long-term interests of its capitalists.[39] Let us turn to examining the evidence; while doing so we can redeem an earlier promise to analyse whether the post-war world economy has helped or hindered Third World states.

There were benefits and costs to the American period of dominance of capitalist society. It would be a mistake to suggest that all the success of the world economy in the immediate post-war years depended upon a 'system' erected by the United States: European recovery, for example, was fastest between 1947 and 1958 when it was not part of a liberal world order, i.e. in those years in which the Bretton Woods agreements were not working effectively.[40] Similarly, it is important to remember that the United States was not altruistic in all its policies; it hoped that its industries would benefit from openness. Nevertheless, any judgement of the period from 1945 to 1971 must recognize that America provided both leadership and services: it came by 1958 to act as lender of last resort, guaranteed peace within the advanced core of capitalist society and tended to pass on investment and growth. At the least, American leadership played a major part in the recovery and democratization of Europe and Japan, and ensured a type of political stability after the Second World War that had not been achieved after the First.[41] Economic growth also took place, as noted, in Third World countries blessed with strong states, and there is every reason to believe that this expansion was helped by investment from abroad and competition in the world market. Even more fundamental, however, was the insistence of the United States, in the immediate post-war years and again at the time of Suez, that the empires of the European powers be wound up. Both these last points stand, of course, in direct opposition to 'dependency theory'. However, the costs of the American-dominated world order lend justification to some aspects of that Marxist theory. Most importantly, weaker states in the Third World do not fare well in the world market. Where a highly educated workforce can adapt to a new international economic situation, a poorly trained workforce, specializing in a single commodity, tends to be at the mercy of international economic change, as Steve Krasner has very strikingly demonstrated.[42] While it would be mistaken to say that external forces always make such states weak, sometimes this is true. Such external action is not always, as we shall see, capitalist in character, that is, it is not achieved by capitalist actors or by states acting for capitalists. However, capital has played some part in the weakening of various Third World states. The sheer size of a multinational like United Fruit or ITT in a small country gives it huge power to interfere with local politics, and to prevent various changes being carried through which would increase state power.

If we are to assess the balance between cost and benefit we need to consider contemporary circumstances. In 1971 America 'came off gold' with the excuse that it was being 'challenged' in two ways.[43] First, various states inside capitalist society have grown at a much faster rate than the United States, suggesting to the theorists of hegemonic stability that economic leadership is again proving to be self-liquidating. The most important of these is Japan, whose balance of trade surplus with America reached nearly 60 billion dollars in 1986; significant inroads into American industry have also been made by Europe and by such Newly Industrializing Countries as Brazil, South Korea and Argentina. Secondly, the Third World has mounted a challenge to the liberal ordering of the world economy. Throughout the post-war period the power of Third World states *has* gradually increased.[44] Third World countries have learnt how to strike better bargains with multinationals, and have nationalized most production of raw materials. Undoubtedly, the most spectacular example of this challenge was that of the oil price rises pushed through by OPEC. This inability of the 'core' to control the 'periphery' obviously makes it impossible completely to accept Marxist dependency theory. However, this is not to deny that this theoretical approach highlights difficulties that are faced by the Third World. Development becomes ever harder as the skill levels needed to operate complicated technical machinery became ever more demanding. More important still, it is worth stressing that many Third World states are not 'strong'. Another way of putting the matter is to say that the post-war world has seen a dramatic increase in the power of rather few Third World states. It is noticeable that those of SE Asia benefit greatly from a literate culture, from nationalism and from a political elite which is honest. These states have political elites, furthermore, of the greatest intelligence and skill. While there is everything to be said for protecting nascent industries, it seems to be disastrous to protect them for too long since technological change in the world economy goes ever faster. It is asking a great deal of any state elite to be able to calculate the opportunity costs of protection with skill; some states do not yet have elites capable of this sort of cost accounting exercise.

At first sight, it seems simply that the period of American hegemony is over, and that the United States has been forced to break its own liberal world norms. It has ceased to provide a stable currency for world economic transactions, as can be seen most clearly in its failure to control the behaviour of international banks in the Third World, something which may yet lead to a banking collapse and which definitely does exploit the Third World, not least because American interest rates increased sharply after the loans were taken.[45] More obviously, the United States has sought to protect its industries from competition; as much of this protection has been arranged via 'voluntary' import quotas its exact extent is very hard to determine. Furthermore, the United States has withdrawn from international organizations such as UNESCO. That this was possible again shows that the key core capitalist state did not depend upon the Third World: it had, in the last analysis, the capacity of managing without it, not least because of the huge size of its own home market. The same generalization can, with the exception of oil, be made for the core of capitalism as a whole: trading figures show that this core does not depend upon the Third World for imports or for markets, and it is sending less and less of its investment there.[46]

A second glance at the current state of American economic power suggests that there is far more continuity than hegemonic stability theory predicted. It is noticeable that there is not, at least to this point, massive protectionism. The United States has not yet completely abandoned its calls for an open international economy. Importantly, the United States is actively pressing for more liberalization in agriculture, services and shipping. In these areas the American economy has a continuing lead, in agriculture because of the heavy subsidies given to farmers! Furthermore, the power of an American company such as IBM is so great that it must make one hesitate to write off the economic power of the United States. Provided that core countries develop new technologies, there is in fact much to be said for them leaving old industries to newly developing societies. In this context, it is worth noting that the parallel drawn between Britain at the end of the nineteenth century and the United States today fails to note a crucial change in industrial organization. British economic leadership was very quickly undermined because its portfolio investment in the Third World encouraged, indeed necessitated autonomous economic growth. American investment abroad has been by multinational companies; these companies represent continued structural power of the core.[47] More importantly, the United States retains a unique ability to control the world economy in its own interest – particularly, as noted, in monetary affairs.[48] American power has enabled it to pass on the costs of the oil price rise through inflation, and there is, as yet, no indication that its allies, most importantly Germany and Japan, are anywhere near refusing to bank in the dollar. Finally, it is becoming clear that the power of the Third World, especially that based on rationing of oil, has been considerably exaggerated. The oil price increases of 1973 and 1979 were more the result of uncertainty caused by war than of any monopoly possessed by OPEC. Importantly, new producers in the core of capitalist society have undermined such monopoly as OPEC did possess. Obviously, OPEC is seeking once again to enhance its power, and has managed to push oil prices up from their lowest level; but it is still doubtful whether they can regain the position of the 1970s. And the United States has distanced itself from the Third World in other ways: it has left UNESCO, cut back its funds to the United Nations, and refused to accept judgements of the International Court. Investment patterns no longer favour the Third World, and American aid is used ever more stringently, as is that of the Soviet Union, to support only favoured client states.

Where does this leave hegemonic stability theory? The theory does not regard itself as refuted. In so far as the United States retains economic power, it is not surprising to discover a continuing attachment to liberal norms. However, further considerations have been added to the original theory which would suggest that openness may be continued even if American economic power slips further. Robert Keohane has argued that international regimes matter because they encourage states to think in terms of mutual interests in the longer term.[49] There may be something to this, although the lack of concern that the United States has shown for its allies when breaking international rules, as when the gold window was closed, suggests that a good deal of scepticism should be directed towards a view which, despite the supposed realism of the game theory in which it is clothed, tends to put hope above experience.[50] Judith Goldstein has stressed, quite properly, that what matters about economics is less the facts than what people believe to be the case; as American leaders, perhaps wrongly, attribute a deepening of the world depression to the passing of the protectionist Hawley-Smoot Act of 1930, it is possible that they may continue to resist protectionism.[51] Other analysts have stressed that openness results from the ability of international banks, which depend upon America, to control their state; it is sometimes claimed that this ability is not just a question of better lobbying but of the objective fact that little profit is now derived from the export of American manufacturers.[52] Importantly, protectionism has been partly defeated by product specification and by movement of production centres; the growth in the world economy has also been sustained by expansion of counter trade agreements.[53] David Lake has noted that total protectionism is not at present rational since it is still possible to strike multinational or bilateral agreements with trading partners; this is to say that the situation of the international economy is *not* similar to that of the 1930s.[54] These are interesting observations; they are, from the point of view of liberalism, very encouraging. But any sense of optimism must be curtailed by considering a point that leads to the major weakness of hegemonic stability theory.

International trade may still be relatively open, but the international monetary system is in chaos. This matters enormously. American policy favoured floating exchange rates, and chose to allow the market to recycle petrodollars in the 1970s. This has proved to be disastrous. Because the American state did not insist on large collaterals for international loans, very unwise lending policies to Third World countries were allowed.[55] This has led to the possibility of a collapse, not just of American banks, but of the world banking system as a whole. If further lending dries up, Third World development may be seriously impaired; this would be likely to terminate most liberalization strategies in the Third World. Equally seriously, the lack of a fixed monetary system is seriously affecting the workings of the economies of the advanced industrial democracies. The title of this section ends with an interrogative because the lack of monetary order may yet seriously hurt the modern political economy. It is important to remember in this respect that protectionism in the inter-war years grew most in response to monetary disorder.[56]

If America is pulling its weight in international trade bargaining, it most certainly is not doing so in international monetary affairs. Hegemonic stability theorists do not make enough of the possibility that a leading power may use the instruments it controls less to lead its allies than systematically to control them; there can, in other words, be use and abuse of power. However, let us leave this harsh judgement, now well understood and anyway easy with historical hindsight, and try and understand *why* monetary reform is difficult.

The United States has tended in recent years to veer between two economic policies. One of these seeks to favour domestic industry by talking the dollar down; this is also designed to encourage powerful international trading partners both to open their markets more to American goods and to help expand the world economy as a whole. The major disadvantage of this policy is that it makes it harder to pay for guns – or, more precisely, for troops. The second approach represents the other side of this coin. A stronger dollar helps the military budget, but hurts the domestic economy; this policy is sustained by high levels of borrowing rather than, as logically if not politically possible, than by the raising of tax levels. All plans for a stable world monetary order depend upon the United States balancing its budget, or at least moving some way towards doing so. This has not occurred, and it seems likely not to occur in the near future. The reason for this is simple. America sees 'the defence of freedom' as its historic task, and this has recently been held to require massive spending on armaments. It is here that the real difficulty of reforming the world economy begins to arise. America resists the neoclassical standards of book-keeping that it wishes others to adhere to on the grounds that it provides defence for all.

It is important to introduce my most severe criticism of hegemonic stability theory at this point, before spelling out the full nature of the difficulty in question. American state behaviour is by no means always dictated by capitalists; the analysis of international trade policies does not lead to an understanding of American foreign policy *in toto*. One goal that matters more to the state elite is that of geopolitical strategy. However, the *ultimate* source of much American state behaviour has been ideological.[57] How different

225

would have been American behaviour towards Vietnam if it had thought of the well-being of its own or of world capitalism, or if it had seriously considered its strategic security! The Vietnam war, of course, had *no* economic or strategic sense to it.[58] It is possible to object to this line of argument on the grounds that economic considerations were ultimately at play: it was not American capitalists but the American state – but the American state consciously pursuing a geo-economic strategy designed to keep world markets open – that was at work.[59] It is certainly correct to say that American state leaders reflect their own social system, and that these geo-economic considerations are sometimes very clearly present in state councils. When such geo-economic strategy can be detected, it is habitually naïve. On the one hand, it fails to realize that the strengthening of states in the third world is necessary for development rather than some sort of evil attack on modernity. Equally importantly, it does not realize the sheer strength of the United States. Only the West has capital and significant markets, and most states, including China, eventually realize that a complete withdrawal from the world market exacts a price which is simply too high to pay. However, such geo-economic considerations do not seem to have been present in the hugely important case of Vietnam. This was an ideological war, so much so as to make one yearn for a complete 'end to ideology', that is, a replacement of ill-considered rhetoric with calculation. The deepest motivation for American ideological crusades is to be found in the nature of American exceptionalism.[60] The earliest foreign policy of the United States evidenced a desire to stay out of the entanglements of corrupt balance-of-power politics.[61] When the United States entered the world scene this distrust translated into interventionist episodes designed to mould other states into the image of America. Such episodes have a very poor record. Would not the long-term interest of the United States have been better served by realizing that any domestically created state is better than none? Would not Iran have been easier to deal with in the long run had Mossadeq not been toppled, and the Shah installed in his place? The consequences of interventionism have been disastrous. All this can be expressed differently. The trouble is that the United States has a limited conception of a community of nations. It has failed to understand that it is the sociological imperative of twentieth-century history and not vice that dictates centralizing power. It has been naïve and insular, and its 'liberalism', most especially its interventions, have betrayed genuine liberal aims. It is appalling that a self-styled liberal state may topple a regime in Nicaragua, admittedly occasionally illiberal but equally capable of providing land reform and certainly of no military significance whatever, and support a despotic, but infrastructurally weak regime such as that of El Salvador. This is a situation of paranoia.

These points can now be drawn together. The United States is weaker than it was in market relationships, even if accounts of its demise have been much exaggerated; but there is no doubt that it remains exceptionally strong in state to state relationships. American policy can be interpreted as trying to cash in its geopolitical/military strength both by demanding freedom of action and by 'taxing' its allies. It is already looking as if this type of policy – if policy it was – is not going to revive America's fortunes: the freedom to veer between a higher and a lower dollar has resulted in huge increases in the budget deficit, and relatively insignificant sums have been raised from the allies. Still more importantly, it has become clear that Europeans and Japanese do not share the geopolitical aims of the United States; they tend to regard such aims as naïve, in this having a wiser view of the nature of a liberal world order. However, the United States tends to regard them as spineless in consequence. Geopolitical mistrust makes it that much harder to arrange economic co-operation.

Two principles of reconstruction recommend themselves. First, monetary instability must be ended. Secondly, it would be best for the nuclear game to continue to be played only by two major actors, and it is anyway certain that Japan and Europe cannot, at least quickly, produce all the means of their own defence.

It is much less easy to operationalize these principles. Europe and Japan should try to prop up the power of the United States. Further defence contributions are required. Serious consideration should be given to playing a stronger role in avoiding general recession. Further agreement to open markets, obviously in Europe and Japan but also in the United States, should be encouraged; to do so is most unlikely to strengthen the American economy, but it may diffuse political passion. All this amounts to offering greater help; it may, however, be a sign of increased cohesion, that is, the threat of rivalry, that galvanizes the United States. For its part the United States needs, in the long run, to accept that Japanese success depends upon quality of goods rather than protection: there may be inequities in the current trading rules, but naïvely 'blaming Japan' would be grossly mistaken. Japan's success is the result of a remarkable capacity to design a cohesive national strategy so as to prosper inside the world market; the elements of its success need to be replicated elsewhere.[62] Above all this means that it will prove necessary to develop industrial policies so as to be able better to compete in world markets; the United States has many lessons to learn in this matter and, although it does not possess a state elite capable of totally directing industry *à la Japonais*, it is noteworthy that it is already protecting its own geopolitically crucial infant semi-conductor industry. Crucially, however, moderation is needed in geopolitical vision. Reagan surely does not believe all the rhetoric about the Soviet Union that he uses; much of it is for home consumption. Such demagogy can unleash sufficient fear to make rational assessment of goals difficult.

At first sight, these sentiments are fairly vacuous. How much, for example, would Europe have to pay for the defence given by the United States? Recompense for the cost of troops in Europe is unexceptionable. But the real core of that defence rests on nuclear weapons. Should Europe help pay for those? Is it anyway desirable that America serve as the hi-tech equivalent of the medieval Islamic Janissaries? It is equally difficult to decide exactly what is to count as interference with the openness of the world economy. Direct protection is easy to recognize, but 'voluntary' export quotas are as bad. At what point does industrial policy amount to systematically distorting the market? Nevertheless, such sentiments are useful if we make a distinction between the short and the long run. In the short run, to increase the climate of co-operation by propping up America will moderate economic problems; this should be used to encourage shared discussion of geopolitical aims. The goal, in other words, must be that of moving from hegemony to a world in which co-operation among the advanced industrial democracies has – as, to be effective, it must – both economic and geopolitical elements. It is not possible to predict what will happen in the longer run. If America does lose a great deal of economic dynamism, it may threaten its military hegemony inside capitalist society.

Conclusion
The most fundamental fact of modern world politics remains the desire for development on the part of countries in the Third World. The sociology of this transition is such as to rule out some of the most cherished hopes of the nineteenth-century liberals. Nevertheless, this transition should be placed at the centre of modern liberal thought; industrialization has the capacity to satisfy crucial tenets of negative utilitarianism to which liberals must be loyal, and major efforts must be made by liberals to try and make this transition, given its potentially destabilizing effects on the balance of world power, as painless as possible. An absolutely crucial consideration in this matter is that of organizing the world market, which remains the engine of growth

and whose salience has clearly gained in significance, so that it can serve liberal aims. The very minimum that this must involve is the restoration of monetary order and retention of an open trading system. A maximalist policy would be more rational. Such a policy would involve securing commodity prices, and providing larger sums of capital for development. This is not to say that the West has the power to create development; on the contrary, many necessary changes must be made endogenously. But there is everything to be said for making the climate within which development takes place more favourable and helpful. The advanced societies of the West need to become much more sophisticated in understanding the nature of state strength in the Third World, and then of finding ways in which that strength can be increased.

To make this happen, intelligent action on the part of state leaders is required. Internal and external policies can usefully be distinguished. Internally, state elites need to gain social co-operation through the provision of those citizenship rights which allow them to prosper in an open international economy; this means allowing old industries to die, in the awareness that the future lies in advanced productivity at home so that the needs of external markets, which will grow as the Third World develops, can be met. The absolutely crucial external rationality that is needed is simple. The United States must gain a better understanding of its long-term strategic and economic interests; a key part in any such move must be a determination on the part of American leaders to educate their public, rather than to conjure up base fears, at least some of which they know not to be true. Similarly, Europeans need to help America with its burdens, not least with a view to influencing its perceptions of the world. In order to achieve these aims, state leaders will need to appreciate the structural processes of the modern world.

One final reflection is in order. My advocacy is for a type of control over the international economy which will serve liberal aims. This is to say that, in an age of nuclear weapons, unrestricted social change, which most certainly includes geopolitical conflict, cannot be viewed as warmly as it once was by liberals. A respect for stability has costs: it means, above all, accepting a large part of the geopolitical status quo, most notably the division of the world between two superpowers. This may not, according to abstract liberal stands, be just; but in current circumstances it is desirable. To endorse realism is not to say that modern liberalism should be passive and conservative. The creation of a genuinely liberal world order requires action quite as much as considered thought.

NOTES

1. E. Gellner, 'Democracy and Industrialisation', *European Journal of Sociology*, 8 (1967).
2. B. Moore, *Social Origins of Dictatorship and Democracy* (Harmondsworth: Penguin, 1969).
3. E. Gellner, *Nations and Nationalism* (Oxford: Basil Blackwell, 1983).
4. M. Freeman, 'Sociology and Utopia: Some Reflections on the Social Philosophy of Karl Popper', *British Journal of Sociology*, 26 (1975).
5. This argument is strikingly put by T. Skocpol, *States and Social Revolutions* (Cambridge: Cambridge University Press, 1979).
6. I am drawing here upon the comparative sociology of Raymond Aron. For a summary, see my *Raymond Aron* (Oxford: Polity Press, 1988), chapter 3.
7. In this paragraph I am drawing heavily upon S. Cohen, *Bukharin and the Russian Revolution* (Oxford: Oxford University Press, 1980).
8. Cf. E. Gellner, 'From the Revolution to Liberalisation', *Government and Opposition*, 11 (1975). A revealing and high-powered exchange over this thesis was R. Aron, 'On Liberalisation' and E. Gellner, 'Plaidoyer pour une libéralisation manquée', in *Government and Opposition*, 14 (1979).
9. Moore, op. cit., p.438.
10. M. Mann, 'Citizenship and Ruling Class Strategies', *Sociology*, 21 (1987).

11. G. O'Donnell, P. Schmitter and L. Whitehead (eds), *Transitions from Authoritarian Rule: Prospects for Democracy* (Baltimore: Johns Hopkins University Press, 1986).

12. S. Giner and E. Sevilla, 'From Despotism to Parliamentarism: Class Domination and Political Order in the Spanish State', in R. Scase (ed.), *The State in Western Europe* (London: Croom Helm, 1978).

13. J. G. Merquior, 'Power and Identity: Politics and Ideology in Latin America', *Government and Opposition*, 19 (1984).

14. Cf. N. Mouzelis, *The Politics of the Semi-Periphery* (London: Macmillan, 1986).

15. A. de Tocqueville, *The Old Regime and the French Revolution* (New York: Anchor Books, 1955).

16. H. Spencer, *The Man Versus the State* (New York: Mitchell Kennerley, 1916).

17. Moore, op. cit., chapter 6; R. Cassen, *India: Population, Economy, Society* (London: Macmillan, 1978); D. Hiro, *Inside India Today* (London: Routledge and Kegan Paul, 1978).

18. Stanley Hoffman does manage to find some room for intervention in the characteristically subtle and careful argument of *Duties Beyond Borders: On the Limits and Possibilities of Ethical International Politics* (Syracuse: Syracuse University Press, 1981). I am influenced here by a brilliant unpublished paper by Caroline Thomas which offers 'An Ethical Case Against Intervention'.

19. A classic statement of this position was A. G. Frank, 'The Sociology of Development and the Underdevelopment of Sociology', in his *Latin America: Underdevelopment or Revolution? Essays on the Development of Underdevelopment and the Immediate Enemy* (New York: Monthly Review Press, 1969).

20. Cf. J. A. Hall, *Powers and Liberties: The Causes and Consequence of the Rise of the West* (Harmondsworth: Penguin, 1986), chapter 8.

21. These are drawn from R. Dahrendorf, *Class and Class Conflict in Industrial Society* (London: Routledge and Kegan Paul, 1959).

22. E.g. J. Scott, *Corporations, Classes and Capitalism* (London: Hutchinson, 1979).

23. J. H. Goldthorpe (with the assistance of C. Llewelyn and G. Payne), *Social Mobility and Class Structure* (Oxford: Oxford University Press, 1980); A. H. Halsey, A. Heath and J. M. Ridge, *Origins and Destinations* (Oxford: Oxford University Press, 1980), especially chapter 11.

24. S. Hill, N. Abercrombie and B. Turner, *The Dominant Ideology Thesis* (London: George Allen and Unwin, 1981).
25. A representative argument of this type is that of J. Habermas, *Legitimation Crisis* (London: Heinemann Educational, 1976).
26. I make this argument about Britain in 'The State', in G. Causer (ed.), *Inside British Society* (Brighton: Wheatsheaf, 1987).
27. J. H. Goldthorpe, 'The End of Convergence: Corporatist and Dualist Tendencies in Modern Western Societies', in his (ed.), *Order and Conflict in Western European Capitalism* (Oxford: Oxford University Press, 1984).
28. L. Weiss, *Creating Capitalism: Small Business and the State since 1945* (Oxford: Basil Blackwell, 1988).
29. D. Stewart, 'Account of the Life and Writings of Adam Smith, Ll.D', in Vol. III of *The Glasgow Edition of the Works and Correspondence of Adam Smith*, that is, *Essays on Philosophical Subjects* (Oxford: Oxford University Press, 1980), p.313.
30. P. Katzenstein, *Small States in World Markets* (Ithaca: Cornell University Press, 1985).
31. I Hont, 'The "Rich Country–Poor Country" Debate in Scottish Classical Political Economy', in I. Hont and M. Ignatieff (eds), *Wealth and Virtue* (Cambridge: Cambridge University Press, 1983).
32. This point was very neatly made in a BBC Radio Three series on the welfare state which was organized by Professor A. H. Halsey. See also P. Katzenstein, op. cit., p.84 and passim; G. Esping-Andersen, *Politics against Markets. The Social Democratic Route to Power* (Princeton: Princeton University Press, 1985).
33. The argument that individualism may now be an obstacle to capitalism is made by N. Abercrombie, S. Hill and B. Turner, *Sovereign Individuals of Capitalism* (London: Allen and Unwin, 1986). On the darker side of Japanese ideology, see P. Dale, *The Myth of Japanese Uniqueness* (London: Croom Helm, 1986), together with the review of this book by I. Buruma, 'Soul to Soul', *London Review of Books*, 19 February 1987. I have relied heavily on the work of R. Dore for understanding the nature of Japanese economic success; see especially his *Flexible Rigidities: Industrial Policy and Structural Adjustment in the Japanese Economy, 1970–80* (London: Athlone Press, 1986).
34. Cf. C. Waisman's treatment of the 'reversal of development' in Argentina via corporatism and a withdrawal from the world market in his *Reversal of Development in Argentina* (Princeton: Princeton University Press, 1987.

35. The classic statement is C. Kindleberger, *The World in Depression, 1929–33* (London: Allen Lane, 1973); the most extended working through of all of the themes involved in the theory, albeit from a very particular position, is R. Keohane, *After Hegemony* (Princeton: Princeton University Press, 1984).

36. It is possible to draw a distinction here between harder and softer versions of the theory. Robert Keohane believes that the presence of international regimes may encourage actors, for rather complex reasons derived from rational choice theory, not to stress self-interest *tout court*; in contrast, Steve Krasner's work suggests that states act more brutally for obviously selfish reasons. On this point, see Keohane, op. cit., and S. Krasner, 'State Power and the Structure of International Trade', *World Politics*, 28 (1976).

37. T. McKeown, 'Tariffs and Hegemonic Stability Theory', *International Organisation*, 37 (1983).

38. D. Lake, *Modern Mercantilism: International Economic Structures and American Trade Strategy, 1887–1939* (forthcoming).

39. The phrasing of this sentence reflects S. Krasner, 'United States Commercial and Monetary Policy: Unravelling the Paradox of External Strength and Internal Weakness', in P. Katzenstein (ed.), *Between Power and Plenty. Foreign Economic Policies of Advanced Industrial States* (Madison: University of Wisconsin Press, 1978). Interestingly, however, Krasner's work as a whole does not consistently hold to this version of economism. In *Defending the National Interest. Raw Material Investment and US Foreign Policy* (Princeton: Princeton University Press, 1978), Krasner demonstrates that the American state has sufficient autonomy to act against the immediate interests of particular capitalist interests. The most sustained and rigorous spelling out of the hard version of economism, i.e. that version which stresses the power of capitalist interests and denies the state any autonomy, has been that of Jeff Frieden of the University of California in Los Angeles. See particularly 'From Economic Nationalism to Hegemony: Social Forces and the Emergence of Modern US Foreign Economic Policy, 1914–40', *International Organisation* (forthcoming).

40. A. S. Milward, *The Reconstruction of Western Europe, 1945–51* (London: Methuen, 1984).

41. C. Maier, 'The Two Postwar Eras and the Conditions for Stability in 20th century Europe', *American Historical Review*, 86 (1981); *Recasting Bourgeois Europe. Reconstruction in France, Germany and Italy in the Decade after World War 1* (Princeton:

Princeton University Press, 1975); 'The Politics of Productivity: Foundations of American International Economic Policy after World War Two', in Katzenstein, op. cit.

42. S. Krasner, *Structural Conflict: The Third World against Global Liberalism* (Berkeley: University of California Press, 1985).

43. J. Gowa, *Closing the Gold Window, Domestic Politics and the End of Bretton Woods* (Ithaca: Cornell University Press, 1983). This book casts considerable doubt on the 'softer' version of hegemonic stability theory represented by the work of Keohane, and mentioned above in note 36.

44. Krasner, Structural Conflict op. cit.

45. H. Lever and C. Huhne, *Debt and Danger: the World Financial Crisis* (Harmondsworth: Penguin, 1985); S. Strange, *Casino Capitalism* (Oxford: Basil Blackwell, 1986).

46. Some figures are presented in Hall, op. cit., chapter 8. Cf. P. Dicken, *Global Shift: Industrial Change in a Turbulent World* (London: Harper and Row, 1986).

47. The distinction between portfolio and multinational investment is clearly made by R. Gilpin, *US Power and the Multinational Corporation* (London: Macmillan, 1976).

48. S. Strange, 'Still an Extraordinary Power: America's Role in a Global Monetary System', in R. E. Lombra and W. E Witte (eds), *Political Economy of International and Domestic Monetary Relations* (Ames: Iowa State University Press, 1982).

49. Keohane, op. cit.

50. Gowa, op. cit.

51. J. Goldstein, 'The Impact of Ideas on Trade Policy: A Comparative Study of the Origins of US Agricultural and Manufacturing Policies', *International Organisation* forthcoming.

52. Frieden, op. cit.; Strange, *Casino Capitalism*, op. cit.

53. S. Strange, 'Protection and World Politics', *International Organisation*, 39 (1985).

54. Lake, op. cit., chapter 8.

55. Strange, *Casino Capitalism*, op. cit.

56. Strange, 'Protectionism and World Politics', op. cit.

57. This is brilliantly demonstrated by S. Krasner, *Defending the National Interest: Raw Materials Investment and US Foreign Policy* op. cit.

58. Ibid., chapters 8 and 9; B. Moore, *Reflections on the Causes of Human Misery and Upon Certain Proposals to Eliminate Them* (Boston: Beacon Press, 1969), chapter 5; R. Aron, *Imperial Republic* (London: Weidenfeld and Nicolson, 1978).

59. H. Magdoff, *The Age of Imperialism* (New York: Monthly

Review Press, 1969); G. Kolko, *The Roots of American Foreign Policy* (Boston: Beacon Press, 1969).

60. D. Bell, 'The End of American Exceptionalism', *The Public Interest*, 40 (1975); R. Aron, *Imperial Republic*, op. cit.; S. Hoffman, *Primacy or World Order: American Foreign Policy since the Cold War* (New York: McGraw Hill, 1978).

61. F. G. Gilbert, *To the Farewell Address* (Princeton: Princeton University Press, 1961).

62. There are many examples of Americans 'blaming' Japan; this is an initial assumption of an otherwise sophisticated paper by J. L. Goldstein and S. Krasner, 'Unfair Trade Practices: The Case for a Differential Response', *American Economic Review*, 74 (1984). For a corrective which demonstrates that Japan's economic success owes most to her political economy, see Dore, op. cit.

AFTERWORD:
A WAGER ON REASON

This book has offered an interpretation of the nature, history and present condition of liberalism. Although much has been made of the failings of liberals in the past, the argument has been that there remain powerful reasons for us to hope that liberalism can survive, and perhaps prosper, in the contemporary world. If this is straightforward, critical attention on the argument as a whole may be best focused by means of some personal reflections. Obviously, authors cannot somehow transcend their prejudices, and so there must be ultimate limits to the usefulness of this approach. Nevertheless, some points do seem clear and worthy of attention.

Perceptions of liberalism seem to change in an almost cyclical manner. Liberalism often seems attractive because it encourages privacy, even apathy. The early proponents of capitalism welcomed it on these grounds, as did the 'end of ideology' school of the 1950s.[1] At other times, activism is deemed attractive in, or held to be necessary for, liberalism. This was true for much of the nineteenth century, and activists, wanting to rewrite liberalism according to their preferences, are among us now. It seems to me a strength to have tried to combine these alternative viewpoints; indeed, even to wobble between the options is less danger- ous than opting entirely for one of them. There is much to be said in favour of peace, privacy and prosperity. Who would not, at least sometimes, agree with Confucius that a happy age is one without history? Private life is exciting enough for my taste; it has its dramas. But herein lies the need for the second approach. It is sometimes necessary to fight publicly to preserve, and always necessary to fight to extend, the benefits of the *Weltanschauung* of negative liberty.

A second reflection is much less happy. This book has not paid nearly enough attention to the complexities of moral life in a liberal world; indeed several issues, partly for reasons of space, have been presented with exaggerated simplicity. One aspect of complexity has been touched on. Bertrand Russell once claimed that 'opinions which are held with passion are always those for which no good ground exists; indeed the passion is the measure of the holder's lack of rational conviction'.[2] To subject one's innermost views to evidence is by no means as easy as Russell imagined: it is a noble aim, but a hard one to realize since it involves tampering with human identity. Faced with this problem, respect for others almost, but not quite, dictates relativism, that is, not interfering with others. But this will not do. The most obvious difficulty – and it is a very great one – that follows from this is that of finding a way to divorce criticism of opinion from person, both as critic and criticized. Less obvious but equally vital dilemmas have had much light cast on them by Judith Shklar in her *Ordinary Vices*.[3] Many of her arguments, perhaps especially the insistence that liberals should dislike cruelty most of all, carry great conviction. However, in one sense, her book is dispiriting. Few people possess Shklar's formidable intelligence; an open moral universe was always difficult, but her discussion makes it seem very hard indeed.

A great deal of suspicion should be directed at the emphasis in this book on the scientific-industrial complex. I have tried to make the reader wary by speaking of a 'logic' that *may* work, rather than of a logic which will have determinate outcomes. There is a good reason for this. Evolutionist arguments are, for excellent reasons, currently unpopular in social science. They tend to functionalism, that is, the view that because something is needed for the 'working' of a social system it will therefore appear. This is facile. There may be objective pressures for something without them being able to succeed. In other words, evolutionary arguments tend to allow hopes to rise above experience. It is useful to remember in this context that the initial emergence of industrial society did not dictate a single institutional pattern for all societies, as some had hoped and expected. Does the discussion in this book of the scientific-industrial complex fall foul of these critical injunctions?

At a formal level, the errors of functionalism have been avoided by the continual stress on the need for agents to recognize and realize social trends. In this connection, much has been made of the importance of elite behaviour. It is proper to see Adam Smith's *Wealth of Nations* as a type of conversation with the members of the political and intellectual elite of his day. He sought to make them understand the beneficial workings of the market in order that they might protect it against the rapaciousness of merchant interests. This book amounts to being a similar sort of conversation. It is based on the hope that elites will see a better way. It is a wager on reason.

This emphasis on elites should not be misunderstood. It is not hard to see that the adoption of the scientific-industrial complex in authoritarian regimes, with all that implies for liberalization, depends heavily upon the attitude adopted by key elites. Such elites monopolize power. They possess something of the repressive apparatus of modernity, and so have considerable, if varying, capacities to suppress movements of which they disapprove. Their policies have led to social rigidities. Liberals may at least hope that authoritarian elites will seek to co-operate with increasingly pluralistic societies in a social contract based on softer political rule. None of this is to say that elites alone count in such societies. Very much to the contrary, the degree of intelligence and skill of social movements, the ability to ask for something but not for everything, to make real gains

239

without creating fear through needless rhetoric, is absolutely vital.

The recognition of a fact should not be taken as somehow implying endorsement of its status; 'is' does not equal 'ought', and description most certainly should not be taken to imply prescription. This can be put more simply by saying that elites not subject to popular control may always make large and disastrous mistakes. But this is not to say that the culture of elites in democratic societies is without significance. In Britain, popular discontent with the economic policies of both major parties has led in the last two decades to continual oscillation. While the ability of voters to punish bad performance remains admirable and indispensable, any reasonably well-informed British citizen cannot help but long for more intelligent economic sense on the part of both party elites. Far more importantly, an elite culture which does not whip up generalized hatreds or fears through dangerous simplifications, as happened in Imperial Germany, is profoundly to be desired. For even democracies can be destroyed by demagogues.

A measure of optimism is justified by actual social developments. However, the hopes expressed for liberalism depend rather too much for my comfort on sociological mechanisms. It may not be true that individuals can build themselves genuine identities. Capitalists may yet become systematically opposed to liberalism in industrial relations whilst their interests may make them proponents of war; they may become absolutist opponents of welfare. It is only fair to note that my position *is* idiosyncratic; the 'crisis of the welfare state' has led many thinkers to abandon evolutionary schemata of every sort! Even if my optimism about these matters is justified, it may be the case that elites are *not* rational enough to see, let alone realize, the long-term interests of their societies; perhaps increasing political competition for votes will increase demagoguery.

If the sociological basis for hope is misguided, then liberalism will have a bleaker, more embattled future. It will distinctively be one world among many; the philosophical foundations of liberalism will continue to appeal to *us*, but little hope will be available that they will seem as attractive to *others*. As it happens, I do not think that the situation is so bleak; but I may be wrong. Accordingly, these hopes are offered without illusions. We have a duty to seek for a better world; we should not fool ourselves that such a world is easy to achieve.

NOTES

1. A Hirschman, *The Passions and the Interests: Political Arguments for Capitalism before Its Triumph* (Princeton: Princeton University Press, 1977).
2. B. Russell, *The Basic Writings of Bertrand Russell* (ed. L. Dennonn and R. Egner) (London: George Allen and Unwin, 1962), p.16.
3. J. Shklar, *Ordinary Vices* (Cambridge MA: Harvard University Press, 1984).

SELECT
BIBLIOGRAPHY

The principle behind selection has been that of encouraging thought about liberalism. Not all the works listed here are by liberals: some critics succeed in laying bare liberalism's problems, others make it look attractive by sheer contrast. Several books are concerned with the social conditions that favour or hinder liberalism in historical and contemporary circumstances. The best history of liberalism remains that by G. de Ruggiero; a useful, easily available and reasonably extensive list of writings by liberals is contained in Arblaster's book.

Arblaster, A. *The Rise and Decline of Western Liberalism* (Oxford: Basil Blackwell, 1984).

Aron, R. *Peace and War* (London: Weidenfeld and Nicolson, 1966).

Aron, R. *Democracy and Totalitarianism* (London: Weidenfeld and Nicolson, 1968).

Aron, R. *An Essay on Freedom* (New York: World Publishing Company, 1970).

Bell, D. *The Cultural Contradictions of Capitalism* (London: Heinemann Educational, 1976).

Berlin, I. *Four Essays on Liberty* (Oxford: Oxford University Press, 1969).

Calleo, D. *The German Problem Reconsidered: Germany and the World Order, 1870 to the Present* (Cambridge: Cambridge University Press, 1978).

Calleo, D. and B. Rowland, *America and the World Political Economy: Atlantic Dreams and National Realities* (Bloomington: Indiana University Press, 1973).

Cowling, M. *Mill and Liberalism* (Cambridge: Cambridge University Press, 1971).

Dahrendorf, R. *Society and Democracy in Germany* (New York: Anchor Books, 1969).

Dunn, J. *Western Political Theory in the Face of the Future* (Cambridge: Cambridge University Press, 1979).

Dunn, J. 'From Applied Theology to Social Analysis: the Break between John Locke and the Scottish Enlightenment', in I. Hont and M. Ignatieff (eds), *Wealth and Virtue* (Cambridge: Cambridge University Press, 1983).

Dworkin, R. 'Liberalism', in S. Hampshire (ed.), *Public and Private Morality* (Oxford: Oxford University Press, 1978).

Esping-Andersen, G. *Politics against Markets: The Social Democratic Route to Power* (Princeton: Princeton University Press, 1985).

Freeden, M. *The New Liberalism* (Oxford: Oxford University Press, 1978).

Freeden, M. *Liberalism Divided* (Oxford: Oxford University Press, 1978).

Gellner, E. A. *Thought and Change* (London: Weidenfeld and Nicolson, 1964).

Gellner, E. A. *Legitimation of Belief* (Cambridge: Cambridge University Press, 1974).

Goldthorpe, J. (ed.), *Order and Conflict in Western European Capitalism* (Oxford: Oxford University Press, 1984).

Gray, J. *Liberalism* (Milton Keynes: Open University Press, 1986).

Hall, J. A. *Powers and Liberties: The Causes and Consequences of the Rise of the West* (Harmondsworth: Penguin, 1986).

Hartz, L. *The Liberal Tradition in America* (New York: Harcourt Brace Jovanovich, 1955).

Herf, J. *Reactionary Modernism. Technology, Culture and Politics in Weimar and the Third Reich* (Cambridge: Cambridge University Press, 1984).

Hirschman, A. O. *The Passions and the Interests: Political Arguments for Capitalism before Its Triumph* (Princeton: Princeton University Press, 1977).

Hobhouse, L. T. *Liberalism* (London: Allen and Unwin, 1911).

Hoffman, S. *Duties Beyond Borders: On the Limits and Possibilities of Ethical International Politics* (Syracuse: Syracuse University Press, 1981).

Howard, M. *War and the Liberal Conscience* (Oxford: Oxford University Press, 1978).

Katzenstein, P. *Small States in World Markets* (Ithaca: Cornell University Press, 1985).

Krasner, S. *Structural Conflict: The Third World against Global Liberalism* (Berkeley: University of California Press, 1985).

Laski, H. J. *The Rise of European Liberalism* (London: Allen and Unwin, 1936).

Lowi, T. *The End of Liberalism: Ideology, Policy and the Crisis of Public Authority* (New York: Norton, 1969).

MacIntyre, A. *After Virtue* (London: Duckworth, 1981).

MacLean, D. and C. Mills

(eds), *Liberalism Reconsidered* (New Jersey: Rowman and Allenheld, 1983).

MacPherson, C. B. *The Political Theory of Possessive Individualism* (Oxford: Oxford University Press, 1962).

Mann, J. M. *The Sources of Social Power. Vol. 1: From the Beginning to 1760 A.D.* (Cambridge: Cambridge University Press, 1986).

Manning, D. *Liberalism* (New York: St Martin's Press, 1976).

Minogue, K. *The Liberal Mind* (New York: Vintage Books, 1968).

Moore, B. *Reflections on the Causes of Human Misery and Upon Certain Proposals to Eliminate Them* (Boston: Beacon Press, 1969).

Moore, B. *Injustice: The Social Bases of Obedience and Revolt* (New York: M. E. Sharpe, 1978).

Newman, S. *Liberalism at Its Wits' End: The Libertarian Revolt against the Modern State* (Ithaca: Cornell University Press, 1984).

Popper, K. R. *The Open Society and Its Enemies*, 3rd edition (London: Routledge and Kegan Paul, 1957).

Ruggiero, G. de *The History of European Liberalism* (Boston: Beacon Press, 1955).

Sandel, M. J. *Liberalism and the Limits of Justice* (Cambridge: Cambridge University Press, 1982).

Shklar, J. *Ordinary Vices* (Cambridge MA: Harvard University Press, 1984).

Skidelsky, R. *John Maynard Keynes*, Vol. 1 (London: Macmillan, 1983).

Skinner, Q. 'The Idea of Negative Liberty: Philosophical and Historical Perspectives', in R. Rorty, J. B. Schneewind and Q. Skinner (eds), *Philosophy in History. Essays on the Historiography of Philosophy* (Cambridge: Cambridge University Press, 1984).

Strange, S. *Casino Capitalism* (Oxford: Basil Blackwell, 1986).

Taylor, A. J. P. *The Trouble Makers* (London: Panther, 1969).

Tocqueville, A. de *The Old Regime and the French Revolution* (New York: Anchor Books, 1955).

Wolff, R. P. *The Poverty of Liberalism* (Boston: Beacon Press, 1968).

INDEX

Index

Index

Index

251

Index

Radicalism, political, 16
Rational actor, 187–8
Rawls, John, 179, 187–8
Reactionary modernism, 78–80, 84, 146, 213
Reason, 11–12, 18
Relativism, 26, 30–31, 170–71, 183, 186–9, 238
Religion, 14, 22, 35, 56–7, 73, 114
Repression, 113
Respect for others, 93
Revolution, 103–5, 116–17, 120, 146, 159, 195, 202
  fear of, 107
  in science, 172
  see also French Revolution
Riesman, David
  The Lonely Crowd, 85
Robinson Crusoe myth, 75–7, 181
Rousseau, J.-J., 18, 84, 91, 93, 184, 185
Russell, Bertrand, 14, 238
Russia, 116–19, 145, 196–9
  Zubatov movement, 118
Russian Revolution, 104, 117

Sandel, Michael, 179, 180
Sartre, Jean-Paul, 84, 85–91
  Being and Nothingness, 90
  Critique of Dialectical Reason, 91
Sayer, Derek, 27
Scepticism, 12
Schmitt, Carl, 78
Science, 18, 22–4, 31–2, 59, 74, 160, 171–8, 199
  and liberalism, 3, 9–10
  and morality, 174–7
  philosophy of, 171–2
  and society, 185
Secularization, 59
Self, the, 83–92

see also Individual
Self-interest, 57, 59, 154
Sensation, 11, 73
Shils, Edward, 164
Shklar, Judith
  Ordinary Vices, 238
Skinner, B. F., 81
Skinner, Quentin, 182–3
Slavery, 35, 38
Smith, Adam, 13, 36–51, 54–6, 59, 71, 105, 182, 184, 193, 202, 210
  his concept of liberty, 45
  The Theory of Moral Sentiments, 40, 45
  The Wealth of Nations, 39, 41, 43–9, 239
Smoot-Hawley Act, 223
Social class, 103–22, 206
Social cohesion, 57–9, 198, 207
Social contract theory, 187
Social democracy, 214
Social determinism, 94
Social engineering, 194–5
Social evolution, 165, 238–41
Social experiments, 55
Social integration, 83–5
Social mobility, 197, 206
Social rules, 86, 88–9
Socialism *see under* State socialism
Sombart, Walter
  Why is There No Socialism in the United States?, 116
South Africa, 201
South Korea, 202–3, 220
Spain, 201–2
Spencer, Herbert, 47, 127, 173
  The Man Versus the State, 203
Spengler, Oswald, 79
Stalin, Josef, 47, 119, 145, 158, 196
Standard of living, 174, 207, 214
State, the, 52–8

252